BENEATH THE WOODLAND STARS

BENEATH THE WOODLAND STARS

Cindy Hobbs

DEDICATION

Dedicated to all the families, friends, and loved ones who tirelessly support someone they love who suffers from substance abuse. May you never lose yourself in the process.

And to Moses for helping me to learn to trust again.

TABLE OF CONTENTS

CHAPTER ONE

April Fools', 2014

I always get a cold sore every time I suck your cock.

The message stared back at me from my husband's phone. A warmhearted chuckle left my lips. *How will I ever top this prank?* This one was world-class. What made it even funnier was how unreal it would be for William to receive a text like this from another woman. Everyone who knew us understood just how devoted my husband of fourteen years was to me.

I began to contemplate my April Fools' revenge. Maybe I'll fill his BMW with balloons and confetti. Or put baking soda in his cherished saltshaker. Or better yet, I'll cover the tops of his drums with shaving cream before he plays them next. Yeah, that's what I'll do. My hand tightened around his phone, wondering who had helped him with this.

Wait . . . is this text real? No. It can't be . . . can it?

As the blinking dots came to a stop, I read more.

Maybe I'll stop sucking it, JK . . .

I squeezed my eyes shut, convinced I was seeing something wrong. But when I opened them again, my knees went weak. The text messages and all their glaring implications were still there.

The high-pitched sounds of our toddler granddaughter and nephews' laughter, stomping, and happy screaming that had cascaded up into my bedroom from the entryway below began to succumb to the overwhelming shock I felt. It took mere moments for the noises to disappear. Inside my bedroom, in my thoughts, it felt like an atomic bomb had just gone off, leaving me deaf and blind. There was nothing here but me and the persistent repetition of the words I'd read on the phone, spiraling out of control in my mind. *I have to be seeing something wrong. This can't be real.*

My throat constricted as my heart leaped into it. I clutched my chest as the immense pressure of a thousand-pound weight began to crush it. My breathing became sharp and rapid until my knees finally gave out, and I crumpled to the carpeted floor. *What just happened?* I knew I needed to move, get up, and do something, but my body would not respond. Everything stopped as if caught in a slow-motion film; nothing made sense. And . . . I didn't want it to.

I reminisced about how I ended up in the closet. Time seemed to exist normally just a few minutes ago. I had gone to our spacious custom master closet, lined with dark oak shelves and coordinated clothing hung perfectly on wooden hangers. Meanwhile, my family continued their laughter-filled foam sword fight in the foyer of our grand hacienda below. I had to change out of my stuffy work clothes into sweats to join the rambunctious kids. It would also be easier to take my turn in the chase if I wrapped my long, auburn hair into a quick ponytail. As I attempted to change, I heard my husband's phone vibrating on the center dresser in the closet.

I had never checked his phone before today; I'd never felt a need to. I would kindly bring it to him from whatever room he left it, which he frequently did. Today, I happened to check it. The insistent buzzing had me worried something might be wrong with his mother. After a recent medication change, her health started to decline. I was also vigilant about our adult children. Whatever the reason, I had a sudden strong urge that something was "wrong." Still, never in my wildest dreams had I imagined it might be this kind of wrong.

10

I gasped for air, realizing that I had been holding my breath for far too long. The laughter and shrills of the children and William returned as if some cosmic unmute button had been pressed and I could hear again.

Forcing myself through the motions of putting on my gray fleece sweats, I felt like a robot trying to change—arm in here, leg in there. Pull up, tighten, and tie. I double-checked myself in the mirror to make sure there were no signs of distress anywhere on the pale skin of my face or body. I could not let the children see me upset! This was not their problem. I was a grown-up. I could control my feelings. I'd deal with this—whatever this was—after the children had gone back to their parents tomorrow. I could hold it in until then.

Some part of me even whispered, "Maybe you're reading this wrong, Cindy. Maybe this is just a big misunderstanding. Perhaps you will ask William why he'd receive such a crude, sexual text, and it will all make perfect sense, and your life will go back to the way it was before." Surely, there had to be an explanation for this. This was so out of character for William . . . at least the William I knew.

"It sounds like you guys are having way too much fun down here," I said as calmly as I could manage, traipsing back downstairs. With a big gulp, I pushed my tears and anger down deep into my gut and forcibly settled into my old, calm, loving, usual self.

I kissed little Mia's forehead as she ran past the end of the stairs, her stomping feet echoing on the terracotta floor, blue sword high in the air. Her golden streaks of hair were neatly tied into two small ponytails on top of her head, and her big hazel eyes resembled teardrops turned on their sides, full of joy.

I snared Justin around the waist as he ran past me. His perfect, wide, flat nose and slanted eyes complemented his straight, tousled black hair, showcasing the beautiful Asian features he had inherited from my sister-in-law. He squirmed as I planted a smooch on his cheek before letting him go to chase Mia with his bright yellow and orange sword, screaming at the top of his lungs, "I'm gonna get you!"

While I was upstairs, William had stepped out of the spiraling circle of laughter and into the side office off the foyer. I took a deep breath and walked into the office, pushing the next swell of emotions down; this was not the time nor the place. *Later, later, later*, I told myself.

But I was also thinking, what if this is my last moment with him? If those texts were really from someone else . . . who is he? Who is this man I've been married to for over a decade? He was supposed to only have eyes for me. I stood in the doorway, staring at him. I examined every detail of William as if time stood still.

He had his back turned to me, his broad shoulders extending far past the sides of the back of the chair. The veins in his bicep pulsed under his tight tan T-shirt. His head was shaved down to the scalp, leaving a perfectly tan oval skull. Even when seated, his towering six-foot-four frame remained tall. My William. My husband. The person I trusted most in this world. Certainly, he was still all of those things?

He turned when he heard me enter the room, smiling widely with full lips, a mix of his Irish/Mexican heritage.

Later, later, later, I insisted as I tried to keep a straight face. *You're the grown-up. This is not the time or the place.* But those calm reminders faded, and I couldn't hold back. My grip on his phone tightened into bright white knuckles. My eyes swelled, and I spoke softly to refrain from screaming.

"You left your phone on the dresser in the closet. It was buzzing a lot, and I thought there may be an emergency, so I checked it." I held the phone a foot from his face, the damning text exchange pulled up on the screen. I kept it there and looked at him silently, letting a single tear escape before inhaling firmly, not allowing any more to release.

"We will not be talking about it while the children are here," I said firmly.

His expression shifted to a frown. "Please, I can explain," William muttered under his breath.

I slammed his phone down, screen first, on top of the desk. At least that felt good.

I hope I cracked his screen.

I ignored William the rest of the evening and the next day, pouring all my attention into the children while trying to control my racing thoughts and heart. I would occasionally catch him looking at me from the corner of his eye. He knew this was not a matter I was willing to discuss with the children present.

After the parents picked up their children and we waved goodbye to them from the front porch as if nothing was amiss, William immediately turned to me. "Cindy, it's not what you think it is. It's about drugs," he stated in an exacerbated breath. "This person on the text exchange just wants to score some oxycodone, and this is the code language we use to bargain."

I scoffed unbelievably. Oxy? William? Until recently, he was a part-time stay-at-home husband and part-time debt collector for our loan business. Neither of those was a profession that led to using drugs. Before he could utter another word, I ran to our brown leather sofa in the living room, collapsing into a blubbering ball. Now that the children were safe with their parents, the hurt could finally be released. It poured out of me like a river that had been damned. Our hacienda's bright yellow and orange walls did nothing to cheer me up. Not today.

William rushed to my side. He sat on the couch beside me, gently stroking my arms and back. I guessed he was trying to comfort me because I rarely displayed such emotion. I shrugged him off. The last thing I wanted right now was for him to touch me.

"So you're not having an affair . . . but you're doing drugs? Dealing drugs? That's supposed to make me feel better?" I expelled in a shaky breath.

Hint: it didn't.

"None of this makes sense, William!" I continued, my voice rising with hysteria in between sobs. "I feel like I don't know you at all. What am I supposed to believe?" Today, it was as if the faucet of emotions was turned on, gushing out of control. William kept moving his head, attempting to catch my eyes, but I kept looking away. Besides, the tears made it impossible to see. His voice, that familiar, deep voice, penetrated my heart. I wanted to believe him, every word, even if his explanation involved narcotics. I tried to think that our life together as a happy, loving, loyal couple was not a lie.

"Believe me. Please, Cindy, I would never hurt you. I would never do anything to jeopardize our family. I have you, Cindy. Why would I need anything more? You are my best friend, the love of my life."

His tone was pleading, his voice strained. His hands kept caressing the sides of my arms, touching my chin, trying to get me to look at him. It seemed like he wanted me to understand, and I tried. But nothing he said fit into the life I thought I'd had with him.

"I got addicted to oxycodone after my foot surgery," he stated softly while stroking my arm with his large, warm hand.

I gasped. I remembered the foot surgery. Had it been four years ago? He had suffered from flat feet for so long. It limited his ability to stand for longer than a few hours at a time. I had been with him every step of the way through the surgery and recovery. And the pain that went with it, so at least that part made sense.

He continued, "But the pain didn't go away, and it was excruciating. So that's why I refused to do the surgery on the other foot."

I remembered being so confused about why he didn't want surgery on his other foot. I figured the pain couldn't have been that bad. It was apparent he needed the second surgery, but whenever I'd brought it up, he would say, "Not now," or, "In a year or two." He had plenty of excuses, saying there was still lingering pain, but as long as he rested, he was fine. And I believed him. I had no reason not to. I trusted William with every fiber of my being.

How did I miss the pain he was in?

How could he have disguised that much of himself?

I couldn't help but wonder at that moment if there could be more to William I didn't know.

He continued, "When the surgeon refused to refill any more pain pills for me, I had to find other sources . . . illegal ones. Cindy, I'm sorry. Please believe me," William pleaded as he reached to touch my hair.

Flinching, I knocked his hand away from me. His touch near me seemed tainted now.

"You swore to me you would never be involved in drugs. When we were dating, you told me you dabbled in them a little when you were younger. You said you had to spend thirty days in rehab and would never touch the stuff again," I reminded him sternly.

I recalled times when William was offered drugs in my presence—peddlers on the beaches of Mexico or during sporting event parties at some of William's friends'. Every time he refused them, pushing them away.

William's head dropped, and he began to sob. I had never seen my husband this upset. But why didn't his pain move me to tell him I forgave him immediately? To reach out and comfort him?

"I'm sorry, Cindy. I am so sorry. I wanted to tell you, but I thought you would leave me. I got in over my head. I couldn't stop. Even after the pain was gone, the drugs still numbed everything. I felt invincible . . . you're always so hard on me," William managed to get out between gasps. "Making me sit on the other side of your desk as we review the bills each month, it made me feel belittled, having to account for every cent I spent on little things, especially since you control it . . ."

My spine straightened in disbelief. So now it was my fault I was careful with the money I earned? Did he not recall how I cleaned up his debt when we met? Or the repeated times I was forced to pay off credit cards he charged enormous amounts to behind my back?

I paused, took a deep breath in, and softly said, "The only reason we have a roof over our head and the things we do as a family is because of how I manage the money. How dare you turn this on me? This is not about me; this is about you."

I uncurled my body, pushed him away, and charged up the stairs to the master bedroom. Closing the door behind me, I firmly locked it before slumping onto the floor behind the door, leaning my back against it.

His footsteps pounded like a herd of buffalo as he climbed the stairs, following me. Did I want him to follow me? I didn't know what I wanted. I just didn't want this life that it seemed I now had.

William tried to turn the locked handle. "Listen. I'll stop. I've been trying to. That's why I got on suboxone to get off the pain pills. Please, Cindy. I would never hurt you. I would never cheat on you. I just need your help."

I felt more tears stream down my cheeks. He'd started taking suboxone for the pain in his feet a year ago, hadn't he? I pulled my phone from my pocket, typing as he spoke into its search engine. *Suboxone is for drug addiction.* Why hadn't I questioned this before? I am a nurse, for pity's sake. The answer was bittersweet and straightforward: because I had always trusted my husband.

"You have to believe me," William pleaded. "I'll go to counseling. I'll take drug tests whenever you want. I'll get off everything, I promise. Please don't leave me . . ." His voice broke pitifully between words.

Images of our first date, a casual lunch at an Italian restaurant, surfaced first in my mind. My aching heart recalled the day he proposed at the altar of the cathedral and the beautiful princess-cut diamond he'd placed on my finger. I reached for the ring now, moving it in a circle with my right fingertips.

Family vacation reflections blossomed in my thoughts, showcasing our blended family of three boys. Our boys... the thought of them suddenly flooded me, causing the tears to come faster.

Mathew, William's only child, now stood as tall as his dad. His thick, dark hair was buzzed short, and a full beard covered his face. The boy who grew into a man was now a father himself.

Then there was Lyle, my oldest son. He was a gentle giant, intellectual, and yet clever. He now towered over my five-foot-five frame, standing just shy of six feet tall, and also kept his dark brown thick hair buzzed short like Mathew. Lyle liked routines and consistency. Coffee came first each morning, followed by a bowl of cereal and then an apple.

Cortland was the caboose of the boys. He stood as tall as Lyle, with an early onset of a receding hairline. He had just finished serving a religious mission in the Philippines. It had been a two-year adventure that had him cleaning up multiple villages after tsunamis and earthquakes.

They were our boys, not his and hers . . . ours.

Our home was the gathering spot for holidays. Large turkeys soaked in brine overnight were baked to perfection with a golden-brown crust. Potatoes with the skins still on were mashed in garlic and butter. The gravy was perfectly seasoned with the drippings from the turkey and made thick slowly with a bit of flour.

The echoing sounds of laughter from our parents and godparents filled the hacienda during these times as they shared stories of their experiences in the army and navy. I couldn't forget the tales they shared of summers long past, when the matriarch women would invite the parish bishops over in the afternoon for mass and, of course, wine. Our siblings would discuss how big our boys had grown from the last time they had seen them as they helped with coffee and cakes for dessert.

These memories made me sob now, the sleeves of my shirt soaked as I wiped my face furiously.

"Cindy, are you still there?" William whispered from the other side of the door.

I had made a commitment to this man, for better or worse. Over the years, we certainly had many betters . . . but this was undeniably "a" worse. Was it also the end? Taking a deep breath, I pushed the memories aside. I needed to be in the present, not the past right now.

This would be hard, the decision I knew I had to make, but I had to try. Not only for the sake of our marriage but also for our family.

I am a strong woman. I can help William through his drug addiction. I had no idea what that would mean or the likelihood of him recovering. I just knew that I wanted my old life back. And that I still loved the man on the other side of the door.

Finally rising, I unlocked the handle and opened it. William was leaning against the railing on the other side. When he saw me standing, he abruptly gained his feet.

I lurched forward, falling into his arms. "I can't lose you, William," I said breathlessly. "I can't lose our family."

CHAPTER TWO

June 2014

Two months had gone by, but I wasn't feeling any better. Even though William and I saw a marriage counselor, I started seeing a therapist for myself. Twenty pounds that I didn't intend to lose suddenly disappeared from my frame. During an extra session that I desperately needed one week, I confessed to my therapist, Nicole, that I had been searching through William's phone while he slept at night.

There was a feeling I couldn't shake, one that wasn't being resolved in counseling with my husband, who, despite his remorse, still seemed to be holding back. Nicole was the only one I could share my recent discoveries with; she would know what to do. I kept what I found to myself for weeks while I analyzed the photos in his deleted folder on his phone.

I reflected on that night of my discovery as I settled across from my therapist, now ready to reveal the images I had found. And yet I pondered about the night I had encountered them. *I stood leaning against the granite in our $30,000 kitchen. That damned kitchen he swore he had to have. I looked at those pictures I'm sure he thought he had deleted, trying not to throw up. Then, I contemplated what I should do.*

When I showed Nicole the photos, she realized she couldn't see the faces of either person. I was aware of this and explained how I'd even printed some of the images and left them on

William's laptop one morning, hoping to see his reaction. But when he found them, he just said they were from a porn site.

Of course, the accusations came that he had such images because we didn't have sex enough. I retorted that with his need to take a pill and wait an hour to perform, any spontaneity had left our sex life years ago. He continued to deny everything in marriage counseling. It was a mess. Finally, my therapist raised her eyes when I dropped the big bomb: I'd hired a private investigator and had him download everything off William's phone.

It was quite an ordeal. I waited until he fell asleep before unplugging his phone and sneaking downstairs with it, placing the phone inside an envelope with password details and hiding it under the doormat. The PI then retrieved it and downloaded the contents of his phone. Once he finished, he snuck the envelope back under the mat, giving me enough time to plug the phone back into William's charger. Soon, I'd know the truth.

Was it really just drugs? Were those pictures just porn, or something more? As terrified as I was, Nicole confirmed what I'd already thought: I needed to hear back from the PI to move forward with my life. Even though I was Catholic and breaking my vows to William with a divorce was not an option after my previous divorce from my first husband, the truth was I needed to both eat and sleep again.

Ding! Ding! The bells tied to the front door chimed, echoing through the foyer of the private investigator's office upon my arrival. I could hear the heavy sound of footsteps coming down the hall. Tables, chairs, and boxes lined the walls in what should have been a receptionist area. The smell of stale lunch lingered in the air. It made my already jittery stomach flip with nausea.

"You made it! Come back to my office; I want to show you a few things," Peter, the private investigator, said a little too cheerfully.

How can he be jovial in a moment like this?

Peter's polo was not entirely covering his overlapping belly today. His bald spot, centered on the top of his head, seemed to have gotten bigger since the last time I saw him three weeks ago.

I followed Peter slowly, my feet unable to pick up a fast pace. It was as if I were walking through sludge, and each step felt like my feet were being pulled back down by sticky glue, leaving me lingering in the hall longer than I should have.

You can turn around right now and leave.

Let the truth stay with William.

You can stop this spiraling quest for certainty, resume the life you had!

I sighed inwardly. It was too late for that. If I was ever going to move forward, I had to know the truth. The matter-of-fact version of me knew what needed to be done.

I had never been into Peter's office before, if you could call it an office. It was only slightly bigger than a closet. A large burgundy desk took up most of the space. The desktop itself was covered in paper, notepads, and Post-it notes. Perched above the sea of paper sat two large computer screens.

I noticed wryly there was nothing on his office walls. Maybe that's how private investigators liked it. Perhaps it made it easier for them to pack up and leave a space if a scornful spouse or a wannabe criminal found out they were following them, tracing their every move.

He motioned to an old office chair against the wall. "Pull the chair around so you can see my screen."

I did as instructed, weaseling my way into the small space behind his desk against the wall, trying not to damage the plaster. When I looked up, I had to keep my gasp inside with a huge gulp. My fingers curled around the armrests, their grip tightening as my body started to shake.

On his screen was a picture I was all too familiar with, but it was now in high definition. *HIGH def.* It was one of the pictures I had found on William's phone. I desperately wanted to look away. I could feel my face droop, a large lump forming in my throat as my heart raced.

I glanced at Peter, who seemed unfazed by the shocking image as if he was looking at a sunset or mountain range.

"Ahem . . ." he said, clearing his throat, "so, when we dove into the pixel count of this image versus the pixel count of a downloaded image from a porn site, along with the resolution, any count with a pixel exceeding 300, with a resolution of . . ."

. . . *wahh, wahh wahh, wahh wahh* . . . His voice turned into the adult voices from the Charlie Brown cartoons of my youth. I knew what he was about to confirm: my worst fear.

"So this could not have been downloaded from any internet site. It is an actual picture taken from his phone," Peter finished, his voice becoming clear again from the fog swirling in my head.

As if I were seeing the picture for the first time, I made out William's filigree tattoo on the side of the man's chest, the lines so perfectly curved. Those were the same lines my fingers had traced over hundreds of times.

There was also the chest hair groomed to a singular line. *William's chest.* The hand holding the edge of that purple thong just below the woman's tramp stamp—well, that was William's broad, thick hand, the one that had traced my lines and curves under the covenant of holy matrimony. Suddenly, it was as if a blurry telephoto lens came perfectly into focus. All the pictures I found, every one of them involved William.

I could feel the blood drain from my face. I leaned back in the chair, my head hitting the wall behind it with a small thud. The room spun, slowly at first, and it then sped up. I knew I could pass out at any given moment.

"Cindy, let me go grab a bottled water for you. You look white as a ghost right now," Peter said before standing, squeezing past me out of his office.

As much as the small space would allow, I leaned forward, willing myself not to vomit. Instead, I swallowed the bile down hard.

My eyes glossed over.

I didn't feel like crying.

I wanted to scream at the top of my lungs until I was hoarse. But I couldn't do it here, not in this office. Not with Peter.

The truth that I had been so desperately begging William for was right here in front of my face, and it had been there the entire time.

"Here," Peter insisted as he entered the room, unscrewing the lid before handing me the bottle. I took it without even looking at him, swallowing two big gulps. Acid rose quickly into my throat as the cold water hit my empty stomach.

I had heard enough. I stood, reached for my purse, and took a few steps. The sludge I walked in on my way to his office was thicker and stickier.

Move, feet. You have to move out of here.

I was sure of one thing: I needed to find out who this woman was.

CHAPTER THREE

The moment I watched William pull out of the driveway and down the road toward his own counseling appointment, I raced to his laptop in the office. Peter had revealed the facts to me that afternoon, but I was determined to finish my heart-wrenching search for answers tonight.

How could one woman ruin the perfect life that took me years to build? But more importantly, I needed to know why *this* woman was better than me in my husband's eyes. Why was I not enough?

The heat of betrayal was coursing through my veins like hot lava from an erupted volcano. I needed to know what kind of hold this woman had on William. I only had an hour to discover more about her before he returned from his counseling session. I had found the pictures William thought he had deleted from his phone. I could undoubtedly find a trail to her.

I slid into the black leather office chair, flipping open the top of the laptop. My sweaty palm slipped as it grasped the mouse, trying to navigate the screen. A surge of urgency quickened my breathing, and my heart sped up with every move I made.

Swiftly, I moved from site to site, scrolling through William's social media pages, looking for a name, maybe black hair like in the photos, of any woman I was unfamiliar with. It was as if I was floating above my body, looking down on a woman I did not recognize. In that chair was a woman who, two months ago, never checked her husband's phone. But today, as I looked down at myself, I saw a woman I never imagined I would become. Distraught, betrayed, and consumed with rage. This person was not me, and yet . . . .it was.

My anxiety heightened when I didn't find anything out of order on his social media accounts. William's appointment time seemed to be ticking faster in my racing mind.

Tick, tick, tick.

I quickly moved on to his email. The login page popped up, and I entered William's usual password.

Incorrect password. Please try again.

"Damn," I muttered quietly. I tried another one of his frequently used passwords.

Incorrect password. Please try again.

"Shit, what is it?" I blurted out with a sense of panic. *When did he change it? Is he on to me? Maybe the printed photos I placed on his laptop gave it away.* My heart was beating faster as the clock kept ticking, as if time itself was also against me.

I put my head in my hand, feeling my pulse race and my breathing increase into short bursts of air, knowing another incorrect attempt could lock me out of the system. My hands sifted through scraps of paper, trying to glean a clue of what the password may be.

The edge of a Post-it note caught my attention beneath a picture of his father taped up on the side of his office wall. I lifted the photo to see the name of a small, remote town in Mexico: Merida. It was a place we had visited often over the years.

I took a deep breath and typed the name of the town. The screen shifted, and Williams's email home page appeared.

I'm in.

I abruptly sorted his emails, BMW announcements, parts from BMW that he ordered, chef knife advertisements . . . until an email caught my eye. It was from Rose69@yahoo.com. The subject line was a simple, personal, "Miss you."

Her name is Rose? Rose. I knew no one with that name; now, it would be a name I would never forget. A name associated with betrayal. I opened it—a picture of a middle-aged woman making a kissing face popped onto the screen. I didn't recognize the overly tan face with prominent wrinkles on her forehead. Pink lip gloss covered her medium-sized lips, her eyes dark, lined with thick black liner and mascara, clumping them together. Her eyebrows were small, stenciled lines. Her thin, black hair hung straight down onto her shoulders. She appeared to be the opposite of my soft features. *This is her?*

I immediately recognized that the hair was the same color and length I had seen on William's phone. Bingo!

I hit reply and quickly typed a question.

Hey, are you there?

Rapidly, I clicked Send before I changed my mind. My heart was pulsating in my throat as I checked the clock. Fifteen minutes was all I had left. I started to nibble on the skin around my fingernail.

My thoughts started racing in quick-fire: *What if she doesn't respond? Do I have time to erase everything from William's email? What if she replies later and William finds it? What other sites would he have used to hide conversations with her?*

I reached for the mouse, ready to erase the sent email and continue my search, when her reply appeared on the screen.

Yeah, what's up?

My heart went into overdrive, pumping blood incredibly fast. My fingers took on their own life, typing my response feverishly.

She knows about us. She found the pictures, and I had to tell her.

If William can't end this, I will. I would make sure that this affair ended if I stayed or left. I could feel beads of sweat forming and running down the small of my back. My palms were wet. I rubbed them against my pant legs several times to dry them, but they remained clammy.

Her reply only took seconds this time.

What the fuck? Sure she knows, but I bet she doesn't know about the last three years and all the drugs?

Three years? This has been going on for three years?

Like a kick to the stomach, I couldn't breathe as memories from the last few years flooded my mind: William's father's passing and our grandson's birth. My college graduation where William recorded me speaking to the graduating class. Family vacations to Mexico and Newfoundland. Thanksgivings, Christmases, and Easter with the entire family gathered around tables of food, laughter filling the air.

Had he been seeing her while he'd been with our family and me for the last three years? How could William have led such a double life?

I took a quick, raspy breath, repeatedly wiping my sweaty palms on my pants. Then, finally, I typed the answer as if I was William back to her.

Yeah, she knows. She's okay with it. We're going to make this work.

Of course, I was far from okay with anything right now! I was an enraged, consumed woman. Rose was clearly complicit. She knew William had a wife, and that he kept his drug-infested and affair-ridden lifestyle hidden from her.

But I didn't have time, nor did I want to have an extended online conversation with this slut. I had mere minutes to end this—minutes to make her feel the pain I felt because of her.

Bullshit, I'm coming up to your house; I'm going to tell her everything.

Stunned, I replied: **Go ahead, she already knows.**

I know now. Would she drive up here? How does she know where we live? Has she been in OUR home? Has she been in MY bed with MY husband?

I could no longer suppress my anger; my hands shook uncontrollably. I glanced up from the screen as I heard the sound of a familiar loud engine revving up the street. William was early. Quickly, I typed:

I have to go. She's home, and she has my phone. Don't try to call it.

I just hoped this response would buy me some time to talk to William before she attempted to contact him. Hastily, I erased the email string and deleted it from all of William's folders. I slammed the laptop screen down and shuffled his papers to the positions he had left them in before I hurried to the kitchen.

Grabbing a wineglass from the cabinet, I wrenched open the refrigerator door. I took a deep breath of the cold air, hoping it would mask my heavy breathing. Then I filled my glass from the spigot of the boxed wine as William opened the back door.

With every ounce of control I could muster, I casually threw a look over my shoulder. "Hey, how did it go tonight?"

"It was okay," William replied, his tone low. "I just don't feel like I am connecting with her. I don't know if I want to continue going." He tossed his car keys onto the counter.

I bit hard on my lip, wanting to scream at him for saying this out loud to my face. *Fourteen years is not worth going to counseling? Our marriage, our family is not worth doing this?*

I guzzled half the filled glass of dry white wine before turning to face him. The refrigerator glass door closed with a thud behind me. My hands were still shaking. I clutched the wine glass tightly, the heat rising in every part of my body.

I no longer wanted to cry. Now, I only wanted to scream.

Behind my tight lips were cries I wanted to release about every lie. For all those times I worked extra hours to provide the things he wanted . . . for allowing him to exaggerate to others about what he did for a living so he could appear to be more prominent in front of others. Instead of letting others see him for who he truly was, a fifty-year-old man financially supported by his wife.

"Can I see your phone for a sec?" I asked as calmly as possible, suppressing my urge to scream. I set my wineglass on the counter, extending my hand, palm open, toward him.

"Why?" he replied, the irritation rising in his voice.

"I just have an uneasy feeling. I want to check one thing," I explained, watching as my outstretched hand trembled.

He had allowed me to check his phone in his presence over the last couple of months. And I kept that façade up. He didn't need to know about the actual manhunt that happened through his phone while he slept.

William slowly pulled his phone out of his pocket, entered his passcode, and handed me the phone.

I wanted to ensure Rose hadn't sent him a text and seek clarification on the email exchange. I scrolled through his texts—no texts from Rose and limited texts from anyone else, for that matter.

I walked around our large kitchen island and opened his messenger account from his social media site. I was unsure how they communicated, but I knew her name now.

"That's enough," William said impatiently. "Hand it back. As you can see, there is nothing on it that should worry you. I told you, I'm not doing drugs anymore." The pitch of his voice raised as he moved around the kitchen island in my direction.

"I just want to check one more thing . . ." I replied, picking up my pace as I continued to walk, keeping the bulk of the kitchen island between us.

"I said, that's enough!" William shouted. He quickly circled the island, lunging in my direction. His enormous hand locked over mine, blocking my ability to search anything further on his phone.

I twisted, trying to free my hand, but his grip was firm and forceful.

I pushed against him with my free hand as he started prying my fingers off his phone. William did not budge. My strength was nothing compared to my husband's six-foot, muscular frame.

At that moment, I no longer cared about Rose replying. I didn't care if she had sent him a dozen messages. I just cared about hanging onto William's phone. It was the item he wanted more than anything else at that moment, even more than me. I wanted to keep hold of the key to his secrets and lies.

I redirected my anger with unbridled passion toward pushing him away from me, keeping his phone in my possession. Grunts filled the kitchen air, followed by the skidding sounds of shoes on the tile floor as we pushed against each other.

Suddenly, William shoved me hard, causing me to fall back against the kitchen sink, thrusting the back of my hand into the sink's sharp metal corner with great force.

Blood instantly dripped onto the floor as the pain seared quickly up my arm. I retracted my hand to my chest and reached for a kitchen towel.

"Look what you did! Are you happy? I'm bleeding!" I screamed, pulling the towel tighter over the cut.

"I told you to give it back!" William said sharply. "You're not going to find anything on my phone. I am not doing drugs anymore."

An avalanche of anger rose within my chest, spilling onto my tongue. There was no stopping me now. "You are a fucking liar! Tell me about Rose. And how you have been with her for the last three years?"

My words sat combustible in the air between us. My chest was heaving, and I noticed so was William's as we stared intently at each other as the seconds ticked by.

William's expression didn't change, and I was determined not to back down. Not this time. I could no longer suppress my feelings of anger and betrayal. It was as if we were two snarling bulls, ready to ram into each other with full force.

And then . . .

William's face changed. The corners of his mouth turned down. His eyes drooped.

"I am so . . . so sorry, Cindy," William said. Tears spilled over onto his cheeks. My husband's large frame softened inward as he approached me, crouching like a small child.

The confirmation of William's apology was a sledgehammer to my gut. It knocked the breath out of me, leaving me gasping for air. My knees buckled, and I crumpled to the cold tile floor.

The truth.

William's confession abruptly lifted the stronghold that my anger had on me just moments ago that kept my tears at bay. Heavy sobs escaped my lips, echoing in every corner of the hacienda.

"Why. . . ?" I tried to speak, but my throat closed off after that single word.

My right hand reached up to my chest while I struggled to take short breaths. I grabbed hold of my shirt in a fist, pushing hard against my rib cage, trying to stop my heart from exploding.

But it was too late. I could feel it shattering like a pane of glass.

"How could you?" I whimpered in between loud howls. "I . . . I thought you loved me. I trusted you! You're my husband." The words were made not only of questions but also statements of what I thought my reality was before today.

"I know . . . I'm so sorry. I wanted to tell you," William babbled as he fell to the floor with me. He wrapped his arms around me tightly, leaning his face against mine. Our tears began to mix, dripping onto our shirts, now wetting our chests with the intensity of lost rivers of hope. Time stopped, but the tears continued.

I no longer had the strength to push him away. Instead, I needed him to comfort me in this horrible moment for some infuriating reason. After all, he had been my best friend, the love of my life.

"Why didn't you tell me?" I asked sternly but quietly. The exhaustion of the whole day weighed on me.

"Rose threatened me over and over that if I didn't continue to see her, she would come tell you everything and ruin our marriage. Ruin my life. So many times I wanted to tell you and have you help me fix it, but I was too scared. So scared that I would lose you, Cindy, and our family; you're all I have," William replied through his muffled tears, still tightly wrapped around me on the kitchen floor.

"And the drugs . . . were there actually drugs involved?"

"Yes . . . I have been addicted to oxycodone since my foot surgery . . . she supplies them to me," William replied faintly into my hair.

How could I have been so oblivious to all of this?

Did I pay so little attention to my husband that he had played out this second life right under my nose? Apparently, that was the case. Still, was he that good at covering up his tracks, his lies? Or did I trust William so much that I believed every reason or excuse he gave me—without even a second thought?

"No . . . No . . . No, this can't be happening . . . our family, kids, grandchildren, parents, siblings . . . our lives!" I exclaimed, still trying to catch my breath. The thought of how this would affect them caused my heart to race faster, restricting my breathing even more.

My sobs became louder as I leaned into William's sturdy frame, his grip tightening around me. Memories of the last three years spun out of control in my mind as if what I knew them to be was no longer accurate. *The life I thought I had was a lie.*

"I know. I am so sorry. I love you, Cindy. Please don't leave. I can't lose you, and I can't lose our family," William replied between his loud sobs. His grip on me became tighter, causing my already restricted breathing to become shallower.

I found myself needing to stand to catch my breath. I eased a hand onto the countertop, pulling myself up. My knees felt wobbly, causing me to lean back against the counter's edge. *Can I even walk?*

William released his hold on me as I stood. But as soon as I was upright, he wrapped his arms around my waist again and rested his head on my stomach. His sobbing continued, and I could feel his tears seep through my shirt onto my skin. I found it odd that our tears were still mingling together, just like our lives always had since we met.

My shoulders drooped under the debilitating heaviness of it all. Yet, the weight of my entire world was resting now on my shoulders.

Dear God, I realized. *Knowing the truth is far worse than not knowing.*

I thought about this rash quest for truth I had been on for the past few months—the sleepless nights, the inner torment, the photos that distorted my world, and knowing each of those images was a captured, intimate moment William had with someone else.

The truth.

"How could you . . . ?" My words trailed off once more.

I reached across the counter for a paper towel. The wetness from every orifice of my face made my already labored breathing more difficult. William's arms loosened their grip around my waist as I blew and wiped angrily at a decade's worth of loss.

Picking up the wine glass I had set on the counter, I gulped the rest of its contents. I needed more alcohol to numb everything. With one hand holding onto the counter edge, I staggered to the refrigerator, opening its glass door and filling my wine glass nearly to the brim. That which had earlier been needed for courage now felt as vital as life's breath. I did not know what to do now.

William stood slowly and followed suit, wiping his face and then stumbling to the bar in the sitting area off the kitchen. He grabbed a bottle of tequila from the cabinet, unscrewed the lid, and took three long swigs as he walked back into the kitchen. He needed liquid sustenance too.

So am I supposed to leave now? I thought as I watched him. *Or is this the part where I ask him to leave?*

I realized that I didn't want to leave. I didn't want William to go either. For some reason, that was the last thing I wanted to happen. No matter how much it hurt, I didn't know how in the world I could live without him.

William strode over to where I was leaning against the enormous kitchen island, staring blankly through the glass doors of the refrigerator. The sun was setting through the back kitchen windows, casting an evening glow onto us. It had once been our favorite view.

My husband snuggled up to my side, tequila bottle in hand. I closed my eyes against the pain. Our sobs were faint now, as if we had hit a lull for a moment, allowing ourselves to catch our breath.

Sliding his free arm around my shoulders, he pulled me into him. My head fell softly onto the side of his chest. The smell of fresh soap mixed with sweat and cologne filled my nose. The only thing I could think to do while my thoughts were in a haze was to ask something of William—something I felt I needed.

"I need to know the whole story, William. The truth—no lies. How did this all begin?" I softly demanded, sipping my glass of wine as I nuzzled into his chest. I felt lightheaded and dizzy but brave enough to demand the whole story.

William took another swig off the bottle of tequila. He continued to grip the bottle, not placing it on the counter after each chug. Apparently, he thought he would need it to get through this. *Good. Let him face this, whatever it takes.*

I waited while William let out a long sigh.

"It all started three years ago, after the foot surgery, like I said," he began, his words hesitant, stumbling. "Once the surgeon would no longer provide me with pain pills, I had to find an alternative source." He paused. "My friend, Marco, knew this doctor who would create a false file with false information. The doc would write as many prescriptions as I wanted for whatever I wanted. Rose worked for this doctor . . ."

Good God! I thought. *Did she?* The tattooed woman worked for a doctor? Obviously, it was a doctor who had traded in his Hippocratic oath for greed. So what did that make her?

I still had so many questions, but I could hardly stand at that point. After suggesting we go to the bedroom to continue the conversation, I let William explain until he thought he was done.

He was not done as 3:52 a.m. glared back at me from the too-bright clock on the nightstand. I could barely make out the numbers through my swollen, puffy eyes. Our talking and sobbing had lasted over seven hours. That was the amount of time it took him to answer my questions.

Still, William continued, as I still had questions, and they would not be denied. When had he seen her last? When had they been wrapped in each other's arms or doing what I had witnessed over those telling pictures on his phone?

"It's been three weeks since I last saw her," he admitted. "Now that I am working, I've been able to use that excuse with her. She is crass, a junkie. She lives in the basement of her sister's house, doesn't work, and lost custody of her children. She is nothing like you."

In the early morning hours, William relayed that the doctor eventually was caught by the Feds. But what didn't stop, what had never stopped, was Rose's ability to find and provide drugs to a few of the clients the doctor was servicing.

She had discovered other ways to obtain pills and knew that addicted people would do just about anything for them. From his words, I pictured her as a black widow catching her prey in a sticky web. At least, that was how William portrayed her.

He revealed many things during the night that I needed to hear, but that crushed my heart further—if that were even possible. She was with him on his trip to Arizona a year ago. Her mother even invited him over for family barbeques since he had been at her place so often. Items in our house he claimed he had found at yard sales were actually gifts from her. It sickened me.

William and I lay motionless in our bed, still in our clothes from the day before. My husband had propped himself partway up on the iron headboard that cradled our king-size mattress. Despite all that I was hearing, my head rested on his chest. His fingers softly stroked my auburn hair. Empty bottles of wine and tequila were strewn about the room, along with the remnants of two entire boxes of empty tissues.

I listened long into the night, though I found a cloudy haze had settled over me. I asked questions, and he answered them. I accepted each answer like a knife cut to my skin. I was covered now in hundreds of tiny wounds.

I was numb. I no longer felt angry, sad, or betrayed. *All I feel is numb.* I realized that I was just a shell of my former self from two months ago. Everything I had known to be my world, to be my *reality*, was just a procession of lies—all of it.

My life, my perfect life, was just one big fable.

My head moved up and down on William's chest to his breathing, shallow and slow. His heart had evened to a steady, if drunken, pace. I could barely move. My mouth was dry, and my tongue was sticky. I could no longer see clearly. Even blinking hurt through my bulging eyes.

"I need to sleep for a couple of hours. Then I have to go to work," I whispered into his chest. *Work.* My first day at a new job. My life was falling apart, yet the world still turned around me.

"Don't go . . . call in, please," William said quietly, his fingers still stroking my hair.

The thought of staying curled up in our bed beside my husband was tempting. But I had never walked away from a new position. An old acquaintance had pulled some strings to get me this side home health nursing job. You don't call in on your first day! And I also knew I needed time away from him to think.

Now that I knew the painful, gut-wrenching, stabbing truth, one final question remained: *What do I do now?*

CHAPTER FOUR

February 2015

"Where has your ass gone, Cindy?" Maggie asked as I entered the restaurant's patio for brunch. She stood and embraced me in a firm hug, even as I felt brittle and fragile in the embrace of my dearest friend.

Nine months had passed, with my husband enduring the daily torment of not knowing if I would be staying or leaving him. I needed that time to see if William might, under all that betrayal, actually be the man I thought he was. The holiday season had passed, feeling like a theater act wrapped in secrets and lies, and then suddenly, February arrived.

It was a warm day for late winter, particularly at noon. The patio had a few patrons spread out over the sea of metal tables and chairs. The colorful array of red and orange umbrellas were perched open, providing shade while guests ate.

The smell of fresh-baked bread, accompanied by bacon and eggs, drifted through the air. At any other time, in any other year, I would have inhaled the sweet smells, tasting them on the back of my tongue, allowing a giant smile to drift across my face.

But not today.

Still, even in the dullness of my world, I couldn't help but notice that Maggie looked radiant. Her dark brown shoulder-length hair was in soft curls, angled inward to accentuate her high cheekbones and firm jawline. Her coordinated leggings and flowy blouse fit perfectly over her petite five-foot frame.

For such a little person, she had a big personality. Maggie's sass was on point today, a trait I loved about her. It was a characteristic we shared, or we used to, before I discovered the truth. Now, I found myself numb, going through the motions of life each day.

Today was the first time I had left William's side, except for work, since I had learned about Rose. Tormenting questions swirled through my mind. *Would William relapse if I wasn't right by his side? Or worse, reach out to Rose?*

Over the years, Maggie was more of a sister to me than just a friend. She was the person I confided in the most, next to William. I had at least shared with Maggie about William's drug addiction since people understood and were even compassionate to people who got addicted to drugs.

But telling her about the affair . . . I knew the news would break her heart as it did mine. Besides, William had begged me not to share the information. He deeply feared how people would judge him.

Upon hearing her greeting in the uncrowded outdoor area, I crooked my head to look at my ass. "It's there, just smaller now," I confirmed with a chuckle.

When was the last time a chuckle left my lips? Nine, maybe ten months ago?

My size 4 jeans that once fit snuggly now hung on me loosely. They were so loose that I had to find a belt today to hold them up.

"We'd better feed you before you get swept up in a strong breeze," Maggie managed with a tinge of concern in her voice. "Tell me, how is William doing? And what's life like in the new place? Because from this view, I would think not so great."

"William is good," I replied with hesitation. "We . . . we found a great counselor for him, and his doctor has him on suboxone, which helps block the effects of opioid medication. He tells me he has been clean for nine months now. And don't be jealous of the diet plan. I may package it up and sell it, make a fortune," I added with another snicker before drinking half of the mimosa Maggie had ordered for me.

I let the coolness of the champagne and orange juice seep down the back of my throat, hitting like a thud into my empty stomach. I licked my lips to savor the sweet flavor a little more before letting the warmth envelop me so I could continue the conversation. I'd need the bubbly liquid courage to share what had happened recently, on top of the addiction and the affair, as if that wasn't enough.

Our lovely home, the beautiful hacienda, was gone.

"The new house is cozy and small but meets our needs. We signed a nine-month lease, which I figured would give us plenty of time to figure out what we want to do next," I began. The memories of the events leading up to selling the hacienda made my breathing and pulse quicken in synchrony.

Due to my hectic work schedule, Maggie had always known that part of William's responsibilities as a stay-at-home husband was maintaining a pool of business loans we had lent to companies in exchange for collateral. We managed deeds and titles to equipment, along with post-dated checks and formal loan documents.

In the beginning, these loans were spread out across multiple debtors. People and businesses that could not obtain loans through usual means, like banks or credit unions, came to us. When our dear friend Marco approached us to help save his cash-strapped drilling company, we felt it would be the right thing to do. Plus, he not only offered but was willing to pay a high interest rate for our loans, doubling our usual charge. We eventually sold off the other loans and focused our lending exclusively on Marco's drilling company.

At that time, three years ago, I still considered Marco an honorable man. That was before I found a video on William's phone through one of my late-night searches. Marco was performing a sexual act with someone other than his wife. It appalled me. We had spent a lot of time with him and his small family: dinner dates, boat trips, and jointly planned parties.

I was torn about telling Marco's wife, but I knew if I did, Marco wouldn't pay back the loans we had lent him, even if we formalized everything. Then, four months ago, things went south anyway: Marco informed William that he would no longer be able to make the loan payments. Marco and his wife had split, and his business would be closing. So when we got the notice from the bankruptcy attorney to meet and review assets, I had no immediate concerns, knowing we had secured all the loans not only with contracts but with collateral.

I was shocked when the attorney read the court document and discovered that only three titles to equipment and vehicles were in our possession instead of the fifteen I thought we held. And William didn't seem surprised at all.

"Are you fucking kidding me!" I screamed at William the moment we got into the Beamer after the hearing. My voice ricocheted off the tinted car windows. "You gave back all of the titles to Marco? Without asking me or, hell, even telling me?"

"I had to," William insisted. "He needed more money for additional equipment for a big job in Montana. And I knew you would disapprove of us loaning him more money. So he threatened that if I didn't give the titles back, his business would go under, and he would have to file for bankruptcy. Then we would never get paid back!" Heat rose in his voice to match mine as he raced his car down the highway at ninety miles an hour.

"Plus," he continued, "you told me you would never forgive me if something happened to these loans and Marco didn't pay. You're always so hard on me."

I couldn't help but notice William's tone raised on the point of "hard on me" as he darted around the cars.

This is not my fault!

Sadness enveloped my rage at that moment when I realized what needed to be done: the only way we could begin to recoup from this devastating loss was by selling our beautiful home.

Even then, I still didn't leave William.

I didn't leave when I found out he was addicted to drugs.

I didn't leave after the truth came out about the affair.

And I didn't leave after he lost the majority of our money.

The pull to stay committed to my Catholic marriage vows was still deep-rooted within me. *I cannot get a divorce, not again.* But why could I not firmly decide to stay in my heart and mind? I knew I needed to say, "I'll stay," out loud to myself, my counselor Nicole, and William.

Why was I still choosing to live in absolute Purgatory, atoning for someone else's sins?

Maggie cleared her throat. "You okay, Cindy?" she asked.

I had been staring at the menu, or through it, anyway. My mind was far away.

"Yeah, sorry, I got lost in thought for a moment." I turned my gaze to Maggie's hazel eyes. "But enough about me and my tragic life. How are the kids and Travis? It has been months since I shared some good news for a change," I said, reaching across the table and squeezing her hand.

CHAPTER FIVE

March 2015

It was a powerful moment when I realized that one of the few things I had control of was me. After months of being stuck, I decided to break out of my vacillation: it was time to move forward. I didn't know what that meant, but I would focus on finding a new home with William for now since the lease on the rental home would be short-lived.

The next three weeks passed with a renewed sense of purpose. The energy I thought would never surface again engulfed me each evening after work. I spent hours searching listing sites for a house that would meet our now very short list of wants.

Our wants . . .

The words lodged in my undecided heart. William and I were still a couple, but I had still not decided to stay or leave my marriage—a verdict that I knew was absolute that I could speak aloud. But since I was still there, with William in our rental, that was an answer in itself.

I recalled the evening a few weeks back when we discussed our checklist of items we desired in our next home. "I don't want neighbors too close," William conveyed as he busied himself in the kitchen with dinner. "No barking dogs, early lawnmowers starting, or garage doors opening and closing at all hours."

My fingers moved fast across the keys of my laptop, capturing every word as I nodded in agreement.

"I would prefer not to be in the city," I added as I continued to type. "Too many people, and the prices are outrageous for homes."

"We will need a gas range to cook and a strong vent. Every time I cook steaks here, the fire alarms go off," William said. He still tried to create culinary masterpieces in the outdated '70s kitchen in our current cramped living quarters. A recent memory of the tiny space filling with smoke as William and I attempted to fan it out the windows and doors with kitchen towels zipped through my mind, leaving a smirk.

"A bit of land would be nice," I fingered, the ideas running rapid-fire in my mind and now onto the screen. "But flat land. No more living on the mountainside either. We're not dealing with extensive snow removal and rock wall maintenance ever again."

"We will need at least three bedrooms and a couple of bathrooms. Space for the workout equipment too," William added.

We continued with a few more items, ruling out some things that seemed too expensive to have or one of us (mostly me) thought were unnecessary.

I stared at the screen, the cursor now just sitting, blinking. In the end, based on our list, our ideal home seemed like a pipe dream: a semi-remote home with enough rooms and space to have the family over, but not too many that they sat empty for long. A bit of flat land, with a kitchen that housed appliances for William's culinary masterpieces and a price tag that would not keep us in debt for years. It all seemed like a difficult, if not impossible, mission.

But it was a mission I was ready for, I remind myself, a task that would keep me moving forward. My online searches hadn't resulted in finding our home yet, but I was optimistic. Plus, searching for a house gave me purpose, steering me away from focusing on things I couldn't change. Instead, it motivated me in the direction of matters I could control—or at least modify.

"What do you think of this house?" I asked William one evening as I leaned over the couch in the rental's family room, showing him pictures on my laptop.

"Is that a split-entry home?" William said hesitantly. "I'm not a huge fan of split entries."

"I don't see it as a split entry; I see it as a two-story home. We'll move the main entrance to the top floor . . . here, and enclose the current front door, make this area into the stairs to the lower level of the house," I envisioned as I pointed and drew the remodel on my screen with my fingertip.

"I thought we agreed that we didn't want our neighbors so close?" William objected. "Based on the pictures, the house has neighbors on all sides."

I pulled the laptop back onto my lap, scrolling through the images. The neighbors were close, and we did agree that was something we wanted less of. I just wanted to keep the costs under control, which William struggled with.

"You're right," I admitted. "I'll keep looking."

As I continued to scroll through the pages, a home caught my eye on a listing site I signed up for. Staring back at me from the screen was a run-down, two-story house with a price tag of $160,000.

I clicked on the link. The house appeared to be a log cabin but was painted a steel blue. The paint was missing and worn in most pictures, but the faded color was apparent. The house was surrounded by mature pine trees towering over the roofline, with maple and oak trees filling the spaces closer to the ground. A large wrap-around porch extended around the front and right side of the house. The white railing was sagging in areas, and some posts were missing. Still, it took my breath away.

I imagined myself with a glass of wine and a delicious book, curled up on a chair on the front porch, gazing at the mountainside in front of the house.

Woodland.

I had never heard of this town—which surprised me, having lived in Utah my entire life. A quick internet search revealed that it boasted a population of 343 people and was fifty-four miles away from Salt Lake City. However, it was close to a town I did recognize: Kamas. At least I knew we could get supplies nearby.

Fifty-four miles up two canyons. With freeways running both ways. The good news was that the commute to and from work would be opposite morning and evening traffic. Still, it would mean 108 miles daily to and from work. At sixty miles an hour, that's about one hour each way. The good news was that the distance of the house would not be too far for our grown children and family to visit, perhaps even stay for the weekend.

The listing stated the fixer-upper had three bedrooms, two and a half baths, a large bonus room off the kitchen, and a loft on the second floor, right off the master suite area. My mouth gaped. It was the exact amount of room we felt we needed when we made our wish list.

Hmm. I assumed $160,000 for the house, which was the listing price, plus another $100,000 to fix it up properly. Minus a small down payment from the sale of the hacienda, it would leave us with a mortgage of $225,000. That would equate to a monthly cost of roughly $1,500.

That was well within our budget, too.

The math was rapid-fire in my head, but what was in my heart was the beginning of a little flame. So warm, I could feel it.

Hope.

CHAPTER SIX

"Wouldn't it be wonderful to have a house up through the canyon? With a river on one side and the mountain ridge on the other? To be in a town with only one stoplight, and neighbors so scarce you could actually hear yourself think?" I asked my brother Charles as soon as he picked up my call, without even saying hello first.

"Don't get me started on too many people," Charles said dryly. "We are overpopulating the earth. All of our natural resources are dwindling; people have children who cannot afford children and then live off the rest of us hardworking, tax-paying citizens. We need to adopt the one-child policy from China."

I rolled my eyes, even though he couldn't see my expression. Charles, "my little brother"—a term I would always use, was now six inches taller than me and thirty-five pounds heavier. It didn't matter; he would always be my little brother.

I had learned to start my conversations with my brother in a way that would hook him before asking for his help. Diminishing resources on this planet was a topic he was passionate about. Charles was a realtor and a talented handyman, along with the majority owner of a house-flipping business he and I had started six months ago. If William and I were to pull off a major renovation project, we would need my brother's help.

"I found a house in Woodland, Utah," I gushed before he could object. "It's near Kamas and about thirty minutes outside of Park City. I really need you to come with William and me to look at it."

"What are you smoking?" Charles asked, and I smiled at the typical response he gave me when he felt I had another off-the-wall idea. Of course, he knew full well I wasn't smoking anything—even though this had become a painful subject in my marriage and was no longer a light-hearted, teasing topic.

"Today, nothing," I shot back smoothly, "but yesterday, I sucked in more smog here in the valley than I care to admit to." I hated the air quality in the Salt Lake Valley. It felt smothering, dirty, and gross—such an oxymoron in such a naturally beautiful state.

"Don't get me started on the smog, the people, and all of their driving!" Charles retorted. "Do they not understand the concept of carpooling and public transportation?" My brother lived on the west side of town, about twenty-five miles from me and sixty miles from Woodland. He would never drive an extra mile to save his life if it meant a carbon footprint.

Still, I pressed.

"So . . . what time can you meet us today to enjoy some smog-free air?"

"Geez," he sighed, then paused. "Around one this afternoon."

Shortly before one o'clock, we made the rude discovery that cellular service stopped working about a half-mile into the mountainous little town of Woodland. Without GPS, our two cars took too many left turns, leading us down an old dirt road into a herd of sheep.

Retracing our steps, we made our way back to the main road, to the two-pump gas station.

"I'll get directions. Wait here," I said to William as I jumped out of our truck, waving to Charles to stay put in his vehicle behind us. As I walked across the parking lot, I couldn't help but think of how the hour-long drive had been filled with shared eagerness between William and me. My cheeks grew hot as I remembered how I slid closer to him on the truck's front seat bench. He then rested his hand on my thigh as he drove. Instead of freezing up, I leaned my head against his broad shoulder. A sense of calmness floated over us, as if we both sensed the possibility of a new future unfolding.

The gas station was empty, except for the large man standing behind the counter. He was Santa Claus round—with a long, brown speckled beard covering his neck.

"Excuse me, sir, can you give me directions to where Maple Loop is?" I asked.

"Well, you see here, ma'am, you go down this here road a bit till you hit the blinking light. Then you make a left. Now you stay on that road and keep headin' east. Go past the cemetery, the buffalo, and the church until you get to the old Camper World. Now, this is where ya gonna turn right. So that there is the loop you be lookin' fer," the gas station attendant said, ending his instructions by spitting tobacco in an empty soda can.

At least, I hoped it was empty.

I thanked him before grabbing some nearby junk food items to purchase. Of course, I didn't need the things, but detailed directions like that deserved some sort of reimbursement!

"I got us snacks, along with directions," I called to Charles and William as I tossed items into their rolled-down windows. "Ready?" I said to William as I climbed back into the truck and popped open a soda can.

"Ready as I'll ever be," he replied, his tone light.

We pulled out of the two-pump gas station and drove down the narrow lane, making a left at the blinking light, with Charles following close behind.

I kept my window rolled down, folding my arms and resting my chin on top of my hands on the windowsill. *It's just how the email described it.* A vast mountain cliff sat to the east, shrouded in various trees, and the hint of spring flowers began to peek through the melting snow that still covered the shady spots.

The Provo River was gushing over its edges from the snowmelt to the west of the road. I caught a glimpse of a fisherman, standing knee-deep in the rushing water in high boots. I watched, mesmerized, as he gracefully moved his fishing pole back and forth. The fine line made loops and folds until it rested gently on the top of the water.

"This is perfect, William!" I cried in delight before scooting beside him, placing my hand on his arm as he drove. I was sitting next to my husband, going down a beautiful back road. At that moment, I felt a closeness to him that I hadn't felt in a while, and it made me believe in the possibility of a future together. It was a connection that I wondered if I would ever feel again. Yet here, in this unfamiliar town I hadn't heard of before today, I felt it. *Absolutely perfect.*

"Yes, it is," he replied, momentarily putting his hand over mine.

"Look, there's the Camper World sign. Make a right." I pointed with excitement. William navigated the turn slowly.

We pulled in front of the driveway, or what we thought was the driveway. It was more of an overgrown weed garden. A rusted chain attached to two posts on either side of the driveway blocked the entrance. The worn "For Sale" sign, just a few feet from the rusted chain, was hanging on with only one ring from the wooden post it was once attached to.

"This is it?" Charles asked a little incredulously as he pushed his truck door closed.

His medium frame sported its usual attire: a T-shirt and khakis. The only thing missing was his tool belt. He had a full beard, speckled with black, brown, gray, and auburn colors. It accentuated his usually serious face, bald head, and sharp nose line.

"It is! I told you it was a fixer-upper!" I exclaimed as I walked over the chain toward the front porch. It took me a few moments to navigate through the foot-high weeds in my eagerness.

The house appeared to be a log cabin in the pictures, painted that steel blue, but the closer I got to the structure, the more I realized that the blue logs were paneling made to look like logs. There was a depth to the rounded pressed-wood form, giving it the appearance of logs from afar. The online pictures had been deceiving. The paneling was worn and far past its prime if it ever had one.

I climbed the steps of the porch, reaching the exterior. I gently chipped away a layer of blue paint with my fingernail. That revealed another lighter layer of blue underneath.

I could hear Charles and William climb the squeaky porch steps behind me.

"What is this? It's not even logs? Is this paneling?" Charles queried, and I turned to see as he pried at a lifted corner of the facade to peer at what was beneath it.

"Apparently, someone wanted a *blue* log cabin," I said.

As I inspected further, I noticed the wrap-around porch had numerous boards missing. It sagged in many areas as if the earth were trying to swallow it, section by section. The railing sloped, curving like a smile versus a straight line, with some posts absent it resembled the appearance of a smiling child with missing teeth.

I followed William as he walked over to the large, cloudy front window. He cupped his hands around his eyes, and I followed suit. An old set of couches stared back at us. The embroidered design of "cowboy and Indian" scenes was something I recalled seeing as a young child at one of my great-grandparents' houses. Unfortunately, these were full of holes, stained, and covered in dirt.

The far left wall inside was covered in mortared rock. The dust had settled in a thick layer across everything, creating a hazy appearance. The back wall was stained a dark yellow, probably from years of neglect. An unfinished wall with exposed two-by-fours blocked our view to the right. Parts of the floorboards were missing, exposing the dirt below.

Interesting . . . I didn't feel the slightest disarray about the house's state.

"This will be a lot of work. A lot. Are you sure this is a good idea?" William said quietly, for only me to hear. There was hesitation in his voice.

"It's a great idea," I replied. I didn't know why. Something in my gut was propelling me toward this house. I had to own it.

"Are you kidding? This is the house you want to fix up? No, this is a house you tear down!" Charles roared as he walked over to where William and I stood, gazing into the window.

"You're not giving it a chance," I coaxed. "Now, come on, work your magic, and find us the key to get in."

William and I continued to walk around the side of the house, to the back, where we discovered another covered porch. It was stacked with broken furniture, firewood, and bags of garbage. A faded brown door, its facade peeling and warped, was set in the middle. To the left was a three-car garage. Like the porch railings, the garage doors sagged in the middle, with overgrown weeds covering the front.

I stopped.

"Can you hear that?" I asked as Charles approached us.

We all stood silent. There it was: a rushing sound, full of crunches and cracks. It was forceful, and it moved my soul. Even though we were on the back porch, the river sounded so powerful, as if we were mere feet away from it instead of yards. I stood there, letting each sound wash over me like a hot shower.

I could feel William as he inched closer to me. He stood beside me, his arm touching mine. "That's amazing," he said softly. The connection to him I felt just moments ago in the truck kindled again, eliciting goosebumps on my arms.

"The lockbox should be over here," Charles said, interrupting the tumult of the water and my lingering thoughts and emotions.

Charles extracted the key and walked over to the brown door, forcing it into the lock. A tiny click resonated as we all fell silent with anticipation.

Or maybe I was the only one waiting with anticipation. I didn't care. I was excited, as if I were about to enter the tomb of a lost treasure. *A treasure that could change my life.* However, the door didn't open with just the turn of the handle. Charles grunted and shoved his shoulder against it until it flew open with a cloud of dust.

"Ladies first," he said, coughing slightly. I knew his sarcastic comment was more directed at the crazy concept of all of this rather than a polite notion.

"Where is the floor?" I demanded as my heart pounded harder. I had almost taken my first step inside. William and Charles stood on either side of me, their attention focused on what had left me open-mouthed.

A giant hole.

It was the size of a soaker tub and took up most of the house's foyer. We all leaned our heads in to get a closer look. I pulled out my cell phone and clicked on the flashlight, shining it into the pit. There, at the bottom, was an old water holding tank. The pipes and tubes that ran under the house, which I assumed it had been connected to, lay in the dirt, broken and bent.

"Well, isn't that interesting?" I said as I straightened back up, carefully keeping my tone light and hopeful. *This house could have the entire floor missing!* I still wanted it.

No, I needed it.

This house would give me a fresh start—a new life. Maybe, being in this space, away from the chaos of the city below, I could learn to trust William again. And then, perhaps, my heart would finally decide.

William straightened up. "A sheet of plywood should fix that up, right, Charles?" William asked as he gazed my way. The comment made me realize he was warming up to the idea of this house. Or maybe he was feeling what I was feeling.

Still hunched over the hole, Charles turned his head toward us, his eyebrow raised as if he were questioning our sanity levels.

I took a few steps back onto the porch and raced forward. I leaped over the hole as if it were just a hurdle at a track race. *Exhilarating.*

"Jump!" I said to both of them after I had landed safely on the other side.

One at a time, they backed up and leaped. Charles landed with a thud. William hit the back of the cowboy couch with his long legs as he landed. A puff of dust exploded in the dimly lit room. He glanced at me as he straightened up, dusting off his pants, a smirk crossing his lips. I returned his smile with one of my own.

The room was a scene from a movie—where a lost, weary traveler finds an abandoned house to weather out a storm or hide from the villains searching for them. It was as if the previous owner had just opened the door to the house and walked away, leaving behind all the belongings he no longer needed for his next journey.

There was an old bench by the entrance. A fishing rod and a baseball bat were perched by the side of the door. Nestled against the far back wall was a dining room table with dishes covered in layers of grime.

A warm, burning sensation filled my chest, casting down to my fingertips. Most people would have walked away, if not run, from a house like this. But I felt a strong pull, like a magnet, drawing me to this house. I was meant to own this house. *This house needs me.*

CHAPTER SEVEN

I continued to walk around the dimly lit living space of the abandoned house. In the corner of my eye, a massive, dark brown beam caught my attention. There were four of them, running east to west across the ceiling. To the right was the wall covered in lava rock we saw from the window, with an antique, rusted wood-burning stove centered in the middle. On the left was an oddly placed set of french doors leading to what appeared to be the unfinished room. The exposed framing and some bare sheetrock had never been finished.

What would possess a person to walk away from this? To leave the items and the house to become a wasted memory?

Charles walked past me, making his way to the unfinished dining room, but he suddenly stopped. He shifted his weight to his left foot and then to his right foot, taking small steps as he did this balancing act.

"I don't think the house is even level," Charles declared. "That means structural issues, which equates to a lot of money, which means we should turn around and walk back out the door."

I added $30,000 to the budget in my head, surprised and pleased that I still wasn't fazed.

I knew what Charles was thinking: this house would be a money pit, or worse yet, a project that would take long hours and many months to finish. We were in prime house flipping season, which was Charles's primary source of income. Asking him to help us with little financial return would be a waste of his time. I would have to make this enticing for him.

William and I walked toward Charles, the floor rising and falling with each step we took.

"It's not that bad," William placated as he balanced on one foot, then the other. "I'm sure it can be leveled easily."

Even *I* knew there was no leveling a floor easily. Charles and I exchanged a quick side glance. Our eyebrows raised, understanding passing between us. We knew how much work this house would need to make it livable again; William didn't.

"Just think of this like a funhouse," I began, lightening my tone. "The ones you went into when the fair was in town. We used to have to pay a dollar to enter, but today, the price of admission is free."

I didn't need to look up to know Charles was now peering at me. I could feel him rolling his eyes at my statement.

"I wonder what's down here," I said as I turned and walked down a dark hall off the living room and makeshift dining area. I could hear William's and Charles's footsteps following close behind me.

The first open doorway led to a room void of all light. We pulled out our cell phones and, in unison, turned on their flashlights. As we scanned the room, an eerie feeling crept over me.

"Be careful," I warned the men with a slight chuckle, trying to lighten the mood. "Freddy and his chainsaw might be hiding in here."

"Which is the exact reason we need to turn around and walk out," Charles said, his breathing picking up pace. But he kept moving forward, shifting his cell phone light throughout the dark room.

There was no Freddy, but a large, rusted water heater stood boldly out of place in the center of the dim room. The walls and floor had brown-stained cabinets lined with sunflower wallpaper scenes. Some of the cabinets were still attached to the walls, while others lay on their sides on the floor, doors pulled off, leaving remnants of old food packages spewed about. This was the gloomiest kitchen I had ever seen. A mouse, caught in the light of our flashlights, scurried past as it clamored for the next place to hide. We all froze momentarily in the room.

"Well, no need to buy pets," I said, letting out the breath I had been holding. "It appears the house comes with them."

I cautiously made my way through the cluttered kitchen, stepping over the garbage and cabinets on the floor to another open doorway on the far side of the wall. This room had windows, allowing sunlight to reveal its disarray. There was also a wall made of lava rock, and in the corner was a free-standing, tarnished, wood-burning stove.

"What is up with all of the lava rock?" Charles commented as he walked over to the wall. William followed, both men tapping away at the stone with debris found on the floor, attempting to gauge how secure the rocks were to the wall. "This wall isn't going anywhere," Charles added.

It was going somewhere, even if it meant chipping away one stone at a time. That plan had already begun to formulate in my head as I walked from room to room.

"Nothing a hammer and pry bar can't get out," William said. He was becoming my ally on this quest; in my heart, I hoped he realized this house was what I needed to move forward.

Making our way back out of the kitchen and down a small hall, we discovered two bedrooms. The rooms looked to be in decent shape. After the floor was leveled and new flooring laid, it would only need a fresh coat of paint.

Walking back down the hall, we stopped at what would have been the hall bathroom. "Well, look at this," I said as I shined my cell phone light into the darkened room. The ceiling and back walls were missing, exposing the joists and studs. Remnants of insulation drooped down from the rafters above.

A strong odor lingered in the air, causing me to pull my shirt up and cover my nose.

"I'm going to skip looking into the tub at this point," I said to Charles, my voice muffled through my clothing. "I don't want to see the source of the odor." Whatever was in the tub, and the tub itself, would be thrown away anyway. A grin crossed my shirt-covered mouth when I realized I had begun planning the remodel of this house in my mind even before I owned it.

I was surprised that nothing I had seen made me scream or run from the house in defeat. In fact, everything I saw made me want it more. Each cringe-worthy challenge that I shone my light on only gave me more desire to fix it. I knew I could build it to be better than it had ever been previously.

Off the foyer in the entry, past the crater-sized hole, was a set of open stairs to the second level. There was no railing, and a few of the planks were missing. I jumped back over the hole and lunged up two or three stairs at a time, trying to avoid falling through the open slots.

"Come on, you two!" I called from the top of the stairs. "We still have a second floor to look at."

"A second floor full of more reasons you should not buy this house!" Charles shouted up the staircase through the slats.

I ignored his comment and began to stride across the loft I was now standing in. An alcove encased the windows at each end of this open space. I walked to the west window and peered out. I could see the river from here, just across the street, beyond its bank.

The water was forceful, raging, and colored with the reflection of the budding trees, gray rocks, and blue sky. Pops of spring flowers in orange and yellow made their way through the dirt. I could hear William's and Charles's heavy footsteps as they climbed the stairs and crossed the loft to where I stood. I left them standing there as they quietly took in the scenery.

I walked over to the east window. The mountainside stood in regal form like a wall that could never be moved. That wall was made of dirt, rocks, and low-lying vegetation in shades of yellow, green, and orange. The mountain ridge cascaded high above the roofline of the house. I could imagine the sunset over the hill, the glow bathing the porch below. There were patches of snow that still lingered in the shady areas. Trees and shrubs had begun to bloom where the sun was kissing the earth.

This was stunning. The warmth of possibility that ignited inside me when we arrived had the fuel turned up. It was now a raging fire of desire for one thing: to own this house.

I had never owned a home with such natural beauty surrounding it like the river and mountain bank here. Like all my previous homes, the windows here didn't showcase neighbors' houses. Instead, they allowed the viewer to glimpse a world void of distractions. This beauty was so innocent it could only be created by Mother Nature and kept that way because mankind did not touch it.

Sure, the house would take a lot of work to be livable again, but the bones of this place were solid. I could feel it. This house deserved to be returned to its former glory, or better yet, a new, renowned brilliance. And so did I.

I walked through a door off the loft to a room lined with shelves and another bay window facing the river. The shelves were stained, with chipping paint. The alcove was a barren slab of blemished wood.

Across from the bay window, in the room lined with shelves, was another doorway. It led into a master bathroom. The sub-floor was missing, leaving it open to the rafters, along with the walls stripped down to the studs. The toilet was missing, and the sink was hanging on by remnants of broken cabinets. Another water heater had taken up residence in the far corner of the room. In the center stood a gigantic, pale pink jetted tub. It was so enormous I wondered how it possibly could have gotten in here. More so, *How am I going to get it out of here?*

I strolled past the men as they walked into the master bathroom. "What the hell is this?" I heard Charles comment to William. "Another water heater? And there isn't even a floor in here. Is that mold I smell?"

I ignored his comments as I continued to walk into the last room. The house could be full of mold, and I still wanted it.

To the left of the room, lined with shelves, the last room was the master bedroom itself. It was small but cozy. The floor was covered in stained, worn, walnut-brown shag carpet. Built-in shelves were nestled on each side of the room. A gigantic chestnut beam cascaded down the center of the ceiling and extended all the way through to the loft. It had insulation protruding around its edges, and at the far end of the beam, nestled against the wall, was a hornet's nest.

The men entered the room as I walked over to the nest, staring at it with awe and glee. It felt like the cherry on top of my new home.

"The entire house needs to be jacked up and leveled," Charles said, a hint of unwillingness in his voice. "That will at least be $30,000. All new plumbing and wiring will run you around $10,000. And who knows what else we will find behind the walls? You'll need a new roof and HVAC system. Add another $15,000 for that. Have I got your attention yet? This. Is. A. Money. Pit."

"Not to mention I will need a whole new kitchen," William interjected, "with gas appliances and a faucet above the stove, including a powerful hood vent."

"See? This is what I'm trying to tell you," Charles barked over at me. "You will sink more money into this house than what it's worth."

Charles knew I would foot the bill for this, and I also knew his heart was in the right place. He was just trying to ensure that his sister didn't get in over her head. But he didn't know the whole truth about the secret I had been hiding for almost a year. He didn't know how much I needed to escape my life in the city, and this house was my ticket out.

I continued to stare at the nest, my breathing becoming slow and shallow, and then my gaze lowered out the window below the nest. I could see the side lot from here, covered in shrubs. A squirrel scurried through the dirt, escaping into a nearby tree. I felt my lips curve into a smile.

"I don't care," I began in a low and firm voice. Finally, I turned around to face them. "I want this house. This house will become our home."

It wasn't a question anymore. I'd just made it a statement of the direction I was going to go.

Charles shook his head in despair, realizing nothing he said would change my mind. William looked over at me, his expression softening as he observed the seriousness on my face. He understood my need to own this home and to flee to a remote town, because he also sought an escape.

"Let's leave Cindy to her daydreaming," William suggested, interrupting the silence between us. "Let's go find the door to the crawl space to get a good look at what we would be dealing with if we bought the house."

I stared back out the window for a moment more. Their footsteps and chatter became quieter as they strode back down the stairs.

I walked across the room, allowing my fingertips to trace the edge of the shelves. I felt warm, giddy almost. The realization that I could be happy again was settling in. I imagined what each room in the house could become. In my mind, I rolled fresh cream paint on every wall, added wainscoting to the living room and hall walls, and knocked down the walls of the makeshift dining room and kitchen, opening the space to allow light to flood every surface.

Next, I envisioned a large farm sink anchoring the kitchen, along with crisp white cabinets and black knobs. I could almost hear the family gatherings now, including glasses clanking in toasts and laughter filling every corner, in every room.

I saw myself sitting on the porch, cradling a long-stem wine glass in my hand. The railing was no longer bowing, and I gazed over the land while the leaves shuffled lightly in the breeze. I could almost hear the birds singing their song in the calmness of the evening and the bustling of the squirrels as they scurried around for food.

I imagined escaping the life I did not want that was thrust upon me in the city below the canyons. Instead, this house gave me hope that I could learn to breathe, laugh, and trust again.

CHAPTER EIGHT

"Sign here, and initial there, and date here," Chris, the escrow agent at the title company, instructed William and me. He turned the papers over, pointing to the areas to fill in. "The money from your lender has already been wired to our escrow account. We'll file the documents first thing in the morning when the county office opens, and then, the house is yours."

I looked over at William and gave him a smile so big I could feel it tug at the edges of my ears. As we signed the last document in the small conference room, my stomach was full of butterflies. Light streamed through the glass walls from the escrow office's front windows, casting a glow over my husband's face. William smiled back, grabbing my hand under the table and squeezing.

It had taken Charles a little over a week to find the owner of the house, Samuel, who had moved to Mississippi to be closer to his family. Samuel had rented the place out for a while, but the tenants had trashed it. After they were asked to leave, the house sat abandoned for several years.

He had received a low-ball offer for the house just five days before Charles called to inquire about the listing. Samuel had not yet accepted it, stating to my brother, "It just didn't feel right." With haste, Charles submitted a full-price offer on our behalf, which was still a bargain. We were under contract that very same day.

"It's ours . . . it's finally ours," I said as we left the office nestled in a strip mall. Hand in hand, we walked across the parking lot. It was a cool afternoon at the end of March, warm enough that a coat wasn't needed, but cool enough that long sleeves were necessary.

Ours. Was the house ours? *Am I finally leaning toward a firm decision to stay with this man?* My husband, the man I had committed to for better or worse. Maybe I was. Or perhaps it was the exhilaration of closing on the house I desperately wanted. Whatever it was, it was ours.

But I still couldn't bring myself to say the words aloud. Something still held me back from voicing the sentence, "I choose to stay with my husband." Was it the lack of trust I still felt toward William? Even though nothing made me question his renewed commitment to our marriage over the last few months. That had to be it—trust, or lack thereof.

"We have a month to get the demolition done," I proclaimed, focusing my thoughts on the present as we both opened the car doors and climbed into the warm cab. "Then, Charles will be ready to help with the rebuilding."

The demolition would be my and William's responsibility. That was part of the deal we made with Charles. That allotted him time to finish the house flip he was working on. William had wanted to tackle the whole project, including the rebuilding, with just some assistance from Charles. I barely considered that plan: As much as I loved William, he was a cut-corners guy, but Charles was attentive to details. I wanted this to be done right. I needed the investment to last.

I chose my words carefully when I responded to William right after we were under contract. "I'd prefer to have Charles do it, with your help, of course," I said, my voice low and soft.

"This will give you an opportunity to learn how to do certain handyman work and help in the house-flipping business down the road. Plus, he has all the tools, something we can't afford right now, what with the project's cost itself."

I knew that wasn't what William wanted. Still, he had already gotten his way with so many things over the last eleven months, including coming and going from jobs whenever he pleased. I no longer needed a stay-at-home husband; I needed a partner, another contributor to the monthly budget.

He had been let go from one job and had quit two other jobs. After studying for months to obtain his loan officer license, he'd only lasted a week at that one. I begged him to give the job another chance. Adjusting would take time since he hadn't worked for a company in years. He didn't. I hated that I had begun to feel that he had no cares regarding money. My husband got to choose the path he wanted, and I was left holding the bag of responsibility in our financial relationship.

William wanted his freedom to come and go as he pleased. He refused to account to anyone that would result in only a measly couple thousand dollars a month. That was the impression I got from his actions, but those couple thousand to me were golden. They meant I was not the only one contributing to the household budget.

But William saw an opportunity to participate in a side business of flipping houses that Charles and I had started. The extra money the company had been making helped recoup some of the losses from the Ponzi scheme we fell victim to the year before.

William saw the profits coming in and wanted a part of it. He felt he could help grow the business by doing more house flips. I figured it was another way for my husband to avoid the corporate rat race of blue-collar work. Still, I could only devote so much time to the flipping business. My full-time job quickly propelled me into senior leadership positions. Charles thought William could help with the running-around work, county auctions, and such.

So . . . I begrudgingly agreed.

The day after we closed on the Woodland property, William went to work preparing for demolition. First, he had a large dumpster delivered in front of the drooping garage of the property, smashing down the overgrown weeds. Then, with the help of a couple of day workers he'd picked up in Salt Lake City, he cleared the house of all the old furniture, garbage, and loose debris from the inside and back porch.

"Look at that!" I exclaimed as William and I turned the corner onto the back dirt driveway of the Woodland house that Saturday, three days after we closed on the property. I could see the garbage protruding past the top of the dumpster edge. "You have this dumpster almost full. And, look! I can actually see the back porch. It's clear and spacious without the junk taking it over."

He parked the truck next to the forty-foot dumpster. I hastily climbed out and went over to the side of the dumpster, hoisting myself up to peer in. It was filled with the old cowboy couch and chairs, water heaters, and piles of wood and garbage that once lay strewn through the abandoned house and porch.

"You got a lot done in just a few days," I said as I jumped down, walking toward William, now standing on the back porch. I grabbed the crook of his arm, pulling him down and kissing his cheek.

"I'm proud of you," I said lightly, my tone filled with joy. Maybe this type of work aligned better with my husband's needs, unlike the past three jobs he tried this year. Perhaps he was meant to become a construction worker type of guy, and I just needed to give him the chance to learn and become better at this skill.

"We are on a tight timeline," William said earnestly before kissing my forehead. He then turned and unlocked the back door, swinging it open. The hole in the foyer had been covered by a piece of plywood, allowing us to walk across easily. Once filled with old furniture and garbage, the house was now clear. I stepped carefully through the foyer, gazing at the amount of space that appeared in its now barren state.

My chest swelled, and my hands tingled. I spun in a circle in the clear, open living space, my arms outstretched from my body. *I was full of excitement and possibility!* I had been looking forward to this day for weeks. This was the first weekend I got to roll up my sleeves and help bring this home back to life.

And in turn . . . I hoped it would help rebuild my life again.

"So . . ." I began as I stopped spinning, walking across the wavy floor to the kitchen doorway. "Do you still agree that we start the demolition in the kitchen first?"

We had spoken that morning, on the drive up to Woodland from our rental, about what room to tackle first. We settled on the kitchen since I could carry out the remnants of cabinets and counters from the demolition, unlike the ginormous pale pink tub from the master bath or the massive lava walls that would take careful chipping stone by stone.

"Yeah," William replied, his tone enthusiastic. "Come help me gather the sledgehammers, pry bars, and stand-up lamp out of the truck." We headed toward the electrical pole on the corner of the lot where the power had been turned on, plugging in our bright orange extension cord and trailing it through the house to the dark kitchen.

William set up the construction lamp and flipped the switch, allowing the 1000-watt bulb to flicker and illuminate the space as if a sun had just risen in the corner of the room. The blaring light highlighted the kitchen's state of disarray. Four cabinets were still hanging on the walls, their open doors showcasing the tattered, stained sunflower wallpaper that lined the back of the cabinet shelves. The bottom cabinets formed an *L* shape along two of the walls. Most of the lower cabinet doors were missing, and the few left were barely hanging on by single rusted hinges. The dilapidated coffee-brown Formica countertop, covered in stains and round burn rings from pans, held them all in place.

What remained of the painted walls of the kitchen were stained a straw yellow, along with brown and black streaks running from ceiling to floor. William and the day workers had cleared the loose garbage out of the room, including the massive water heater.

Before grabbing the sledgehammers, William and I put on white coveralls, goggles, and masks. We paused for a second, looking into each other's cloudy eyes behind our goggles. "Are you ready?" William mumbled.

"Ready as I'll ever be," I replied, my voice muffled.

With all my strength, I thrust the sledgehammer into the side of one of the hanging upper cabinets, watching the hammer knock it off the wall with a loud thud. It crashed to the floor, breaking into several pieces. *That felt good.* A portion of the anger, betrayal, and hate I held onto was finally released with that first swing.

This is exhilarating.

William swung, and a sizeable double cabinet clattered to the floor, shattering into pieces.

We're on fire! We took turns thrashing the hammers into the rest of the upper cabinets, stepping out of the way as they tumbled to the floor with a thundering clatter. In no time at all, we carried all the broken pieces out to the dumpster, tossing them over the metal side into the pile of rubble.

Without pause, we turned our attention to the lower cabinets. I thrust my hammer down on the old Formica countertop. It acted as a springboard, shooting the sledgehammer back up. I stumbled backward, falling on my caboose.

"You okay?" William asked through his mask, concern racing through his eyes. He stepped toward me, but I put my hand up to stop him. And then . . . I burst into laughter. It was a loud, booming, deep-belly laugh as if it had been bottled up way too long, which it had.

"I'm fine . . . more than fine, in fact," I spewed between my laughter. "This is the best therapy any money can buy. We should have done this ten months ago."

William reached down after my laughter slowed, hoisting me back up. "You have a morbid sense of humor, love. But you're right . . . this does feel good."

The floor cabinets came next, and even though I was just as eager to smash them, they were not as keen to move as the top cabinets were. Something kept those old cupboards stuck in place even with our combined strength. Inch by inch, William and I pried the cabinet up, then stood back to catch our breath. Small tunnels made of debris formed part of a nest beneath where the cabinet had been.

"Is this what was holding the cabinet firmly in place?" I questioned, walking over to get a closer look. "A rodent's nest?"

William walked to my side. "Apparently so."

We continued the slow process with the rest of the lower cabinets, prying, pulling, and loosening each one until they all toppled over. Standing hunched over, laboring to catch our breaths, we pulled our glasses and masks down. "That was brutal," I said through gasps. "There is no way a rodent's nest could have been that strong to hold them in place like that."

But then I noticed an intricate maze plastered in the now-open space. Whatever rodents had claimed this space as their home had carried in twigs, dried leaves, foliage, stuffing, and debris from the couch. They created their own community of sorts. The pathways and nests that wound around the back two walls where the lower cabinets once stood were a work of art. I stared in amazement at the intricacy of the tunnels, following their paths to the different areas where food was stored, nests were built, and openings appeared to the ground underneath.

"These had to have been here for years," I whispered in awe as I reached down with my gloved hand to touch one of the tunnel walls. It was firm and solid, almost as if mortar had been poured over the twigs and debris, holding them securely in place. Of course, there was no mortar, but the rodents knew how to pack a wall tightly.

I let the nest lay exposed as we carried the pieces of the broken lower cabinets out to the dumpster, and then, like everything else in my life, I began to clean it up. I scooped the maze's walls up with a flathead shovel, placing them in a garbage bag.

As the sun set over the west mountainside in front of the house, casting an orange glow through the front windows, William and I stood back in admiration of the now barren state of the kitchen. Everything in the room had been torn down, including the sheetrock, leaving the exposed studs ready for rebuilding. The full dumpster of rubble from this morning was now overflowing with the added remnants of the kitchen.

We packed the tools into the truck's bed, and as I pulled my aching body into the cab, I realized this was just the beginning of this project. Day three, in fact. And yet, every cramp, cut, and ache I bore on my dirt-covered body felt good.

This, I realized, was what moving forward felt like.

It took a little over four weeks to complete the demolition of the house, clearing it down to the studs in most areas. The forty-foot dumpster was filled and emptied three times during April. Throughout the destruction, the recent inhabitants of the house were relocated or given proper burials. The lot included two dead cats, three gophers, two raccoons, one skunk, and many, many mice. Okay, maybe the mice just got tossed in the dumpster; there were too many to count.

Every layer we took off of the house revealed hidden secrets to fix. Tube-and-knob wiring was discovered throughout the main floor walls. Within all the bathrooms, the plumbing was connected to nothing. The guest bathroom had three tile layers; the previous owners had added another layer to the top instead of removing a layer.

The unfinished dining room walls were torn down, along with the studs that separated the kitchen and living space. The west mountain sunlight illuminated the open space in its destructed state. It was beautiful. The home was becoming a blank canvas, waiting for a masterpiece to be created.

The two walls in the house covered in lava rock were the most challenging project of all, and William waited until the end of the demolition phase to remove them. Each stone needed to be chipped out individually due to the amount of mortar used to secure them in place.

I happened to be in between meetings when he was doing this task. My phone buzzed on top of the stack of patient charts I was holding while walking to a conference room.

Does this look bad? the text from William read.

I set the stack of files down on the conference room table, picked up my phone, and zoomed in on a picture of William's face. His eye was entirely red, vibrant red. It looked as if every blood vessel had popped, and what was supposed to be white was now a pool of blood contained in a globe.

What happened? I typed back, concern overcoming me as I zoomed in and out of the picture on my phone.

I think I hit a bullet with the hammer and pry bar while removing the lava rock.

I replied feverishly, trying to wrap my head around what I saw. **Like a bullet from a gun? In the mortar that surrounded the lava rock? Who would put ammunition in mortar?** I replied, thinking through if he needed to rush to the emergency room or not.

Yeah, a bullet that you put in a gun. I was chipping away, and then, BAM, a blast threw me to the ground. Do you think I should go to the hospital? I can still see, and it only hurts a little.

I was surprised to read that response from him. William had always been the type to make a big deal if he got hurt, even for minor injuries.

You may need to. You're not having any blurry vision at all? I asked.

No, I can still see, it's not blurry. So I think I will keep going. I almost have the front room wall done.

There is this item I heard of, goggles. You should try wearing them. I'm told they protect your eyes. And if your vision changes, even in the slightest, you better call me, I replied, my worry subsiding a bit.

You're funny. I'll let you know if my vision changes. See you tonight.

William's eye stayed red for weeks, yet he still chose not to see a doctor. "As long as my vision is okay, I want to finish the demolition on time," he answered me one day when I urged him to go to the clinic. I hadn't seen William so driven to work on something in years. The lingering thought I had that first Saturday cascaded through my mind again.

Maybe he is cut out to be a construction worker. Perhaps this is what he is meant to do.

Whatever William was meant to do, we did finish the demolition on time. That final weekend, William cleared what remained of the mortar from the lava rock. I went around the house, pulling out the remaining staples and nails from the walls and floor.

"Whistle while you work, do do do do do do," I softly sang through my mask as I swept each room and between each stud. It surprised me that I was singing again, even if it was a *Snow White* song. The laughing, singing, and hope were pieces of myself that I thought had died. But this house was already transforming me as we began to restore it.

When the sun finally set and the tools had been packed away in the truck, William and I walked through the house, discussing the vision of each room. "The two guest bedrooms at the end of the hall on the first floor," I said, my voice firm with direction, "just need a fresh coat of paint on the walls after the floors are leveled. Then a good cleaning to the original tongue-and-groove wood ceilings will do wonders."

We continued to walk down the hall on the first floor. "The guest bathroom will be off-white," I continued, pointing at the barren walls in the room, "with subway tiles surrounding the deep soaker tub, one with high walls for the grandchildren to wash in after a long day of playing in the dirt and river."

We strode to the kitchen area, which would become the house's focal point. "Are you still okay with floor-to-ceiling white cupboards with black knobs, along with a farmhouse sink?" I asked, glancing at William as he stared out the front windows to the west.

"As long as I can have a big gas range with a high-power fan for cooking, you can do whatever you want with the cupboards and sink," he stated, not looking at me.

"And here we will put in french glass doors, allowing the western sun to spill in and illuminate the space," I said excitedly, pointing to the area on the wall where they would go.

William didn't seem to be as excited as I was. But I didn't care; I was electrified for the first time in months. "And just look at the original hearth made from river rock you uncovered under the old lava rock. We will have a real wood-burning fireplace," I continued, walking over and touching the exposed rounded gray and brown stones.

I stood there before the fireplace, thinking about the upstairs rooms. The loft would be converted into an office on one end and an exercise area on the other end. The dressing room would house custom shelving for our wardrobes, and the window alcoves would have cushions, perfect for curling up with a good book on a cold day.

The master bath would showcase a clawfoot tub under the window, where the bank of mountains to the west could be gazed upon while soaking. There would be double vanities on each side of the door, with a corner glass shower stall to the far right and a toilet room to the far left.

I cleared my throat, turning to where William stood, getting his attention. "Let's walk the lot and discuss what we would like to do out there," I said, my mood more subdued now.

"Of course," William responded, following me out the back door, his tone less lively.

"Maybe we could have a small guest house someday to the south of the house, on the side acreage." I trudged a few paces faster than William to the area. "Perhaps a horse with a stable. Chickens. I surely needed a chicken coop up here!" I exclaimed as we walked. My excitement soared again like a child on Christmas morning. There were so many possibilities, and they all meant the same thing: I was moving forward.

"I'm just going to stroll over to the edge of the lot and gauge how much land we have," William said neutrally, staring into the distance.

My joyful mood came to a sudden stop. *Something's off with my husband* . . . he usually looked at me when he spoke and held my hand as we walked. But tonight, I watched him step away from me, his right hand twitching. He stopped at the far southwest corner of the lot, then crossed his arms around his midsection. *Was he sick?*

"Are you okay?" I yelled over at him. Concern, along with an uneasy feeling, drifted through me. He shot me a wave without turning around.

Something is definitely wrong.

I retraced our steps over the last month. We had both worked long days, spending our weekends in Woodland doing the demolition. Was he just exhausted? Was this project turning out to be too much for him? Was he still mad that Charles would be leading the rebuilding? Whatever it was, that uneasy feeling began to grow inside me. It was the same uncomfortable feeling I had felt only twice before: the night I found the text on my husband's phone and the night I learned the truth.

CHAPTER NINE

May 2015

"Hey, you're home. How was your day?" I asked William over my shoulder as he strolled into our rental a little after nine pm. We were a week into the rebuilding of the Woodland house; May 7 had just passed. It had been a little over a year since I found the fatal text on my husband's phone and five weeks since we closed on our major DIY project.

But tonight, in the late evening hours, I didn't *really* care about how William's day was, nor did I want to talk about mine. Asking was the polite thing to do. My attention was focused on my laptop, which contained the work I still needed to finish. I was in a sour mood, having been interrupted earlier in the evening.

"Those floors will be the death of us," William replied, his words coming out fatigued, just like his slouching shoulders as he heaved off his work boots. "Charles and I finally got the jacks under the house, but the three metal I-beams are heavy and difficult to hoist into place with just the two of us."

"Well, we knew the floors would be the biggest challenge," I replied, my eyes not leaving the screen in front of me. "I made some chili dogs. They're on the stovetop," I added, hoping my short answer and the fact that I did not turn to look at him would end our conversation. I was in no state to talk tonight. I was tense, uneasy. My pulse had been racing all evening.

"Thank you. I'm starving." William trudged past me in the dining nook, kissing my cheek on his way to the kitchen. I wiped the kiss off my cheek as he walked away. He didn't notice since his back was to me.

The disturbing call from Charles replayed in my mind from earlier that evening:

"I think you just need to find someone else to rebuild this house," Charles stated abruptly as soon as I picked up the line. His tone was dripping with frustration. "This will take months, and William—he is a pain in my ass! First, we had to redo two footings before placing the jacks under the house due to *his* sloppiness. He knows better. Second, your husband broke one of the jacks, which just about killed us both because he didn't put his end of the I-beam in correctly."

I sighed, but he didn't let up.

"Not to mention that man takes way too many shortcuts, which resulted in one of the interior walls cracking when he was jacking up the house! He did not bother showing up again until 10:30 this morning when we agreed on 8:30. And then he took a fucking two-hour lunch break! Cindy, if he is supposed to be helping me, he needs to be here."

"Well, did you talk to him about this?" I replied, irritated that he had interrupted my intense evening work deadlines to complain about William.

I had recently been promoted to a nursing leader role. It was a role I needed, not because I needed the extra load of reports to complete and charts to check, but because the money was vital. More compensation for my time would allow us to pay for the rental we were in and the Woodland house with its ever-mounting remodel expenses. Working late had become the norm for me.

"No. He's your husband. You talk to him," Charles replied, his voice snide.

"You do realize I'm his wife." My voice rose, matching Charles's frustration. "I'm not his mother, nor am I the foreman of this job! You are."

"Maybe we should let him work on the house in Woodland by himself. The two-hour drive each day is killing me already."

"No, I don't trust him to do it right; I trust you. We have an agreement." I paused, taking a deep breath before replying more calmly. "I'll talk to him and remind him we agreed you are the one who would guide the work; he is to be there to learn and assist. I'll emphasize the 'be there.' Look, I have to go. I have work to finish. I'll call you tomorrow."

And with that, I hit the End button on my screen. The last thing I needed was for Charles to stop working on the house because of William.

But even as I tried to refocus on the work I desperately needed to finish, Charles's words lingered in my mind. *Plus, he did not even show up until 10:30 this morning, and then he took a two-hour lunch break.*

Something was off about that. As I stopped and pondered it, the hair on the back of my neck stood up, and a cold chill shivered down my body. *Why was my husband showing up late?* He was getting ready each morning well before seven, just like me. I had assumed he left for Woodland shortly after I left for work. *And why such a long lunch?* My mind raced back to the week before when we walked the lot after the final demolition day. His hands had twitched, and he'd clutched his midsection in the distant corner of the lot. A pit formed in my stomach.

Please, Lord, not again.

Charles's frustration continued through the following month of the remodel. I heard from him almost daily. It was either to voice his frustration about the project itself or tell me something I needed to do, like pick out tiles or light fixtures. But most often, it was to complain about William.

I would try to mediate the complaints about William. *My brother, the perfectionist.* The guy who must think through things thoroughly, measure ten times, and cut once, was attempting to work with my husband, the "let's just get it done the first time" guy and "consequences be damned."

But William's lateness and long lunches continued sporadically. I found myself looking through our phone records again, trying to locate numbers I didn't recognize. I wasn't prying now—I had long ago told William I would do so in order to build trust with him again. But the phone records held nothing out of the ordinary.

Am I just being paranoid?

I tried to bring things up in conversations with William subtly: "Charles needs us to pick out the flooring, so he called me on his way home. He also said you didn't show up until eleven this morning. Everything okay?" I was careful to pose my question as a concern versus a witch hunt.

"Yeah, everything is fine. I just had to run by Mom's house to help her with her washer," or, "Of course, remember, you needed me to get the oil changed in the truck," he would reply, his voice almost too calm. Some of the errands made sense, but others didn't quite align. *When did I ask him to get the oil changed?*

None of it mattered: the reasons or the answers.

Something just *did not* feel right.

The gnawing ache in my gut would not go away. I knew Charles struggled to work with William, and I knew William felt the same about Charles at times. But it was more than just that. More than just friction between them. Something more was going on; I could feel it.

The two most important men in my life had gotten along for over a decade. Could it be this house? Or perhaps it was how William had edged his way into the house-flipping business that Charles and I started. Could that be what drove the wedge between them? Or could my brother have picked up on something that was bothering me, too?

I continued to remind myself of the advice Nicole, my counselor, had given me in a session months ago. "Trust is given easily at the beginning of a relationship. But when trust is broken, rebuilding takes a lot of time and consistent actions."

It was true—I still didn't trust William. I knew it would take years to rebuild that trust if it ever happened. *Maybe all of this is in my head?* Rebuilding a house takes a toll on the people involved. And my recent job change had left me in a position of needing to prove that I was leadership material, which equated to working long hours.

Maybe this was why I couldn't decide whether to stay or leave William. Perhaps trust, or lack thereof, was the real barrier. That had to be it.

The first two weeks of the remodel could have been a "what not to do" show on TV. We chose to forgo the expensive $40,000 bid to have a professional contractor level the floor and foundations. Instead, we watched hours of online videos and read numerous how-to websites.

The house was currently standing on fifty-year-old piles of stones for support. It wasn't hard to see how much they had deteriorated, with the subfloor gone in most places, revealing the ground below which I found myself becoming intimate with, having fallen through the beams to the dirt on more than one occasion.

It was just the three of us doing the work, and I could only help on weekends. It was painstaking to dig ten footing holes two feet down and place twenty fifty-pound footing cinder blocks in the tiny three-foot crawl space. But that's what the videos and websites recommended. Each jack had to be strategically raised millimeter by millimeter while a laser level inside the house measured the accuracy. Next, six heavy-duty jacks were placed to hold three massive I-beams to support the sagging floor. When the house was finally level and the new subfloor was laid, walking across the flat surface through the main floor was exhilarating. Step one, done.

Step two was to rerun new electrical wiring through the house and remove the old tube-and-knob wires uncovered during the demolition. Roles of wire were strewn across the house as we tugged and pulled through the exposed and not-exposed framed walls. That lasted for days. Then, finally, we could turn the power on in the house, making it easier to use the tools that required electricity for the rest of the remodel. Next would be plumbing, followed by sheetrock. The list continued to grow as more items to fix were uncovered in the rebuilding process.

On a mild June Friday night, I could finally take a breath. The sun slowly crossed the eastern sky, casting shadows through the rental's living room window onto the sofa. As the gentle June breeze blew through the open window, I heaved a deep sigh of relief. William would prepare steaks dripping in butter and garlic, served alongside golden-brown steak fries. I would prepare sliced baguettes toasted lightly in olive oil and chopped romaine lettuce, drizzled with Caesar dressing.

I picked up the phone and called William, which had become a habit of mine after a few weeks into the Woodland project. I didn't know if it was just because I wanted to hear his voice and how his day went in an attempt to rekindle the flame I had felt with him when we started this project. Or if it was my sly attempt to check up on him, making sure he wasn't taking a detour where he shouldn't be on his way back to the rental. I sighed as I dialed, realizing it was probably a combination of both.

"How far out are you?" I asked once he answered. I walked over to the cabinet, pulling down a wine glass, phone balanced on my shoulder.

"About an hour," William replied, his tone light yet tired. "Will you take the steaks out of the fridge so they can start getting to room temperature?" I was going in that direction anyway to find wine. Juggling the phone on my shoulder, I pulled the steaks from the refrigerator and placed them on the stove. I found a corked bottle and set it on the counter.

"Of course. Anything else I can prepare for you?" I asked, pulling the cork out and pouring the bottle's contents into the tall, stemmed glass.

"No. You can help me with the rest when I get home."

"Sounds good. I have a few more things to finish for work, but I should be able to get it all done before you get home. I'll see you soon," I said, and hung up after he said goodbye. I didn't have things to finish. Not work things. William's late arrivals and long lunches that Charles continued to share had started weighing on me heavily.

The phone bills turned up nothing, but I felt myself falling back into detective mode again since the intuitive ache in my gut would not go away. I took a large gulp of wine and leaned against the counter.

I imagined a tiny angel and devil from the *Looney Tunes* cartoons of my childhood materializing on each of my shoulders as I leaned against the Formica counter, sipping the cool white wine. My hurt and betrayal pooled to the surface, prompting a need for action so that I could move past these feelings.

The devil's voice whispered in my left ear, "An hour would give you enough time to check a couple of his online accounts just to ensure he is still faithful."

"I would not do that, Cindy. You need to learn to trust him; this is not the way to get there," the angel's voice whispered in my right ear.

"The only way to rebuild trust is to check up on him!" the devil said sternly.

The angel softly uttered, "The only way to rebuild trust is to ask him."

"She can't just ask him!" Now, the devil was nearly screaming. "He lies and hides the truth! She needs to take one little peek. If there is nothing there, she'll feel better."

"Fine," the angel conceded with a huff.

I pushed myself off the counter and walked over to William's laptop on the table. *Do I really want to do this?* I turned and walked back into the kitchen and began to pace. The pressure in my chest was building. My need to know was like an itch that had to be scratched. I walked back over to the laptop, flipping open its lid.

William knew I checked his online activity from time to time, an agreement we had made in one of our come-to-Jesus talks. Logging into his email easily this time, I scrolled through dozens of messages. Heat rose in my chest and onto my neck. My breathing sped up. Maybe the angel was right, this wasn't a good idea, but it was too late to turn back.

I kept scrolling through mundane communications: confirmation of BMW parts being ordered for his car, a new nail gun for the flooring install, and a few recipe emails for meals I assumed he wanted to make in the new kitchen.

I let out a long exhale of air, not realizing I had been holding my breath. I raised my hand to close the laptop lid, relief washing over me, and then something caught my eye.

Again.

A message notification from one of his social media accounts.

From Rose.

A lump formed in my throat as I opened the email to read the message. "No worries, I still have a lot of 30s when you have time."

I reread it . . . again and again.

30s . . . fuck. Oxycodone.

I minimized his email and clicked over to his social media page, reading the message there. And then I deleted the message from his social media account and the email notification.

I stumbled into the kitchen, finding another bottle of wine in the refrigerator, dumping more into my glass. I gulped it as if it were water before I doubled over on the floor in front of the fridge. I had just been kicked in the gut once more. I started panting, unable to catch my breath, water welling in my pulsating eyes.

My heart was pounding hard and fast as if it were about to burst through my rib cage and plummet to the ground. The theater act William had been performing over the last year was a bunch of lies.

More lies! He's had no intention of stopping the drugs or seeing her. He has not changed at all.

I leaned my back against the fridge, taking the wine bottle and drinking straight from its rim this time—no more need for a fancy glass.

Why? I screamed inside my head. *Why the hell would he do this? Why would he tell me he stopped when he hadn't at all? Why didn't he just leave me and live the life he apparently wants? Obviously, one full of drugs and loose women.*

I raked my fingers through my long, auburn hair, tugging furiously when I felt a knot. Why did he feel the need to stay and lie endlessly? To torture me? Because I was his security? This surely could not be because he loved me! I knew I couldn't cause someone I cared about this much pain.

I sat slumped on the cold linoleum floor, realizing this time was different.

Not for him, for me.

This time, I didn't feel a need to hire a private detective. I didn't have the obsession to slip his phone away in the night. Then, as if I had been waiting for it all along, the other shoe dropped.

I was done. So done! *Well, that's it then, isn't it?* So that would be my decision: to leave.

I was through with all the lies and deceit. And I was definitely finished with trying to hold a marriage together based on what it used to be and what I longed for when he obviously wasn't. No matter how hard I tried, it would never be that way again. To stay now would not only be idiotic on my part. It would be unthinkable.

I picked up my cell phone and dialed her number—*Rose's number*—the number I had memorized after looking at phone records over and over last year.

"Hello," she said as she picked up the line.

What am I doing? Making things worse? You are better than this, Cindy.

"Hello, is anyone there? William, is that you?" Rose asked.

My hand holding the phone dropped. I stared at the screen as I ended the call. Of course she would think it was William. I wanted to confront her, or at the very least scream at her for ruining my life. But suddenly I knew it wasn't all her fault. She might be those awful things that William had told me or not. But I realized she was being led by a man who was good at lying.

I slumped to the ground again. This was going to be a long night.

The hour passed quickly. I was sitting at our small pine kitchen table, tucked neatly into the rental's makeshift dining room corner, when I heard the truck pull into the driveway. An empty bottle of wine sat in front of me. I was cradling the wine glass back in my right hand again, the stem between my first two fingers.

I heard William open the front door and pull off his work boots, including the thudding sound as they hit the floor.

"Honey, I'm home," William said, excitement in his tone. "Let Friday night begin!" He came around the corner into the dining room. "Aww, there you are. Did you take the steaks out?"

he asked. As he walked by me, he kissed my cheek, as he often did on his way into the kitchen. I sat motionless, answerless, cradling the glass in my hand.

"Yes, you did. Just look at these cuts! I cannot wait to grill them up," William exclaimed.

I didn't move or say anything. Instead, I took a long sip of wine, letting it linger in my mouth. The light flavor of grape and pear seeped into my tastebuds, and then I swallowed down his treachery, followed by my resentment.

"I saw a message from Rose tonight on your social media account," I said calmly, almost a whisper. The words were as light as a casual conversation before I took another sip of wine.

I saw him pause at the sink from the corner of my eye, his back to me. He had pulled the potatoes out and was beginning to wash them. William stood there for what seemed like minutes, but it was only a few seconds.

"You must have seen something wrong. I have not spoken to her in over a year. You know that," he said, not even turning around, just continuing to wash potatoes.

"I *thought* I knew that," I said bluntly. "But tonight, I realized it was all another set of lies. This explains why you were always late to Woodland and the long lunches. How are you even passing your drug tests anymore to get your Suboxone?" I asked, since it was a requirement he had to maintain to get the medication.

He took out a cutting board, placed the potatoes on it, and retrieved a knife from its wooden block. "I pass my drug tests just fine," he said without even looking in my direction.

"Another set of lies," I said, still calm, talking low. "When will you stop, William? When you lose it all? Or will it continue after that?" I paused. "Maybe that's all you know how to do: lie."

I took another sip of wine, holding it in my mouth again for a few seconds before swallowing. I was calm, unusually calm.

Shouldn't I be screaming and hitting him? Maybe even throwing all of his belongings onto the lawn?

He turned to the stove and placed oil in a pan. He let it pop before adding the potatoes.

"I told you, I am not seeing her!" he said in a raised voice.

"You can't even admit it now, even when confronted with it. You can't even look me in the eye when you lie anymore, can you?" I asked. My tone rose, too. I was getting impatient with his lies.

He turned at that moment, facing me as I sat at the table. "I told you, I'm not seeing her or doing drugs. What are you trying to stir up?" he asked matter-of-factly. "Between you and Charles, I feel like I am getting beat up all the time," he added curtly before returning his attention to the stove.

I rose to my feet. *I was not going to allow the truth to be twisted this time.*

"You still don't get it, William," I began, my voice level and firm. "All I ever wanted was the truth. I had no intention of leaving you. I just needed the real story, the real you. That's all I ever desired. But I guess that's too much to ask of you."

"I'm not in the mood to argue with you tonight," William said, agitated. "I'm hungry. You always have such perfect timing. Ruining the one night a week that we spend together."

"Are you fucking kidding me? Pardon me for ruining your night! I'm *not* hungry. You can eat for both of us. I'm going for a drive," I exclaimed before grabbing my car keys and purse off the table. I pushed through the front door, letting it slam back in place.

After starting my car, I shifted the gear into reverse and peeled out of the driveway, my tires screeching against the asphalt. My blood was boiling and coursing through my veins as my heart pounded against my chest wall.

"Damn you!" I screamed, hitting the steering wheel repeatedly with the palm of my hand.

I realized then I was driving too fast through the neighborhood. I knew I shouldn't be driving at all, with an entire bottle of wine in me.

I didn't care.

I veered off into the empty high school parking lot at the thought. Pressing hard on the gas, I sped past the light posts that ran the center of the parking lot.

Fifty . . . seventy . . . eighty-five.

I slammed on the brakes, skidding the car to a stop, only feet away from the concrete barricade surrounding the football field.

I screamed at the top of my lungs, pounding my palms again on the steering wheel over and over. Finally, I put the car in park and turned the engine off. I was no longer breathing heavily, but panting, trying to catch my breath. The windows inside the car quickly fogged up.

"I am so fucking done! I am done with covering your tracks and supporting your sorry ass. Done with making excuses for you. I am done with it all!"

I sat in the car, head on the steering wheel, windows completely fogged up for an hour as I sobbed. Then two. Finally, my shoulders slumped, and my hands released their grip on the steering wheel and rested back in my lap. My breathing eventually evened out, allowing the top edges of the window to defog slightly.

I had done my research in the beginning about what the path to recovery looked like for a drug addict. But until you are in the moment, realizing it could also ruin your own life, you can never be fully prepared. William hadn't hit rock bottom, but I could no longer stay and wait for impact.

Before William, the only experience I had with drugs came from my childhood. My brother, Tim, five years older than me, took control of the house and reigned in a complete rage. He was always angry. He fought my mother for her last few dollars each week. She needed those few dollars for milk or bread since that was all that was left after paying bills in our almost poverty-stricken home. But he did everything he could to force it from her so he could buy drugs. Of course, he only did this when my father was not around—not that my father could control him. No one could.

"Give me twenty dollars, now!" Tim would demand of my mother, the walls so thin in our run-down house on the west side of town. We never needed to strain to hear an argument, even when my mother tried to make Tim keep his voice down.

"No! That's the last money we have for food and gas to last us the week," my mother would say.

"Give it to me now, or so help me, I'll kill you," my brother would reply, a steely, cold edge to his voice that no one wanted directed their way. *Instead, it said, "I can and will do this."*

To make matters worse, sometimes I'd hear a slap or a small cry that would make me shudder since I was helpless as a young girl to answer. "Let go of me," I'd hear my mother whisper . . . or wail.

In due time, my mother always gave in. The threats and violence wore her down. I saw it in her face, her puffy eyes that spent many nights crying. I was only eight at the time.

I could never forget how strong of a woman my mother was. She worked a full-time job and ran a strenuous household of five children from three different fathers. I never saw her sit for longer than ten minutes unless it was to sleep. But she relinquished to Tim's demands; she could not manage him as strong as she was.

Just hours later, a strange smell would seep through the floorboards to the room my younger brother Charles and I shared. Maniacal laughter would spiral up through the vents. In those moments, Tim was happy. Happy only on drugs.

Those happy moments never lasted that long, maybe a day or two. Soon after, anger and violence crept back again, like a returning thief threatening our sense of safety.

With my breathing calm and the windows no longer covered in haze, my mind drifted from thought to thought. The things I imagined would take place in Woodland—William cooking gourmet dinners, the family gathered around the dining room table, wine, games, conversations . . . it all started to fade from my vision and my dreams.

What do you want your life to be like, Cindy? It's now your turn to choose.

I let a slow, exhausting sigh out in the quiet of the car.

"I choose hope," I whispered softly as I lifted my head off the steering wheel where I had been resting it to think, pressing it back against the headrest.

I knew what I had to do.

CHAPTER TEN

"Where's William?" Charles asked me with a quick side glance. He was standing in front of a table saw, pipe in hand, set up in the living room just off the foyer of the back door of the Woodland house. It was Sunday, two days after the other shoe dropped. William and I were meant to help Charles with the plumbing today. But there wouldn't ever be a "William and I" again.

"I need to tell you something." I paused, even now hesitant to reveal the bitter truth. "I've kept a secret from you for the last year. Come sit with me on the porch, please."

Charles looked over at me, more appraising this time. His eyes went tight and worried. I noticed both his eyebrows were raised in surprise when I came into full view in front of him. My hair, messy in a bun, only accented the bags under my bloodshot eyes. I didn't bother more than a glance in the mirror that morning. My shoulders were slumped in defeat.

My brother put down the piece of pipe he was ready to cut and followed me to the porch.

We sat on the unfinished stairs in the shade that led to the south yard behind the sagging garage, which was still covered in foot-high weeds. The well-top pipe that had been recently replaced protruded through the tall green vegetation a couple of feet from the back garage wall. The space was surrounded by towering pines, oaks, and maples. There wasn't a cloud in the sky. Instead, a cool breeze drifted past us.

"I'm not sure where to begin," I said quietly. "It all started a little over a year ago." I took a deep breath and then proceeded to tell him about the last fourteen months of my secret life.

"Fuck!" left Charles's lips a few times as the vivid parts were revealed.

The information took him by surprise, which I knew it would. My stalwart brother got up and paced, kicking at the house wall with his boot tip as I finished talking.

"I knew there was more going on than just drugs," Charles blurted out with rage. Like my friend Maggie, I had told Charles about some of the drug issues early on. "You lost your home because of his stupidity, and now it appears it may have been tied to the drugs and the distraction of this other woman for three years. Three fucking years! All that time, you were working your ass off to support this deadbeat, and he was off doing this shit?"

"Yes, I suppose so," I said, my shoulders curling further with the weight of Charles's words.

"So, what are you going to do?" Charles demanded. As he continued to pace, his jaw was clenched tight. "And what about this house? We can't leave it unfinished, and you can't sell it right now in this market; you would lose money. And sure as shit, William is not coming back up here."

"I'm leaving him," I said, my head bowed. Saying the words out loud to someone other than William made it seem final, and it was. The tears I had thought were dried up over the last few days of crying began to swell up in the back of my eyes again. "And I'm moving up here to Woodland by myself. Starting a new life, I suppose. But I'll need your help to finish the house."

I couldn't meet his eyes, but this was my plan. After hours spent sobering up in my car in the high school parking lot on Friday night, that was the decision I had reached. William had no real job, per se. He couldn't afford the payments on this property, nor would I allow him to have it. I promised this house I would restore it, and in return, it would restore me.

Charles leaned against the side of the house, his hands balling into fists. "Where is he right now?"

"At the rental," I said, sniffing up the tears that attempted to drop as I looked up at Charles's face. "He needs to figure out what he's going to do with his life since he will no longer be a part of our business and will not be working on this house . . . my house."

My house. It stung to hear me say it out loud, but there was also a sense of relief. This *was* my house, and now, this was just my life.

"Well, I'll need help." Charles unballed his fists and spoke in a calmer tone. "We may have to hire Peter or Clay to help me with the work that requires two people."

"I fully expected that—and one more thing. I will be moving into one of the bedrooms as soon as one is mostly done," I said firmly, with no hesitation or pause in my voice despite my heavy heart and sore eyes. "I don't have the energy, time, or money to move twice. So I'll stay here while we finish the house."

Charles looked down at me, his eyebrows softening along with the corners of his mouth. "Okay."

For the first time in my life, my brother didn't push back. He knew my mind was made up. There would be no sense in trying to talk me out of it.

"Are you ready to work?" I asked, breaking our silence after a few minutes.

"Only if you want to," Charles said, his tone low matching mine.

We stood and walked back into the house. I was more than ready to work today and eager to let physical labor consume my weary mind. I was ready to move on.

CHAPTER ELEVEN

July 2015

"Jose, please put that box in the top bedroom, on the far back wall. Pedro, that table will go mid-center in front of the kitchen, along with the chairs. And put the treadmill under the stair rail in the foyer for now," I said as I directed the day workers unloading the moving truck in Woodland.

"Do you need my help?" Charles asked, coming out of the utility room where he was installing the tankless water heater. He stepped into the empty living space where I stood.

"Nope, best you stay in there and finish that install," I said, conjuring a smile. "It would be nice to have hot water for a bath later; I'm sure I'll need it." Certainly, I needed hot water, but what I needed most was peace. Keeping Charles inside the house and William outside seemed the most peaceful thing.

Charles's eyebrows raised, along with one side of his mouth, before he turned around and retreated to the utility room, adjusting a wrench as he walked.

On that blistering hot July morning, William and I sorted through fourteen years of combined stuff in just three hours. That was what it was to me now, just stuff. I wanted to walk away from all the material items that would remind me daily of when we bought it and what room we thought it would go perfectly in when we were creating a life together—or at least I thought we were. But I couldn't exactly afford to walk away from all of it right now, what with the remodel and having to split the small savings I had with William.

At least William had offered to help me with my move. But why, exactly? Was this his way of putting closure to everything? Or did he want to spend the last few remaining moments he could with me before I was gone? Was he simply being nice? He had pleaded with me over and over the last few weeks not to leave. He felt I wasn't giving us enough time—that we could still work it out. William had no idea of the war inside my head, which had already consumed me for over a year. And he had no clue about the peace I felt the day I decided to leave. It was what I needed to do.

The last month living with William in the rental, knowing I would leave, was bittersweet. I no longer cared what he did, who he saw, or even where he was; that was freeing. I had already grieved. I had already experienced the loss of him. Now, all I felt was freedom. The month for me was merely a formality. It was a month to take care of business.

William and I discussed who would get what large furniture items, how retirement accounts would be split, and who would keep particular debt, credit cards, and business accounts. There was also the formality of filing the divorce papers. Conversations with the children, family, and friends were filled with shock and surprise. It was the last thing anyone expected.

From the outside, we were perfect. No one knew all the secrets I kept for over a year. And no one needed to at the moment. Charles was the only one who knew it all, which was why it was best for him, heavy wrench in hand, not even to see my soon-to-be-former husband.

But now, as the July sun kissed my skin, I was pleasantly delighted that it was at least fifteen degrees cooler here than in the city below the canyons. The trees surrounding the lot were covered in bright green leaves that shaded parts of the property and the house. Only a few yellow flowers, hiding in the oak tree's shade, remained from spring. The river was more of a soft hum in the background since the rage of the spring runoff had already passed.

William stayed outside in the truck bed, handing the items down to the day workers to have them brought inside. The moving truck had been pulled in front of the garage by the house's back door, which seemed to be sagging more since the last time I saw it.

I noticed that William made no effort to go inside the house. I imagined this had to be hard for him. But I didn't ask. I didn't care anymore. That man had made my life hard for far too long. It was hard to remember the good times and love we once shared. Those moments were now hidden in a heavy, dense cloud of betrayal and hurt.

The house was not done. Nor was it in a state that any person of sound mind would live in, I reminded myself as I grabbed one of the boxes from Pedro and sent him back for more. The exterior was still covered in a white sheet of plastic wrap. As I walked back inside, I knew the rooms had only the first layer of primer covering them, and if luck would serve, I might have hot water at day's end. I just needed one room. I had told myself that over a month ago and had scurried Charles to get things this far. And one room was all I had. I set down the box on the black walnut dining table, one of the items I claimed I needed in my new life this morning, and strode back out.

"William, please hand me those iron candlesticks and the large vase; I'll take those in," I said as I headed toward the truck bed.

I wanted to move this along so the final part could be done. The tension in the air had been like a thick cloud all day. It had been a day I was anticipating and a day William, I assumed, was dreading.

"Are you sure you can take them all at once?" William asked as he handed them down to me. We were cordial with each other and had been over the last couple of weeks. It was almost as if we were finishing a business agreement, not ending a marriage.

"Of course. In fact, hand me the other brown vase too," I said, squeezing the vases into my arms and holding them tight to my body while carrying the heavy iron candlestick holders.

It took a little over an hour to unload the limited number of items and furniture I felt I needed into the unfinished house.

"Senorita, you want us to unpack for you?" Pedro asked in his broken English.

"No thank you," I replied, smiling with kindness and gratitude toward the men who had worked so hard already. "I want to do that on my own." I knew the last bout of emotions would surface as I unpacked the boxes and traced my fingers over each item, carefully sifting through the memory of where it sat in our grand hacienda. Nobody needed to be here to see that.

"You told them two hundred each for this job as we agreed?" I asked William, pulling him aside from the men while they drank cold water straight from the hose. Fifteen degrees cooler or not, it was still a hot summer day, and I hadn't the faintest idea where the glasses were in the boxes.

William had graciously gone down to the Home Depot corner and hand-picked these men at my request that morning. He knew how to pick the hardest workers and had a soft spot for the Mexican ones. He always wanted to ensure they got paid a little more since most of them sent money back to their families across the border.

"Yes," he confirmed.

I quickly counted six hundred dollars from my bag and handed the bills to William. That was officially the last time I would hand money over to my husband so he could pay for something, making it appear to others that he was the family's wage earner and not me. He hated it when he didn't pay. He said it was unmanly. I always felt that was an old-school way of thinking. I could have just walked over and compensated the men myself . . . but I was in no mood to deal with William.

Besides, this was the last time.

Charles stepped out the back door onto the cleared back porch. A box of firewood lay to the left of the door, and a pinewood bench that once sat in the courtyard at the hacienda found a new home to the right of the back door. He leaned against one of the poles that held up the porch roof, wiping his hands on a rag, peering in the direction William and I were standing on the side of the truck. He obviously did not heed my advice about staying inside.

Before turning to the men, William and I exchanged a half hug of sorts.

"Gracias. Thank you for your help today," I said as I waved and stepped onto the porch next to Charles.

My brother shot a hand up, acknowledging William's parting. William did the same. I had seen these two men exchange hugs and have conversations filled with laughter for fourteen years. With a heavy heart, I realized that now, it was all they could do to be in each other's line of sight. But at least they were being amicable. I admired Charles's restraint.

Charles and I watched as the moving truck, with William inside, pulled out of the driveway, down the long, tree-filled lane, and essentially, out of our lives.

"So you're actually going to do this?" Charles asked as we walked back inside, a hint of concern in his voice. "Stay here, by yourself, before the house is even done?"

"Yes, I am going to do this," I replied, picking up part of my king bed frame to carry upstairs. "Can you help me put the bed together before you take off, please? That is the only thing I can't do by myself."

Charles followed me up the unfinished stairs with his socket set. The brown, rustic iron bed frame William and I had carefully picked out for our hacienda lay in pieces on the floor of the master bedroom. It still smelled of fresh paint and new carpet. It was a third of the size of my bedroom in the hacienda, but I didn't care; it fit me perfectly.

I looked down at the large pieces. Years ago, it took William and me months to find the right bed frame. We searched dozens of stores before entering an import furniture store. We looked through hundreds of pages of a catalog of beds in their back room until it appeared on a page. It was the perfect combination of masculine and feminine. The iron filigree leaves wove in and out of the intricate design on the head and foot frames. It was the kind of bed that would last my lifetime and many generations after.

"Pick up the side rails first. Then, I'll hold the base and put the screws in," I hastily added, pointing at pieces on the floor. "We can tighten them all once we have them in place."

"So . . . did he say anything to you, try to talk you out of coming this morning?" Charles asked as he steadied the heavy iron side rail.

"No. We just went about dividing everything up," I said flatly.

It wasn't the whole truth. My husband had asked me that morning when we woke up if I was sure about moving and getting a divorce. He wondered if I wanted to wait a little longer before making this decision. But my mind had been made up. There was no turning back and no sense talking about it either.

Once the screws were secured in the heavy frame, Charles and I heaved the new box springs and mattress onto the assembled iron frame. The bed was the one splurge I allowed myself since our custom mattress was now William's. Good riddance. I didn't want to take the energy of the years spent sleeping beside him with me into the new-for-me house. I wiped my hands off each other, a subtle signal to my brother that we were finished.

"That's all I needed," I said, nodding to Charles. "Thanks for your help. I can take it from here." I desperately hoped my brother would take my hint that I was ready to be alone.

"What have you got to protect yourself?" Charles asked.

"Protect me from what? Mice, squirrels, stray cats? I don't need anything. I'll be fine." There were neighbors on this small lane, just a few, all of us on about an acre of land. I hadn't officially met them, but I assumed they were as harmless as the gophers burrowing holes in our lots.

Charles shot me his "Seriously?" look. I knew it all too well. He was obviously more worried about me than I was. "Let me go see what I have in the truck," Charles said as he turned and trotted through the rooms and down the stairs.

I located the box on the far wall of the bedroom labeled "master bedroom bedding." I opened it and pulled out sheets, throwing them on the mattress top. I was tugging the corners of the fitted sheet taut when I heard Charles coming back up the stairs. I glanced up at him as he entered the room, curious about what he might have found for me to protect myself. He was holding a two-foot-long metal pipe.

"Take this," he said, holding it out to me.

"A metal pipe?" I laughed. "You expect me to beat some poor criminal?"

"Yes. The cell service will be spotty up here until we install a booster. You're a single woman in the middle of nowhere! Are you not getting this?" he said, worry dripping from each word.

Maybe I'm not getting it.

Maybe I don't care to get it.

Maybe being up here alone in an unfinished house is better than everything I faced in the valley below.

"Okay, okay," I said begrudgingly. I grabbed the bar from his outstretched hand and placed both hands on the end, clutching it like a lightsaber sword from *Star Wars*. I swirled it around as

I moved my feet to a fencing stance, showing him that I had the Force.

Charles rolled his eyes at my performance. That was how I felt about the metal pipe. But really, I was grateful that my brother cared so much for me—more than I cared for myself just then.

"I'll be okay," I said in a low, reassuring voice. I leaned the metal pipe against the wall by the bed before walking over to him, placing my hand momentarily on his arm. "I promise."

I walked Charles to the back door and watched him drive away before going upstairs to finish making the bed. Once it was finished, I paused for a moment to admire it. The smooth cream sheets and blankets were flawlessly folded down from the headboard, and the four pillows with fresh cases leaned against the filigree frame. The aroma of lavender, emanating from the pillow spray I had picked up while shopping last week, adding a subtle yet cozy fragrance to the air.

I turned around and let myself fall onto the freshly made bed, landing on my back, arms outstretched, ignoring my aching muscles. My bed, in my house. I stared at the newly painted ceiling, the dark beam still running down its center. I let the quiet stillness of the empty house wash over me. I was finally here. Alone.

Just then, my eyes clouded over, forming pools of water that spilled onto the side of my face, running down onto the freshly made bed. Relief cascaded through me. Those tears were not of sadness. Those had already been expended, over and over.

I exhaled a long breath of air.

CHAPTER TWELVE

Rebuilding a house is easy. Walls are framed with studs spaced sixteen inches apart. Water lines run cold to the right and hot to the left using red and blue tubing. Electrical wires are color-coded, matching red to red and black to black, and outlets are placed every four feet, ten inches from the ground. The tile is secured with mortar and tiny spacers. A tile saw is used for the last few pieces that never quite fit, even though you measured ten times so you wouldn't have to cut tile.

Houses are finite. You follow a specific set of codes and rules; someone draws a plan, and you just need to follow it.

Not life though. Life has no blueprint or set of plans. No building inspector comes out and passes you when you do things right—or tells you what to fix when mistakes happen. But a house . . . that was exactly what I needed right then. A finite set of items that needed to be done, in a particular order, in a specific way to completion, with something tangible to show. You could lose yourself in work like that, and gratefully, I did.

To be honest, rebuilding the house also became my reason to say "no" to any social events. It was a cut-and-dry answer. Its simple beauty allowed me my space, with very few comments back. Who could argue with that reason?

It was a much easier answer than, "No, I can't go to coffee, my life is falling apart," or "I'll take a raincheck on the gala—I just left my husband and don't have a plus one." Those reasons would inevitably result in too many questions to answer or the sympathetic responses that followed when people didn't know what else to say. It was so much easier to use the house excuse, and it wasn't a lie, just not the entire truth.

But at night, when the house was quiet and my hands were still, with just my thoughts to keep me company, the mourning of my past life and the uncertainty of a future commenced. Tears would build and then spill out as I drowned them with wine. Each night I escaped to my sagging front porch, a quilt wrapped around my shoulders, my long-stem wine glass clutched in my left hand. Taking my spot on the wooden porch steps, still waiting their turn for repair, I huddled in the last of the grieving I thought was done.

I wished it didn't take long, but it did.

Night after night.

Why was I not enough for William?

Was the connection I had with him all in my head? It couldn't be. I felt it from the beginning. I sensed it when he took me to meet his family for the first time. When he proposed to me in the cathedral behind the altar. And on our wedding day, it was full of electricity as if it pulsed through us.

One late evening, as the stars stretched across the sky like diamonds on a velvet blanket, I realized I had lost that bond with William somewhere along the way. *When did my connection with William stop?*

My thoughts took a sharp turn toward a memory of William and me at an event. We had been married a little over two years, and to me, he was perfect. I stood proudly next to him that night at the gala, with my arm looped through his. His rugged, flirtatious cologne occasionally caught me off guard, making my knees weak.

William looked fetching in his dark gray, non-pleated dress pants; black button-down shirt undone to mid-chest, accentuating his well-built physique; and tasteful silver cross necklace he wore most days. I had chosen a mid-calf-length black dress with large embossed red roses across it. It was form-fitting, accentuating my then thin yet voluptuous curves. Moreover, it was the kind of dress William liked to see me in.

We were standing in a circle with several other couples we had just met, each holding a crystal glass of various shapes and sizes. The contents reflected our individual choices from the overpriced cash bar. The function was a charity event to support the battered women's shelter in the area. Yet, they had spared no expense to ensure this gala was high class. It felt more like a show-and-tell display of the rich and famous in Utah, each person trying to one-up the other in dress and success.

As the conversation continued in the circle of couples William and I were standing in, the customary, "What do you do for a living?" question came up. You could see the men stand up taller, their shoulders squaring as if they were ready to enter the ring. All right then. I'd been playing this game for years. So when it came to our turn, I was giddy to share.

I wanted to blow all of these couples' minds by explaining the non-traditional role reversal William and I had in our relationship. As I was about to speak up and describe the success of my business, I was caught off guard. William squeezed my hand tight and moved it behind my back, pulling me closer to his side as if to halt my answer, which it did.

And then, he did the unthinkable.

"Cindy and I have a successful lending company," he began, squeezing my hand and nudging me with his elbow. "I've been in lending for over a decade, and our product is in high demand. We've expanded into the additional western states, trying to keep up with all the requests. I travel all over . . . Idaho, Wyoming, even into Arizona marketing our products while Cindy ensures the office runs smoothly."

I couldn't believe what I was hearing! His words and actions were nearly as neanderthal as saying he went out to slay dragons each day, while I was home, barefoot and pregnant. And here's the thing: if it were the truth, I wouldn't have been bucking like a wild horse inside as I was at that moment.

William was taking the credit for the company I had worked so hard to build. At four in the morning, *I* was the one up drafting materials, documents, and forms before marketing for the day, on top of making sure the office ran smoothly! I was the one who signed the deal with the banking institutions for exclusive rights to sell their products. I was the only name on the articles of incorporation and business license.

Me. Not William.

He glanced down at me in that instant, pulling me even tighter to him, with a menacing glint in his eyes as if to say, "Don't embarrass me in front of all these people."

At that moment, a realization hit me like a ton of bricks. I knew my husband didn't accept me fully for who I was because he did not accept who he was. I recognized our love now had conditions. He wanted to appear successful, and I was his cover. The connection I thought we shared based on trust and honesty was a mirage.

That night, William took full credit for my successes—and worse—I let him. I stayed silent and smiling as the rest of the party proceeded in the conversation, not wanting to call him out in front of all those people I didn't know because he was my husband. In my mind, back then, I thought it was a one-time occurrence, William trying to show off in front of the other men. However, it continued sporadically over the years we were together.

But I stayed. My Catholic vows had deep roots. The pope himself had to give his approval for William and me to marry. You don't just walk away from something like that.

But now, in the solace of the warm end of summer nights in Woodland, my mind wandered. Finally, I knew precisely what I was missing in my life and realized exactly when I'd lost it.

It was with that first lie from William.

I glanced up at the stars, so bright they lit up the ground beneath them and vast, their glow extended for miles. There were so many that I felt I could reach up and touch them. Stars like this did not exist in the city, with too much light and smog to compete with and cover them. But here, void of all barriers, with just the faint chirp of the crickets lingering in the background as my soft lullaby, they sparkled for me every night, keeping me company.

The Woodland stars.

"God, are you there?" I asked, tears streaming faster as I turned my face to the starlit cosmos. "I know I don't talk to you enough, and I'm sorry about that. But I need your help, maybe a little guidance. How do I find a true connection, unbridled trust, and acceptance? I mean, do they even exist?" Pausing, I took a deep breath in, sniffing up the tears with it. "I just need to know if I will ever find anyone who will accept me . . . for me?"

As I spoke the words of this invocation, a star in the western sky grew bright, so vivid it appeared to be a small sun in the night sky. Just as suddenly as it flashed brightly for me, it shot across the sky, leaving a streak of brilliant and breathtaking light in its wake before it was gone.

All I could do was utter two small words with my face still tilted to the stars. The tears were now subsiding. "Thank you," I whispered, knowing I was not alone underneath the Woodland stars.

The canyons between my house in Woodland and my office in Salt Lake City began to change color as the fall months made their appearance. Deep orange, bright yellow, and brownish red covered both sides of the mountainous banks, making it a feast for my eyes during my travels. I was also on my ninth book on disc, a mystery novel set in Ireland. It was a guilty pleasure I discovered one Saturday afternoon while exploring the small, quaint library in town.

The library was once the courthouse. The musty smell caught me by surprise when I first entered it. I made my way through the compact rooms now filled with shelves of tattered books, waiting for someone to take them home and open their now browning pages to explore a world that could only come to life in someone's imagination. The books on disc section was also adequate, helping ease my mind each day on my drive as I entered another world for a time, away from my own.

My Friday-night date nights with William had been replaced with long soaks in my pedestal tub, with the mountain bank peeking out over the top of the window shade. A glass of pinot grigio sat on the stool beside me, and music, soft R&B, cascaded through the steam of the hot water. I realized I had stopped listening to music when I discovered William's affair. Every love song I'd heard stung like the nest of angry wasps unintentionally found under the wooden porch. But now, I felt the songs conveyed a possible unforeseen future. Maybe my future.

The fall months became all about finding new routines in my life. I woke early, then drove an hour down the two canyons back to the city to work all day before driving the hour back home to hastily change my clothes and help Charles work on the house. Day after day, week after week, that became my familiar routine.

One mid-October evening after work, my brother enlisted my help to install the new metal roof on the house. The challenge of doing something new and figuring out how to do it right was enticing. It was thrilling even, because after seven months, the house was almost finished. There were just a couple more items to complete. I couldn't wait to hear the pitter-patter of rain on the new chocolate-colored roof once we were done. The roof effortlessly completed the home's exterior, covered in whiteboard and batten, with new efficient brown-cased windows and bright red back door. It was a far cry from the old blue log paneling we'd found it in.

The metal sheets were heavy and awkward, especially since just the two of us were doing the installation. Charles and I hoisted the six-foot-wide, twelve-foot-long metal sheets up as far as possible from the ground to the roofline. I steadied each one while Charles scurried up the ladder, grabbing it from the top. Then I darted up the ladder after him to help pull it the rest of the way up. He then led us to where the sheet needed to be placed on the roof. I held it tightly while he put the foam spacers and screws in, securing it to the black tar paper. We were in for quite an afternoon, with sixteen sheets to be installed.

The cooler temperature in Woodland at least made the roof installation bearable. I couldn't imagine doing this in the city sun; the rays casting back the heat from the metal sheets would be excruciating. As if in answer, a deliciously cool breeze swept across the roof as we worked. It dried the beads of sweat that attempted to form on my back.

"I think I'm ready to go out on a date," I blurted out to my brother as he continued to screw in the metal sheets with bouts of exerted air escaping his lips.

I looked at him, a little hesitant. I had been considering this for the last month, worried if I did it too soon, it would appear I was rushing into something. But, on the other hand, it had nearly been four months since William and I separated. I did not want to hurry into being in a relationship; I hardly wanted more than one date at that point.

I was genuinely concerned that I hadn't been on a date for fourteen years. William had been my last date. How do people date in their forties? With technology the way it is, what are the ways of meeting people now? I had no intention of replacing my husband's role anytime soon; maybe I never would. I just felt like I should try one date to see if this new version of me even liked it or not.

"Really?" Charles replied, trying to catch his breath as he pushed the drill down into the metal sheet. "Why's that?"

I didn't want to tell him the whole truth. I didn't want to reveal that I got lonely here alone, even though it was what I had chosen, that my friends lived far and were all in relationships. As beautiful as it was, spending time with my children and grand-children only helped fill one small void in my life. Or the fact that almost every night after Charles was gone, I wandered the house clutching a glass of wine with a blanket wrapped around me. At some point, I always ended up outside, on the unfinished porch steps, inhaling the hardy pine smell accompanied by drift-ing campfire aromas, allowing my tears to flow under the stars.

Instead, I told him, "Because I'll have to do it at some point, I suppose, to at least see what it's like." My words also came through quick bursts of air while competing against the pulsa-tion of the drill. "That way, I can decide if dating is something I even want to do. Or if adopting eight cats and living as a hermit makes more sense."

Charles let out a chuckle. "That's what I would do if any-thing happened to Lucy—minus the cats, of course," he replied as he pushed the drill down hard to secure a screw.

Lucy, my sister-in-law, was a dutiful, soft-spoken Asian woman. I knew she tolerated my brother far more than my brother tolerated her.

"Well," I huffed as I twisted the metal to align with the roofline, "I may not even find anyone to go on a date with. Who wants to drive to a small town in the middle of nowhere and have dinner at a local café before driving another hour home?"

I pondered my statement for a moment. I actually might not find anyone who wanted to go on a date with me. But, if I did, would I meet them in the city or ask them to come up here? Was there a local dating site for Woodland men? Full of cowboys with big buckles and tobacco pocketed in their cheeks?

Charles glanced over his shoulder while screwing in the last screw through the sheet of metal I was holding. "Do whatever you want, but we have to finish this house. These twelve-hour days are killing me," he said with a snort.

He was right. I did commit to being here every moment I was not working to help finish this house. I knew full well Charles was doing me a huge favor. Even though I was paying him a little, it wasn't enough to compensate him for the extensive amount of time and effort he gave me.

The Woodland house was almost done, though, and another place had already been lined up in the city for Charles to remodel. I was in no rush to go on a date with a man I didn't know. I could wait until we were done with the house and Charles moved on to the next one. Maybe I would change my mind by then and live my life as a recluse.

Maybe.

Charles sent me a text late Friday afternoon, close to the end of October. Halloween was just a couple of days away. The leaves on the trees that surrounded my house had mainly fallen, and the few left were deep orange and yellow, barely holding on with their browning stems.

I'm leaving at five today; you can have the night off. I promised Justin I would take him to a movie tonight. I left the stain and brushes for the stair planks in the backroom for you to finish tomorrow, and I put some temporary boards on the stairs so you can at least get upstairs for now.

I snickered under my breath. As if I needed my brothers' permission to have a night off! But deep down, I did. I was happy he was spending time with his only child, Justin. Charles's son was closer in age to my granddaughter, which made me feel like he was one of my grandchildren versus my nephew. I knew I was spending more time with his son than he was lately since my brother was consumed with getting this house done.

In fact, Justin had expressed to me on my last sleepover with him, "I never get to see my dad because he is always at your house!" Those words stung. Thank God we were almost done—just a couple more items—and then Charles's life could return to normal. And mine, well, without the house as a distraction, it might be time to have a social life again. But was I ready? Ready for the onslaught of "How are you doing" questions?

The isolation in my home and the work that needed to be done to finish it had been a sanctuary for me, a protected glass bubble of sorts. But if I wanted to truly figure out who I was and what I wanted for my future, I had to expand past my four walls. I had to go out into the world and try.

This is how you move on, Cindy. You try.

Earlier in the week at work, a conversation about online dating ensued, one I was eager to eavesdrop on. A couple of the more seasoned coworkers had told stories of how they'd met their spouses through sites where you had to fill out more substantial information about yourself—not just a picture and quick message, which seemed more like a hook-up than a date.

So that night after my Friday routine of soaking in my tub was done, I shuffled to my desk in the loft area, since I had the night off, and typed their recommendation into the search engine. Pages of information exploded in front of me. "Over two million people have found love," "Site that will most likely lead to happy relationships," "Highest-quality dating pool," "Dating advice tips," I read aloud before scrolling through the plan options available, deciding on the lowest-cost plan for now. No need to spend a lot of money for one test date.

The profile questions popped up instantly after I picked the plan.

"What does a perfect date look like?" *A local café diner in the middle of nowhere?*

"Happy hour at a local brewery," I typed.

"What do you do in your spare time?" *Hoist large sheets of metal around.*

"Explore other worlds in the contents of books."

"How financially savvy do you feel you are?" *My ex-husband just got a third of everything, so not bad.*

"My credit score is 720."

"Have you been married previously?" *Think of it like Bewitched; the role of Darrin has been played twice.*

"Yes."

"How do you feel about kids?" *Mine are all raised, and yours better be too.*

"I adore children."

I answered the remaining questions with ease, pausing on the last one: "What age range is acceptable for you?" I turned forty-four that year. Forty-four years old and now single. What was an appropriate dating age range for a woman my age? I certainly didn't want to go too young. That would feel like I was on a date with one of my sons. Nor too old, either, where the conversation would be all about hearing and vision loss. Hmm . . . 38–50 seems like a reasonable range for a test date.

"38–50."

"Please attach three to five appropriate pictures to gain more traction with your profile," I read aloud from the last page. I scrolled through my phone, realizing I didn't have a lot of pictures of myself. There was the unfinished kitchen, the guest bathroom tile being installed, wood flooring choices, pictures of the grandchildren baking cookies, and more photos of cookies.

I finally decided on three that I thought were acceptable: my work headshot, a picture of me with my three sons that I cropped William out of, and one of me with my girlfriends at a winery. That one was the money shot.

"Thank you, your profile has been submitted," I read after clicking Submit.

Suddenly, I wheeled my chair back from the desk a bit while I raised my hands high above my head as if I were on a roller coaster and getting ready for the ride.

Here goes nothing.

CHAPTER THIRTEEN

I lingered in bed the following morning, allowing my body to stretch out across the king mattress that I alone occupied. A golden ray of light peeked through the edge of the blinds, streaming across me as a chorus of birds chirped in unison behind the windowpanes. It was such a far cry from the barking dogs and lawnmowers in the city that I felt as lucky as a Disney princess. I stared at the brown wood beam running across the ceiling. Bits of insulation still seeped out around the edges. *Okay, maybe not a picture-perfect princess. I really need to fix that.*

"Maybe I'll go buy trim today," I said aloud in a slightly hoarse morning voice. "Nail it up around the edges." I had resorted to talking aloud to myself more and more. It broke the deafening silence that was becoming a constant in my nearly finished converted French country cottage. And I figured, as long as I didn't answer my own questions or have an argument with myself, it was fine.

My phone buzzed on the nightstand. I glanced at the clock behind it and saw the glorious sleeping-in time of 8:47 a.m. on a Saturday staring back at me nonjudgmentally. I pulled the phone from the table, unplugging it from the charger. Then, tapping on the screen, the number of messages in my email box appeared, causing me to blink with shock.

Thirty-seven new emails! I had never woken up to that many new emails in my personal email box. I had to be seeing something wrong. I hastily scrolled through the messages.

All of them were replies from the dating site I'd just signed up to.

I jolted upright, my hair falling out of the messy bun I had slept in. "Cheese and biscuits! Is this normal?" I abruptly blurted out. "I am not awake enough for this yet. I need coffee!"

I threw on a robe and stumbled down the jimmy-rigged temporary stairs Charles had put in place yesterday. Hastily, I made a large mug of French roast dabbed with sweet cream. The robust, bitter, yet sweet aroma instantly made my taste buds tingle, awakening my foggy mind.

I carried the steaming cup back up the makeshift stairs to my loft, where my office was located, just off the master suite. I felt like a young girl on Christmas morning. The anticipation of what could be in the wrapped packages was more exciting than the packages themselves. That's what those emails were: packages of possibility!

I took a deep breath, sat down in my black fabric office chair, wheeled it closer to the desk, wiped my now sweaty hands on my robe, took a sip of coffee, and then . . . I opened the lid of my laptop.

"You've got mail!" I said aloud, realizing the movie came out in 1998, and it was now 2015. *Classics never die. Maybe I am just a classic.* Another thought struck me: *Maybe dating won't be so bad in my forties.*

My fingers paused before clicking on the Enter key to open my email page. My heart began to pick up pace, my hands becoming clammier. *Damn.* I felt suddenly nervous. I took several deep breaths, holding each one for as long as I could before exhaling.

"It's just a test date, Cindy. Calm down," I whispered to myself, shrugging my shoulders with the absurdity of it all. I took another long sip of coffee and hit Enter on my laptop. The first email instantaneously opened.

Bill: "Do you like wine?"

That's all he's got? Just one statement in an email.

How do I reply to that? Should I even reply at all? It was a good observation on Bill's part since it was listed on my profile. But such an astute character could have at least asked if I preferred red or white wine—something to make me think he was capable of more than an acknowledgment of what I had listed in my profile and that he could carry on a somewhat captivating conversation. Nope. I hit the Delete button before moving to the following email.

A picture of a more prominent man in his late forties, even though he looked in his fifties, popped up with his message: "You're sure pretty."

"You're sure pretty"? Really? That was very nice of him to say, I thought, but what dialect of English was that? And does someone in their late forties, really fifties, actually say that to someone online they don't know?

Next!

This time, a picture of a man in his mid-forties flashed on my screen, proudly holding the head of a freshly killed deer.

Gross! Next.

I opened all thirty-seven emails but didn't reply to a single one of them. A heavy feeling settled on my chest. Disappointment. It reminded me of the little girl who opened all her Christmas presents to find that she didn't get the one thing she really wanted. This was going to be more complicated than I thought.

However, I did reach a conclusion about men on dating sites: they took too many pictures of themselves playing sports. Helmets and glasses covered their faces as they exerted themselves down a biking trail or a ski slope. Or there were plenty of facial expressions of strain as they jumped over other men to get the layup on the basketball court. There were also a few water-skiing shots where the wave took over most of the picture, hiding any resemblance of a man holding onto a rope.

By far, the hunting pictures and bathroom selfies were the most entertaining. Shirts off, a dirty shower in the background, an open bottle of toothpaste on the counter, and phone at mid-point as they tried to flex a pose. There were too many more men dressed in camo, kneeling over the carcass of a freshly killed animal or bird, with its eyes all bugged out, fresh blood seeping. *Eww.*

Do other women actually like these types of photos? Maybe I am being too critical. Too vain. I pondered it for a minute. No, I was not being too critical or too vain. Let's face it, dating online starts with an attraction to a picture and a few words to intrigue someone, as shallow as that may be. But the men who put absolutely no thought or effort into what they were portraying were just not my style. Even though I had no clue what my style was, I knew it was not that.

My hand reached for the lid of my laptop to close it, feeling the need to get to work staining the stair boards. Defeat weighed on me like a giant rock on an anthill. Then another thought crossed my mind: *Maybe I am just being too picky? Just pick one, anyone.*

I heard a "ping," as if on cue, alerting me of a new email. My hand sat frozen on the laptop's lid I was about to close. "Maybe number thirty-eight is the lucky one," I voiced aloud. I hoped so anyway, for my sake.

Pulling the lid of the laptop fully back open, I read:

Hey there, I'm a sassy attorney looking for a fun night out. Are you up for it?

Todd

Todd. *Sassy? Well . . . I am fluent in sass!* His introduction was short, brief, to the point, and yet intriguing. I clicked on his photo, a close-up of his face, head, and neck. His chin rested in the palm of his hand. He was bald, but in a good way, giving him a regal look instead of someone past their prime. His eyes were a bright, piercing blue. There was a softness to his expression that

I liked. Without saying a word, that look somehow conveyed that he was a kind man.

I hit reply: Sounds great, but first, you must pass a quiz.

I smiled and hit Send. Then suddenly I realized: *Crap, now I actually need a quiz!* I pondered that one for a moment. How in the world do you prepare a quiz to see if someone could be engaging through a couple of hours of date time? *I know!* A random set of questions to see if his sass and intellect would continue through an evening and keep me interested.

I bit the edge of my finger as I waited to see if Todd, Mr. Right Now, would respond. Then I started questioning myself. Maybe I answered too quickly and boldly? Maybe men in the dating market now like subtle women? I sighed in resignation, disgust, and more disappointment. *Perhaps I should just go on a date before I start inventing my own rules.*

Just then, my email chimed.

I'm always up for a challenge, he replied.

I felt the corners of my mouth turn up and my chest fill with butterflies.

I hastily typed:

First, if you were a wine, which one would you be?

Second, Bert or Ernie?

Third, favorite comedy movie?

Fourth, white bread or wheat?

Fifth, pie or cake?

I hit Send before clamoring down the stairs to refill my empty coffee mug. The familiar "ping" of my email rang as I started to climb the stairs back to the loft.

Interesting questions, sassy Cindy, white, sweet wine, please, since I'm still acquiring a taste for it. Bert because he is the more sensible one. My all-time favorite comedy movie, BIG, I'll tell you why on our first date.

Clever, he is leaving a hook for me.

Wheat, because nutrition is vital at my age, and pie, any kind of fruit pie, it's my kryptonite.

Oh, Todd was good . . . ingenious and intriguing. His answers had me longing for more.

Excellent, you passed this round. We award you an inquisitive dinner full of comedy and reflection with a spirited lady as your prize. See you in Park City tomorrow evening, at seven pm at the 360 restaurant?

I hit Send and then realized it sounded more like a demand rather than an ask. I jotted down on a sticky note *less sass and stipulations upfront* and pasted it on the side of my office wall. Who wants to spend an evening with an assertive, bold, auburn-haired lady who is already demanding?

I breathed a little sigh of relief as his reply popped up within seconds:

See you then.

I stared at the screen in wonder. *This guy may be as saucy and off-kilter as I am.*

My brother and I worked through the following day, Sunday, leveling the sagging garage doors, even though my mind was elsewhere the entire time we worked. I was over-planning the date I was to attend that evening. *What should I wear? How should my hair and makeup look?* It had been over fourteen years since the last first date I had been on.

I eventually settled for jeans with holes with a blazer and tee, a look I thought revealed my young yet classic side. My makeup was light, allowing my auburn curls to cascade loosely down my back and take center stage. I hastily darted to my car with a breathless, "See you later," over my shoulder to Charles. He was still puttering around with the garage door frame. I was in no mood for a stranger-danger lecture tonight. My nerves were already on edge.

Park City was the closest city to Woodland with actual restaurants, not just a café. It was a bustling Swiss town replica, a destination spot for local Utahns and tourists since the snow and skiing were top-rated in the winter months. Boutique shops, galleries, bars, and food establishments lined each side of the main street. Parking was always challenging, but I hit the timing perfectly tonight, securing a spot just as someone was backing out of one on a side road, a mere five-minute walk to the restaurant.

I let out a long exhale as I turned off the engine. Then, reaching up, I pulled the rearview mirror down to check my appearance. I dabbed more lipstick on my already rose-colored lips before re-fluffing my hair. "You will be fine, Cindy. Baby steps, remember?" I reassured my reflection.

I pushed my way through the large wooden-framed glass doors of the 360 bistro. The smell of fresh-baked bread hit me as I gingerly squeezed through a few waiting couples in the black-and-white tiled entryway to the host station.

"May I help you?" the twenty-year-old girl asked, looking up from her clipboard. She was dressed in all black with a well-positioned blonde ponytail.

"Yes, I have reservations for two," I began, raising my voice so she could hear me over the crowd in the foyer. "It should be under Cindy. I am a little early and was hoping I could wait in your lounge area."

"Yes, there you are. Let me show you the way to our bar." She turned from the host station toward a small hall, expecting me to follow. I moved around the podium, sprinting to keep up with her.

My mind wandered as I walked. I'd already planned the perfect meeting between Todd and me. I would be sitting at the bar, a glass of white wine in hand, facing the bottles of whiskey and bourbon on the back shelves while catching glimpses of my appearance in the mirrors behind the bottles.

I would fidget with my hair in the back bar mirror, readjusting it to ensure each strand was ideally in place. The host would then direct him to the bar area when he arrived, where I would be waiting. Once I saw him in the mirror approaching, I would turn in my stool, allowing my auburn curls to whip around lightly before our eyes locked. I had seen this scene a hundred times in the movies, and each time it made me chuckle, but deep down, I admired it.

"Ma'am, here we are," the hostess stated as we entered the lounge, jolting me back to the moment.

"Thank you," I replied, glancing at the row of stools. "I'm waiting for a gentleman by the name of Todd. Would you mind directing him this way when he arrives, please?"

"Of course," she stated before turning and walking back down the narrow hall.

The dark mahogany bar anchored the room against the far wall from the entrance off the foyer. The room was quaint, filled with warm brown furniture. A half dozen bar stools lined the front of the bar, and in front of me were a handful of small tables and chairs. A few patrons sat at the tables, sipping cocktails while conversing, waiting for their tables to be ready in the dining area.

My breathing began to speed up. *Dang nerves.* I needed a drink before they got the better of me. I slid onto a stool in the center of the bar, placing my clutch on the counter.

"What can I get for you?" a way-too-young blond man asked as he placed a white cocktail napkin down in front of me. *If only I was twenty years younger . . .*

"A glass of pinot grigio would be lovely," I replied.

"Coming right up," he stated as he walked back down the bar, glancing at the array of bottles lined up until he came to the right one. I peeked at my reflection in the mirror, pulling ever so slightly at the skin around the edge of my eye. The tautness made the small lines that were becoming more prevalent each year disappear. Always on my birthday. But there I sat, a forty-four-year-old woman. Single, with crow's feet. Waiting for her first date in over a decade.

"Here you go, ma'am. Would you like to start a tab?" he asked as he placed the drink in front of me. *"Ma'am." Ugh.*

"No thank you," I replied, grabbing my credit card from my wallet and handing it to him to ring up.

The wine worked its calming magic after a couple of minutes. My breathing slowed, and my shoulders slumped back to normal, not realizing I had tensed them up. I was more alert now, even with wine in me, waiting with anticipation as I turned my head slightly when I heard a man's voice enter the room. Todd should be arriving any minute.

One by one, guests left the lounge area as their names were called. The clock ticked closer to the top of the hour. I could now hear soft band music overhead, good ole Frank Sinatra and his soothing tone. Soon, the foyer grew quiet until the sound of the large front doors opening and closing could be faintly heard. Then, the sound of my name came echoing down the hall.

"Of course, she is waiting for you at the bar," the hostess stated, her footsteps becoming louder down the small hall.

This is it! I glanced at my reflection in the mirror behind the glass bottles. And then—I spun myself around on the stool, allowing my long, auburn waves to flip and cascade off my shoulder. It was perfect, just like I had seen in the movies.

Instantly, our eyes locked. My jaw dropped.

CHAPTER FOURTEEN

I quickly closed my gaping mouth, lowering my gaze to take in Todd's full appearance. Before me stood a tall man, mid-forties and thin as a rail. He was so thin that I was worried that if I stood too fast, the wind I would create might blow him down or knock him over a few feet.

His light brown khakis were so loose that he had to cinch his worn black belt tightly to keep them up. His dingy, white button-up shirt hung on him like a child playing dress-up in their parents' clothes. Under his sagging khakis, his black dress shoes were worn and scuffed, showing signs of long use.

This is Todd?

I fixed my expression to a soft side smile as the bald man with piercing blue eyes gazed down at me on the stool I sat on.

"Cindy, I assume?" Todd asked, a smile crossing his face.

"That's me," I answered briskly, sticking my hand out to welcome him. Todd placed his balmy, sticky hand into mine, causing me to loosen the usually firm signature grip I had mastered over the years. It always took men by surprise at work, but it was a limp fish at best tonight.

He looked nothing like his picture except the color of his eyes.

Wait . . . his picture was only a close-up of his face and neck! *Was I supposed to ask for a full-body shot to ensure the head was attached to something I may be semi-attracted to? Was that a protocol I hadn't been taught yet in online dating?* I caught a glimpse of his smile growing broader as I turned my expression-less gaze back toward his face.

"You look way better in person," he stated once my face was in full view.

I couldn't help it; I grinned, feeling the warmth rise into my cheeks. I was sure they were a light rose, even though I couldn't see them. They always turn shades of red when strangers compliment me. A sudden surge of guilt seared through me. I wished I could return the same compliment to him, but I couldn't. It would have sounded disingenuous at that moment.

Cindy, remember his feisty personality? The one he showcased through your witty email exchange? Remember Bert and wheat bread? I realized I needed to focus on that, not his appearance or what I expected him to look like. *You know better than to have expectations.* Just relax, breathe . . . this is only a trial run, not an altar for a shotgun marriage!

I could feel the tension in my arms begin to relax, then my shoulders. The sensible Cindy in my head was right. I needed to focus on what brought me here: his ability to intrigue me with his words.

Todd slid onto the stool beside me, looking down at my drink. "What are you having?" he asked.

"Pinot grigio," I answered, swallowing the last of the yellow-tinted liquid that lingered in the bottom of my glass.

"Excuse me, sir," Todd quietly asked the bartender, whose back was turned to us. The young bartender's wandering eyes surveyed Todd's physical appearance when he faced us, sizing him up. Todd hadn't seen it, thank goodness, so he continued, his voice unsteady. "Could you get the pretty lady here another one of whatever she was drinking and one for me too?"

"Coming right up," the bartender replied as he turned and walked back down the bar where the wine was stored.

Point for Todd, I thought as I placed an imaginary notch on a chalkboard. *When was the last time someone actually bought me a drink?* It had to be at least nine, close to ten years ago, when William was still employed. Either way, I was glad to see chivalry had not been lost or forgotten.

"This will be the third time in my life that I have tried alcohol," Todd stated as the bartender poured wine into two tall, stemmed glasses down the bar. I could feel my eyes get as big as saucers. Then I quickly glanced down, not wanting my expression to cause alarm.

"I'm trying something new," Todd continued as he fidgeted with the white cocktail napkin the bartender had placed in front of him moments earlier.

"Well," I began, meeting his gaze again, realizing he was nervous, "my advice is to sip sparingly then." *Please heed my advice,* I thought hard, imagining what it would look like if I had to throw Todd over my shoulder and carry him out of the restaurant in a drunken state.

The hostess came back into the lounge area at that moment, firmly announcing, "Your table is ready."

"We'll add these to your table charge," the bartender stated, setting our drinks on the bar top at that exact moment. Todd and I grabbed our glasses and followed the hostess to the dining area. I picked up the pace, walking a few steps ahead of Todd to allow myself a sip or two more of wine before reaching our table to reduce the pressure that was beginning to build in my chest.

"Here you are," the hostess said. She extended her arm out like Vanna White, in a gesture that only hosts could accomplish because it wasn't apparent that we were standing in front of a table that was meant to be ours.

"Thank you," I replied, sliding into the right side of the maroon plush booth.

Todd nodded his head toward the hostess. "Yes, thank you." He then slid his slender frame into the booth next to me, catching me by surprise. Across from me was an entire empty booth where he could—no, more like *should*—have sat.

My shoulders instantly tensed up. I could feel myself becoming rigid.

Isn't it customary to sit across from one another on a first date? I had seen that a dozen times in movies. That was the right way. The only couples I had seen sitting side by side were those who expected to be smooching all night, which was certainly not on the agenda! I began to hyperventilate as if I were in an elevator and the walls were closing in on me. *Think, Cindy. You can't be stuck here all evening.*

"Excuse me, Todd," I asked as my breathing picked up speed. "I should have stopped at the ladies' room before we sat; may I get out, please?"

"Oh, sure," he replied, standing to let me by.

"Thank you. I'll only be a moment." I hastily turned back down the foyer, rushing past the numerous other patrons seated across from each other. *I knew it!*

As soon as I found the ladies' room door, I opened it with a quick pull, happy to see that no one else was in the white-tiled room. I almost tripped over myself as I frantically strode to the sink, placing my purse on the counter above it. Grabbing both sides of the white porcelain bowl, I hung my head, peering into the drain. *Maybe I'm not ready for a date. Perhaps this was way too soon.* I took a deep breath, raising my head to look at myself in the mirror.

"Baby steps," I firmly stated to my reflection, trying to convince myself I could do this. "This was your pilot date for a reason."

I turned on the faucet before dispensing soap into my hands. My mind played out a skit similar to something I'd seen on *Saturday Night Live.*

In this week's episode of how to do online dating in your forties, we bring you tips and tricks you should never forget:

1.   Get a full-body shot without maimed animals, ski masks, or sports equipment.

2. *Have a conversation on the phone with the person first.*

3. *Add to your bio that you are not here to help people through their midlife crises.*

I let out a little chuckle as I dried my hands on a towel before exiting the restroom.

Todd stood as I approached the table, another point for him on the chalkboard of chivalry. Then, taking a deep breath, I knew what I needed to do. "If it's all right, I prefer to sit across from you. That way, we can communicate better and get to know each other."

"Of course," he replied, motioning for me to sit with his arm. "Great idea."

I slid into the maroon booth opposite him with a small sigh of relief, placing my clutch next to me. I picked up the menu, glancing over it as Todd did the same. It was eerily quiet between us.

"Ahem. So, Todd, tell me about yourself—work, kids, family," I asked, thinking that was how you begin a first date.

"Well, where do I start?" he replied, putting his menu on the table before clasping his hands together. "I am just finalizing my divorce now. It was an arranged marriage of sorts. We had been together for twenty years, but, in the end, it didn't work out. We have three kids, two of whom we adopted, and the third was a surprise since we were told we couldn't have kids of our own."

My eyes widened, but I didn't have a chance to respond before he continued.

"I am, or should I say, I have been Mormon, since I assume everyone wants to know that on the first date in Utah," he said. His cheeks turned pink as he added, "But I'm trying something new, expanding past those boundaries to explore."

I nodded, that much being apparent by his new adventures in drinking. The hostess returned, placing two glasses of water on the table next to our wine glasses before walking away. Todd picked up his water, sipping from the rim, and continued.

"My wife—I mean, soon-to-be ex-wife—is a Filipino woman who told me a few years back that she didn't want to have sex anymore. In fact, she stopped doing many things, including cooking and cleaning. She left the kids and me to fend for ourselves a lot. Not that I don't mind cooking, but not all the time, since I worked outside the home, and she didn't."

I swallowed hard on the sex statement; my saliva lodged in my throat. *Is this what conversations look like on a first date? Do people reveal the most intimate issues with someone they just met?* I couldn't imagine divulging William's and my secrets on a first date, not even on the tenth date.

Out of the corner of my eye, I could see the waitress approaching our table again. "Are you ready to order?" she asked, stopping in front of us and pulling out a pad and pencil from her apron pocket. I was grateful for the interruption as a wave of urgency seared through me to move the date along quickly.

"Yes," I replied, not even glancing at the menu. "I'll take your house salad with the dressing on the side, please."

"And . . . I'll take your salmon with the asparagus tips," Todd replied. He folded his menu and picked up mine to hand to the waitress.

As the waitress turned, walking back down the row of tables, I picked up my wine glass to indulge, noticing that it was almost empty, but Todd's glass looked full still. *Well, at least I won't have to carry him out of the restaurant if he keeps drinking at this rate.* I could have suggested he start with a sweet drink, something with an umbrella and fruit, if I had only known he was new to alcohol consumption.

"Are you not liking your wine?" I asked as I set my glass back down on the table. "I noticed personally that wine and beer are acquired tastes. When I first tried alcohol many decades ago, I started with a tequila sunrise drink. Sweet with a bit of fruit. They also have sweet wines; they may be more palatable if you prefer to stick in the wine category."

"No, no . . ." he insisted with a pause. "I'm okay, just nervous." He fumbled with a napkin on the table. "You're my first date since my separation, and, if I can be honest, I'm not being my usual self."

In an instant, my shoulders eased down, and my body slouched in ever so slightly. I was his first date, as he was mine. And to be frank, except for the conversations I had with myself in my head, I was not myself either.

"Well," I said, placing my hands in my lap, "to be honest, this is my first date, too, after my divorce. So we have that in common. Tell me more about your children," I prompted in a soft, low tone.

As Todd spoke about them, he began to relax. He leaned in with his elbows on the table as he shared stories of their adoptions, the sports they liked, and the musical equipment they played. He even took another sip of his wine.

"Here we are," the waitress stated, interrupting one of Todd's stories as she approached our table carrying a tray of food. She placed our meals in front of us before asking the customary waitress question, "Everything look okay for you all?"

I nodded lightly. "Yes, thank you."

"So, tell me about you," Todd said as he cut his asparagus into bite-size pieces. "Do you have any kids? I think I saw a picture on your profile with three young men, but they have to be your brothers. You are far too young to have boys that old."

That was a gracious comment, another point for Todd on the chalkboard in my mind. I placed my fork on my salad plate, pausing before taking my first bite to answer. "Well, I do, in fact, have three grown boys, two daughter-in-laws, two grandchildren, and two more grandchildren on the way. Twins, to be precise." I picked my fork back up, placing a bite of lettuce in my mouth after dipping it in the dressing.

"Twins! Well, isn't that exciting? I assume you must live around here if you picked this spot for dinner?"

"Kind of. After splitting with my ex-husband, I moved to a small, remote town about thirty minutes from here. Not many people have heard of it. Woodland."

"Can't say that I have," Todd answered before slicing his fork into the salmon. "What bigger city is it by?"

"Kamas. If you can call that a bigger city!" I chuckled. "If you continue driving east through Kamas, you will hit Woodland. Population 343, but I think that number may include the sheep and buffalo."

"Buffalo?" Todd asked with a look of surprise.

"Yeah, a herd of a hundred or so, I would say," I answered through the side of my mouth, trying to quickly chew a bite of salad and swallow. "Not sure how they got there though. I haven't had a free moment to research them yet. But I enjoy their presence and stature on my drive each morning."

"Interesting . . ." Todd rested his chin in the crook of his hand for a moment. "You'll have to update me if you ever discover how they came to be in this small town you live in."

I would have liked to update him, in a way. He seemed to be a kind man, but I already knew I would not be seeing him again. I didn't want to give him any hope by saying out loud I would let him know, so I let his statement linger in the air between us as I looked over at him with a smile.

The rest of the meal was pleasant enough. Todd's sassy side, the one he showcased in our email exchange, never fully came out in person, which I chalked up to nerves. He did ask the formal dating questions though: "What do you do for a living?" "What are you reading right now?" "And why did you get divorced?" Unlike Todd, the divorce question I cut short with a simple, "Our future paths were not aligning anymore." He also asked about my house in Woodland, which led to a discussion about the remodel, a subject I was happy to discuss.

Maybe this dating thing is not so bad. It was nice to have someone to talk to besides myself, someone who was interested in me and curious about my life.

We finished dinner and passed on the dessert menu. "It's getting late. I suppose we better call it a night since I'm sure your alarm clock goes off bright and early like mine on Monday mornings," I said with a slight yawn. I wasn't exhausted . . . and yet I was. It wasn't the date or the later hour on Sunday, but the preparation for this night.

"Um, sure. I suppose," Todd replied, shifting his eyes to his wristwatch. "May I walk you to your car?"

"Yes, that would be nice, thank you," I agreed as he obtained the check, and I insisted we split the bill. We left the restaurant, walking side by side down the narrow, almost empty main street of Park City. I glanced in the shop windows filled with the latest trending ski gear. I savored the sweet smell of caramel and chocolate as we passed the candy store before turning down the side road to where my car was parked.

"This is me," I said, pointing to my red Mini Cooper nestled in a spot a few cars ahead of us. A lump began to form in my throat, realizing that I had not rehearsed the goodbye scene of this date in my head over the weekend. I was certainly not ready to kiss anyone yet.

So how do I end this? What if he asks if we should do this again sometime? What if he asks for my number? I certainly didn't want to hurt his feelings. A wave of panic seared through me as if a teacher had just announced a pop quiz I hadn't studied for—yet I needed to ace this to not hurt someone but end with my self-esteem still intact.

We stopped in front of my car, and I fumbled around for the keys in my clutch, thinking of the best way to conclude the evening.

"I had a great time tonight," Todd said with a light tone, standing a few feet away from me, tipping back and forth on his heels as I kept searching through my clutch.

"So did I," I said, finally pulling my keys out before turning my face up to smile at him. "Thank you for such a lovely evening." That, at least, wasn't a lie. I prepared to turn away to unlock my door.

That was when Todd did what I feared most: he leaned down with his lips puckered to kiss me. Terrified, I dropped my keys as a diversion. *Clunk.*

"Oops!" I said as I bent down to pick them up.

Think fast! How do I get out of this? While still crouching down, I took a few small steps back, pretending to fumble for my keys on the ground. When I stood back up, there was a two-foot space between us. I tried not to huff in relief. Todd was no longer in kissing range.

I outstretched my hand. "Thank you," I said, plastering on a pleasant smile. Todd's face, however, shifted to a soft smile once he realized what the end of our date would look like.

He took my hand and shook it gently. "Thank you, Cindy. Maybe we could do this again?"

I didn't want to lie, nor did I want to hurt his feelings. "We will see," I said, and turned to open my car door, hastily climbing in and starting the engine. Todd took a few steps back onto the sidewalk, his soft smile disappearing. I hesitated, waving through the closed window as I pulled out.

I slumped into the seat of my car once I was a few miles down the road, letting out a breath I hadn't realized I had been holding.

Test date: check!

CHAPTER FIFTEEN

November had officially made its rich and glorious appearance. The last orange and yellow leaves fell from my property's maple and oak trees. I had kept my promise to Charles, so besides the one date with Todd, I focused all my spare time on finishing the last of the renovations on the house before attempting another date.

The house, *my* home, stood in front of me in regal form as I raked up a pile of leaves on the small grassy patch in the front yard. The exterior was covered in pristine white board and batten, complementing the chocolate-rimmed windows and roof. Now straight as an arrow, the porch railing accented the recently placed brown wicker furniture on the deck, covered in earth-toned cushions.

Apart from Charles's obvious hard work, every bit of the renovations also had my signature. There wasn't a square foot without my imprint, which left me feeling satisfied and accomplished . . . but also lonely. This house with all its bedrooms only had me wandering through it, reveling in its beauty.

I placed the leaves in a large bag and carried them to the back porch, depositing them in the garbage can. Turning the knob of the vibrant red back door, I entered the foyer. A smile crossed my lips, remembering how I'd had to jump across the dangerous, crater-sized hole that was once there. It was now covered and tiled over with brown ceramic stones. On one wall, there was a small wooden bench with storage for shoes. The open loft stairs I had stained just the right shade of espresso cascaded to the second floor against the other wall.

I removed my shoes and padded through the living room with its restored original fireplace, complete with a river rock hearth. Then I went through the finished dining room, the walls now covered in cream paint and wainscoting, along with my magnificent dark oak dining table that once filled the dining space in the hacienda. I paused for a moment. How wonderful that this table only brought good memories now. I couldn't wait to celebrate the upcoming holidays with my children here. They were used to their mother doing crazy stuff, but this remodel should knock their socks off.

Finally, I entered the vibrant kitchen with floor-to-ceiling white cabinets, complete with glass fronts and black knobs. They were accented by gray-textured granite countertops and a large farmhouse sink in the center of the kitchen island. The golden light of fall poured in from the new french doors in the dining room, illuminating the entire space.

I placed the kettle on the new stovetop, turning the knob too high. A day like this deserved a cup of tea! Finally, my renovations were complete after nearly eight months of nonstop work. Now I had some time to reflect on dating—in this decade. I grabbed the yellow notepad on the counter, which held a list I had started, and continued adding tips for online courting. So far, it contained the following:

1. Obtain a full-body shot from any prospective suitors.
2. Conversation on the phone first (block your number before calling). Inquire about any midlife crisis the potential date may be going through.
3. Dating is not a scene from a movie—don't overthink it.
4. Set the ground rules before the date: opposite sides of the table, no sex talk, and absolutely NO kissing on the first date.
5. Always meet the date at a predetermined location. No

one needs to know where you live. (Remember the movie *Fatal Attraction*)

I knew my list would grow. After my date with Todd, I decided dating was a lot like finding a job. Or maybe I tend to compare most things in my life to the one thing I relate to the most: business. When you're young, you apply for many positions, but as you become older, you become more focused on finding a career where you can live out your professional goals and eventually retire. I was young in my dating life again, applying for many positions, which equated to sorting through hundreds of dating profiles, trying to figure out what tickled my fancy. This reminded me that I needed to add to my dating tips list:

7. Verify potential date has a job via an online search.

As the weeks passed, courting got easier. Conversations flowed over drinks or dinner with suitors, and my nerves settled. Unlike with my first date, I avoided the dreaded end-of-night kiss by communicating my ground rules ahead of time. I had realized an important thing about me: I was in no rush to settle down again and replace the role of William before his side of the bed was cold—even though the bed was always cold every night in Woodland, thanks to the twenty-degree temperature difference from the city.

All I truly wanted was a night, or two, where someone was interested in what I had to say. Someone to keep me company, who could hold my attention with riveting conversation and humor. Someone, even for one night, to tell me I was pretty. But even deeper, I had a longing for someone to make me feel that I was enough, which was something I had been missing in the last eighteen months I was with William before the split.

By the time I had my ninth first date, I had realized I was finding my stride. Finally. Jake and I met for drinks after exchanging messages filled with sarcastic banter. We spoke on the phone, and I was able to see a full-body photo of him. No sports pictures or freshly killed deer with bulging eyes, but a regal image of him in dark blue jeans and a classic blazer.

We met at a brewery in the city for drinks after work. The front windows of the uber-modern establishment highlighted three large copper vessels. I arrived a few minutes early and went straight to the bathroom to recheck my appearance. I had spruced up the black dress I had worn to work that day by adding red open-toe pumps and a red beaded necklace. Before leaving work, I touched up my auburn curls and applied black eyeliner to my lids, followed by another coat of mascara.

As I exited the brewery's restroom, Jake stood at the hostess station.

"Jake?" I asked as I came around the back of the hostess, facing them both.

"Cindy?" His eyes lit up with recognition.

"Yes, that's me," I confirmed, taking in his large frame and perfectly styled short gray hair. "Nice to meet you in person." I outstretched my hand, and Jake grasped it. I instantly firmed up my grip, causing him to firm his. *Touché.*

The hostess led us to a neatly tucked table in the back corner under the stairs. The dialogue throughout the date with Jake was easy. It flowed like a classical piece of music. Drinks were soon accompanied by appetizers on top of another round of drinks.

"So, I can see that you don't have fake nails on," Jake said pointedly, giving me the once-over with his grayish-blue eyes. "And by the look of your lashes, those aren't fake either. What about your hair? Is that all yours?"

"All mine." I chuckled as I ran my hand through my hair, allowing it to skim down to the scalp, not getting caught once. "You must have a pet peeve about fake items on a woman?"

"I just prefer natural girls, with no preservatives added," he stated with a side smile. His sass was on point tonight, a trait I discovered I truly enjoyed in men.

Hours later, when the dinner date ended and he walked me to my car, I was pleasantly surprised by the light hug he gave me. His wide-framed body was pleasing to the touch, solid in a protective way.

As I drove back to Woodland, my insides were filled with butterflies and rainbows. That was how I equated the fulfilling emotion inside me. The evening had given me optimism that the swipe left or swipe right power I had at my fingertips was not as terrifying as I had imagined. Maybe, just maybe, I would enjoy the convenience of this new way of dating.

The drive home didn't feel like a drive at all. Instead, it felt as if I was flying. "I'm bringing sexy back, yeah . . . something, something you don't know how to act" blared through the car speakers, and I was singing along in full force. Tonight, I felt sexy. Jake had commented on how rare it was to find a woman these days with natural beauty. He had shared his experience in online dating, which left him feeling most women didn't look anything like the pictures they posted on dating apps, and how nice it was to be finally proven wrong. I'd beamed back at him, enjoying a handsome man's genuine set of compliments.

When I reached the turnoff to the narrow two-lane road leading me home, a light snowfall had begun to drift down. It blanketed the ground in a white sheet, reflecting the moon's glow. I slowed down a bit, feeling the car slip here and there on the icy roads, but it did nothing to dampen my mood and the car karaoke I was performing.

"Look at those hips . . . dah, dah, dah . . . you make me smile," I continued to sing, just a little quieter now, focusing on the road.

With the lane void of streetlights, the darkness quickly engulfed my car. As I climbed a bit higher in elevation, there was no mistaking the increase in snowfall, blocking my ability to see farther than ten feet in front of me. I had no choice but to slow down and lower the music. The muscles in my body tensed up a little as I strained to navigate through the thick blanket of white.

My car started slipping around each turn, making me grip the wheel tightly to keep it straight. My heartbeat sped up as my nerves heightened. I took shallow breaths, feeling my anxiety rise. A sharp curve in the road was coming up, a bend forced to be there due to the protruding mountain cliff. I eased around the bend cautiously.

Well, kind of cautiously. I was still reveling in the great night I had in the city. Then, as I rounded the last turn, I panicked, screeching hard on the brakes. Something was blocking the road in front of me.

"Shit! Shit! Shit!" I screamed as the object came into focus in the car's headlights through the now-thick cascade of snow. A brown cow stood like a statue on the road. Startled by my headlights, she raised her head, allowing the beam of lights to reflect a red glow in her wide eyes as my car barreled toward her.

With both hands on the wheel, I jerked the car to the right with all my might, away from the mountain cliff and the giant beast.

My car plunged down the embankment like a giant sled, skidding across the fresh, wet snow. I could feel the underbelly of the car crunching, being torn apart, as it slid across the brush and boulders that lined the road edge. I was headed toward the dark field in the distance, where somehow I knew the rest of that cow's family was safely grazing.

I screamed as the barbed wire fence came into view in the car lights.

"AHHH!"

I pressed my foot hard on the brakes, pumping the pedal up and down. But that only made it worse, causing the car to slide out of control. I was now an unwilling passenger in my rebellious Mini Coop, like a child careening downhill on a sled with no way to steer or stop.

I could feel my blood pulsing through every vein. My heart-beat was wild, fast, and bounding within my chest, wanting to burst through my rib cage. Every nerve in my body was on fire, alerting every heightened sense that I was in imminent danger.

I crashed into the barbed wire fence despite my foot stomping hard on the brakes. "FUCK!" I screamed. Shattering glass filled the cab as a pole holding the barbed wire cracked my windshield.

All I could do was hold on for dear life. My hands had a death grip on the steering wheel, my knuckles turning white. My foot feverishly pushed up and down on the brake pedal, willing it to stop. But the car didn't stop. Instead, it continued to slide through the cow field, dragging the barbed wire and poles along with it.

"Stop you stupid hunk of metal, stop!" I screeched. Yet, as if to spite me, my car turned in a circle, sliding backward into the middle of the field.

I turned my head sharply, trying to see the car's direction while still exerting more force on the brake. I was rapidly approaching a herd of cows with no chance of stopping, and with even more speed and force than I had on the road above when I avoided the first one.

I pushed the brake against the floorboard, grabbing the emergency brake simultaneously. My taillights reflected off the herd's dark eyes, cascading their red glow back at me. I braced myself for impact but was mesmerized entirely at that moment: in slow motion, I watched every one of those cows jump out of the way.

What in the world . . . ? Who knew cows could jump?

And then, suddenly, mercifully . . . the car stopped.

I sat frozen.

There was no way I could release my grip from the steering wheel. My racing heart and fast-paced gasps were the only sounds echoing inside the car. Bewildered, I watched the jumping cows staring at me and slowly moving farther away from my car. Their loud mooing now resonated through the car's interior. I couldn't tell if they were annoyed because I'd disturbed them or were laughing at my panicky winter driving.

The moon may have been covered with clouds now, but I'd just witnessed something I never thought I'd see. Abruptly, the old nursery rhyme of cow and moon made sense. Still, I could not move or even laugh. My nerve endings tingled with the sheer terror of what just happened, that was just now catching up to me.

Finally, and only when I was sure that my car had, in fact, come to a complete stop, I let out a long, drawn-out breath. I also managed to release my painful, white-knuckle grip from the steering wheel. *Am I okay?* I thought as I slowly moved my hands up to my face, feeling for any cuts from the shards of glass that used to form my windshield.

I felt nothing. Slowly, I moved my hands down my body, patting my arms, then legs, checking for further injuries. "I'm okay," I breathed aloud after realizing I wasn't hurt. I couldn't believe it. I turned my eyes toward the windshield. It was shattered on the right, along with barbed wire strewn across the left.

But the car was still running, giving me a glimmer of hope. *Maybe I'll be able to just drive out of this whole mess!* I turned off the engine, left the headlights on, and noticed they were the only light source for miles around. Everything else was utter darkness, which was now engulfed by heavy snowfall.

Reaching for the door handle, I tugged briskly, shoving the driver's door open with my shoulder. When I stepped out of the car into the darkness, my red pumps instantly sank into the mud. *At least, I hope that's mud!*

I pulled up each foot with great effort, stepping carefully onto the balls of my feet as I walked around the car. A muddy substance entwined my toes as I braced my shaking body with my hand on the vehicle. I couldn't see much.

I glanced around in the snowy darkness of the field, then back toward the street I had just slid from. It had to be a quarter of a mile away from me and only illuminated by my car's head-lights. Tall, dark trees surrounded the vast field in the distance. I could hear the river flowing softly, realizing it must be a hundred feet away. My tire tracks were covered up with the falling snow that was now becoming a flurry.

The cows had moved so far off in the distance that I could no longer see them. The faint mooing sound was the only thing that made me aware they were still there. The headlights illuminated the scratches and dents from the barbed wire and stakes on the hood and roof of my Mini Coop.

At least the car was facing the road, which was a positive thing in this messy situation. Positive. Luck. *Tshh*! I knew it was facing this direction because I had just spun several times around mere moments ago. I tried to think quickly through the adrenaline still raging in my body.

Maybe, just maybe, I can get back in the car and drive myself out of this field.

In the distance, I could see the hole in the fence where my car had skidded through. My shoulders slumped, and I sighed, realizing I needed to fix that damn fence before any of the cows got out! Yes, amidst my own turmoil, I still thought of the innocent animals that had started this mess. Or maybe their owner, who would be enraged if all of his cows were wandering on the road.

I moved to the front of the car and pulled at the wooden stakes entangled around the windshield, along with the barbed wire. Unfortunately, as I tugged, I lost my footing. My red pumps were no match for the wet snow.

I shrieked as I fell, unable to catch myself, until I landed with a *thwack* in the cold mud, right on my butt. I sat there for a second, glancing down at my once pristinely pressed black dress and expensive red pumps, now covered in mud and debris. My perfectly curled auburn hair was soaking wet, clinging to the sides of my face.

I couldn't hold it in any longer. My amusement erupted into a loud, boisterous laugh from deep down. I laughed and laughed until I felt the presence of a few cows looking at me curiously.

When I could finally stop, I grabbed hold of the car's hood, pulling myself back up. I wiped my hands on my wet, grimy dress, grasping the wire once more and tugging again. I dug my high heels into the mud to anchor myself this time. They were now a tool I was going to use to my advantage.

"Come on, get OFF!" I demanded of the tangled wire that would not budge. My hands slipped as my grip became slick from the snow. I could feel razor-sharp bites as the wire cut through my fingers, causing warm blood to pool in my palms.

But I didn't care. *I have to get out of here.*

Wiping my freezing hands again on my dress, I wrapped the wire around my fists. This time, I braced a muddy foot against the car and pulled. To my surprise and relief, it began to loosen inch by inch. "That's right, you pain in my ass," I huffed through excreted breaths. "Get off my car."

I thought through what my next steps would be as I pulled. *First, I'll drive back up through this field to the opening I chaotically created and back onto the road. Then, I will immediately jimmy-rig the fence together tonight, so cows don't get out and I don't make an enemy of my neighbor. Afterward, I'll come back in the morning and fix it properly. Lastly, I will go straight home and directly into the tub, clothes and all.*

I was determined to rinse this accident right off me, and the image of my victorious soak in the warm water renewed my strength.

"Great plan," I said aloud as the last bit of wire screeched off the car's metal.

Finally!

I fell back against the driver's door, pressing my bloody, scratched-up hands against my sopping dress, feeling icy rivulets run down my bare legs. I stayed there for a while, hands pressed against my dress, catching my breath.

Climbing back into the driver's seat, I turned the key in the ignition. The engine revved to life. A wave of relief washed through my cold, sore body, allowing it to sink into the seat. *Salvation!* I turned the heat up, placing my hands against the vents to defrost.

Once the tingling subsided from my extremities, I put the car into drive, pressing lightly on the gas. I could feel the car move forward a couple of inches; then it stopped. I pressed my muddy foot harder on the gas pedal, but it didn't budge. Instead, the back tires spun ever so slightly. Frustrated, I threw the car in reverse, easing on the gas again. Just like before, I felt it move mere inches before stopping.

"Come on, for the love of all that is holy!" I shouted, pounding my hands on the steering wheel. My hand reached down, desperately searching the car's floor that was now covered with the items that were once in my purse. "Found it!" I exclaimed as I drew my cell phone up to my face.

No Service.

Of course.

I was in the dead space zone. The small road from Kamas to my house never had cell service available, just like the day we came to see the place many months ago and got lost in the sheep field.

Opening the car door, I illuminated the area with the flashlight on my phone and walked toward the front tires. I knelt in the mud, shining the light into the space.

"You have got to be kidding!" I exclaimed. The tangled wire came into view. Wedging my way deeper into the space, I could see that the barbed wire had wrapped around the axel, of all things, like a tightly woven spool of thread. I reached in, pulling at the wire with my hands. But it was so firmly wound around the steel that I ended up cutting my hands more.

Frustrated, I leaned back on my heels, turning my face upward to the drizzling dark clouds.

"A little help would be nice!" I roared to the sky.

Using the car to steady me, I pulled myself back to standing. The fight-or-flight mode that gave me energy moments ago was gone. The throbbing pain from the cuts on my hands and bitter cold that now seeped down into my bones had taken its place.

As I was about to grasp the door handle, I saw headlights coming down the lane. I watched as they slowed down, and eventually stopped in front of the fence opening I'd created. My blaring headlights cast a bright spotlight in the direction of the road, highlighting their arrival.

Thank you, Jesus!

A feeling of liberation overcame me as I raised my hands in greeting. Then I hesitated. A quick surge of instinctual panic filled me when I saw five men emerge from the truck and start down the embankment. *Oh, Cindy . . . is this about to go from bad to worse?*

Only as they got closer did their shapes morph. Two of the men remained tall and looming, but three got smaller. With a long exhale, I realized the three were just boys, and I knew now I would be okay. One of the men shone his flashlight in my direction as he raced through the field. "You okay, ma'am?"

"I'm all right," I called back, the threat of terror now gone. I didn't think my body could take much more adrenaline bursts tonight. "I just got my car stuck, is all."

As they approached, their flashlights revealed the extent of the damage to my vehicle and me more clearly. I glanced down and found myself indeed covered in mud, with my hair wet and limp around my face and dried, bloody palms.

Once the men and boys were a few feet in front of me, I could see their Boy Scout uniforms under their coats. *Great, I am about to become the service project for a new patch! Something I can cross off my bucket list, even though it was never on my list.* My headlights captured their expressions as they grimaced at the car.

"Are you *sure* you're okay, ma'am?" the shorter man asked with a slight country drawl, his flashlight quickly darting between the car and me. "We can call the medics and sheriff if you need us to. In fact, Sheriff Clark is John's pappy o'er there." The flashlight shifted in the direction of a small blond boy who waved hastily in the light.

"I'm fine, really," I replied in a reassuring voice, patting myself up and down so they could see I had nothing broken. "I just need to get my car out. The engine still runs, but the barbed wire is wrapped around the front tires. It won't budge more than a couple of inches."

The two men and one of the boys knelt down in front of the tire well, shining their flashlights in the dark space. "Yeah, that is wound pretty tight," said the shorter of the two. "Boys, go fetch me the pliers from the truck's glove box and snag the blanket in the back for the missy here."

The boys arrived back quickly with the pliers and a blanket. The blond boy brought the covering to me, which I eagerly accepted, wrapping it around my shivering upper half.

"Thank you," I said softly.

The small man climbed as far as he could into the wheel well while the taller man held the flashlight for him to see. Grunts echoed along with the occasional snip of pliers. "That's twisted skintight," the small man echoed back from the wheel well. "So dang tight that I can't get a grip on most of it with these small pliers." He climbed back out of the tire well, peering in my direction.

The men explained that they were on their way back to the church to drop off the boys for pickup after attending an event, which made sense with the uniforms, and the hour was not that late. It was slightly past eight, but it felt much later with the snowfall and daylight saving time change. The other man had left his truck at the church and carpooled with the group. He had a set of heavy-duty wire cutters in the back of his truck at the church, having just been cutting fence lines earlier.

They asked me to ride with them, concerned for my well-being alone in the field. I pondered the invite for a moment before accepting. I reasoned that if I was with them, they had to come back and help me with the car. Plus, I felt safe now. If the Boy Scout uniforms were not enough to prove it, the men's kindness certainly was. Besides, the last thing I needed or wanted was for the rancher to show up in the morning, scratching his head, angrily pondering how a car got into the middle of his field.

We trudged up the field as the men led the way, trying to find the flattest patches for me to walk on in my ruined red pumps. The snow flurry had slowed by the time we reached the truck, thank goodness. The drive was short, and small talk was exchanged, mainly about the upcoming winter season.

Apparently, the weather would only worsen from here on. The men informed me that ten to twenty feet of snow would drop in mere days during the winter season in Woodland. Thank goodness I had purchased a maroon Jeep a few months back, which did me little good right now since it was sitting nice and comfy in the garage at home. But it did give me a little comfort, knowing it was there waiting for the rest of the treacherous winter weather to come.

The boys hastily jumped out of the truck once we parked in the church parking lot, echoing their goodbyes over their shoulders. The men efficiently retrieved the tools they needed from the other truck before driving the couple of miles back to the field where my Mini Coop sat in defeat.

We arrived back at the opening of the fence leading to my car. Squinting in the darkness, I was relieved that none of the cows had yet wandered up to the break in the fence. They were still off in the field, probably sore from all the jumping. The short man insisted I wait in the truck as they untangled the wire.

I adamantly refused. "Nope. I'm coming with you. My mess. My responsibility," I firmly stated.

"Suit yourself." He shrugged as they opened the doors and leaped out of the truck. On the other hand, I slithered out of the truck in my grubby dress, the blanket still wrapped tightly around me.

We slogged to the car, and the men got straight to work. Soon, the sharp snap of the pliers echoed into the now almost clear evening sky. It was as if the snow came and went in an instant, only making an appearance to dampen the mood I was in after what I thought was a great first date. Looking up at the sky, I mouthed, "Thank you for the reminder that life is still not good!"

At least I found pleasure in the sound of wire being cut. It was music to my ears—a means to an end of a now exhaustive night. They did the driver's side first, then the passenger side. Finally, after a few minutes and a lot of grunting and huffing, the short man sat back on his knees in front of the tire.

"I think we got it all, ma'am," he announced through an exhaustive breath. "Hoist yourself back into the car and see if it will move for ya now."

I eased myself into the seat, placing the key in the ignition and my foot on the clutch, turning the key. The engine revved to life right away. Lightly, I pushed on the gas, allowing the car to move forward, preparing for it to stop after a few inches—but it didn't. Soon, I was fifteen feet in front of where my car once sat.

A long sigh escaped my lips before I pulled up the parking brake, letting the car idle as I opened the driver's door. "You did it! I can't thank you enough!" I proclaimed as they approached where I stood on the driver's side.

"Our pleasure, ma'am. I'll guide ya to the main gate over yonder," he stated, pointing to the far end of the dark field. I was unsure how far it was in the shadows, but I knew that was the direction I needed to go. "My friend here will jimmy-rig the fence back up so none of the cows get out."

They guided me slowly through the field with just the light from my headlights and a small flashlight, careful to make sure I did not drive over any boulders that would thrash the underbelly of my car more than it already was. Once we reached the gate, they opened it, letting me out.

The short man came over to my window, which was still rolled down. "Okay, ma'am, we're going to follow you home to make sure you get there okay since that windshield is pretty torn up and I don't know how well you'll see through it."

I really didn't need to be followed home. I knew I would be okay driving with my head out the window, at ten miles an hour. But I also knew these weren't the men you say "no" to under these circumstances. They were country gentlemen, and they would follow me anyway. All they wanted to do was make sure I got home, and after what they had just done for me, I owed them that.

"That would be nice, thank you," I said softly.

Turning on my hazard lights, I eased the car onto the two-lane road, peering in my mirror to ensure the truck followed me. The road was empty besides the two of us. Our headlights cascaded off the light blanket of snow that now covered the fields and cliffs to the east and west of us. We passed the church that was now dark, and I realized then that getting my car out of the field had taken hours, not the minutes I'd assumed.

Reaching the turnoff to my lane, I watched as the men's truck signal appeared in my rearview mirror. I turned off my hazard light as I drove past the few houses that shared the street with me before turning onto my now lightly snow-covered driveway. I opened the garage door with one click and eased the car inside.

Climbing out of the car, I strode back to the men's truck that had stopped at the top of my driveway.

"This is your house?" the short man asked with surprise through the truck window he had rolled down. "You're the one who remodeled this house?"

I nodded. "Yes, my brother and I are the deranged individuals who took on this project."

"Well, you did a great job," he continued, nodding his head in appreciation. "It looks nothing like the old run-down place it was! All the townsfolk thought this should have been torn down years ago, but you proved us wrong."

"Thank you," I said warmly, "and thank you again for everything tonight." I felt the last bit of energy seeping from me. "I don't know what I would have done if you all had not shown up."

I waved, then dragged my exhausted frame to the back door as they pulled out. I jerked off my ruined red heels in the foyer. They landed with a thud on the tile floor to thaw. As promised, I ascended the stairs to the loft and climbed directly into the master bath in my destroyed dress. I turned the faucet to warm and let the water cover me, oozing into every cold, aching joint. The water became a medium brown color. *Just like me to make my own gravy.* I stepped out, stripping the wet clothes off to finish washing in the shower.

Dressed in warm fleece with a hot cup of tea in my swollen, scratched hands, I dragged myself into my bedroom, pulling down the brown comforter. As I was about to climb in, a knock sounded at my back door. A wave of panic seared through me. *Who could it be at this hour?* My heart began to beat faster as I glanced over at the clock on my nightstand: 10:23 p.m.

Slipping a robe over my pajamas and my feet into slippers, I crept down the stairs to the back door. I peered through the window at the top, which my brother insisted I needed to see who was on the other side before opening it. I spied two policemen in wide-brim hats.

Questions ran in rapid fire in my mind. *Did the cows get out and the rancher called it in? Did the kind men who helped me inform the police of my incident and ask them to check on me? Or worse, did they report an accident between one Mini Coop and a stretch of barbed-wire fence?* Whatever it was, I knew the officers would not just go away.

I opened the door a foot, sheltering most of my body behind it. Then, taking a deep breath to control my now pounding heart, I asked, "Good evening, gentlemen. How may I help you?"

"Good evening, ma'am. I'm Clark, the sheriff here in Woodland. This is Officer Mike. Are you Cindy?"

I nodded. Somehow, they knew who I was, so I decided to ask the obvious question, not wanting to blurt out my night's adventure. "Is everything okay?"

The sheriff pulled out a muddy, bent-up license plate from behind his back and held it in front of him in his gloved hands. "I believe this belongs to you, ma'am."

I looked down at the sorry piece of steel, a wounded version of its former self.

How the hell did they find this in the middle of a muddy, snow-covered cow field?

My eyes darted down to their shoes. There wasn't a speck of mud on them.

I held in a laugh, realizing it wouldn't help my situation. *Whatever "this situation" is.*

Please, come in, Officers," I stated, swinging the door open. Then I motioned them to the living room with an extended arm.

The sheriff was a medium-built man. His uniform was crisp, sharply pressed, and his jaw was square—firm, in fact—on his clean-shaven face. He removed his hat as he entered the foyer. His sandy brown hair was perfectly combed to the right with a precise part, even with a hat on. On the other hand, the officer was a tall, lanky man. His shirt was not as neatly pressed, and his dark hair was more tousled and a bit too long for a policeman, I thought after he removed his hat.

Before they could even ask what had happened, I recapped the critical events from the evening while holding my damaged license plate. I could tell I was talking fast, but I wanted them to know it wasn't my fault. In fact, if there was any fault, it should be on that big brown cow! That's who they should be talking to.

"So you see, Officers," I stated as I concluded with sweaty palms, wondering what punishment would be cast down on me, "this was just a small weather and cow incident. No one was hurt, and no one else was involved." I said, slightly smiling.

They listened intently, asking questions here or there as they jotted notes on their pads. "You must have had significant car damage since we found this plate quite far out in the field, past large boulders and flattened waist-high bushes?"

Do I ask them how they found the plate? Did they have a drone search party with spotlights searching the field for clues after whoever tipped them off? Maybe it was that darn brown cow!

"No, not that much damage," I said, downplaying it. I realized, however, that I hadn't taken stock of all the damage to the car when I arrived home. I'd made my way straight to the tub, and part of me was instantly glad that I'd at least been able to clean myself up before these men showed up on my doorstep. Still, I added cheerily, "I was able to drive it home."

I clasped my hands together in my lap as if what I was about to say should conclude the meeting. "So, Officers, as I have explained, it was an accident involving just me; no one was hurt, not even the cows, and minimal damage to a fence, which I am fully prepared to fix."

"Can we see the car, ma'am?" Sheriff Clark asked.

Should I refuse? Once they saw the car, they would ultimately decide the event that I described was of a much grander scale. But if I refused, they would be suspicious that I was trying to hide something.

"Of course," I replied, not wanting them to become wary. In my mind, I hoped my car didn't look too bad in the dim garage light. Then, standing, I led them to the back door as they both placed their hats back on. The unattached garage was just to the side of the covered back porch, which shielded the walk to and from the house from the weather.

Unlocking the garage door, I swung it open with ease. I clicked on the switch, and the fluorescent light sputtered to life. Once the garage was fully illuminated, I could feel my jaw drop slightly, hesitant to look over at the officers' faces.

The entire front, sides, and top of the car were covered in large, claw-like scratches as if a herd of hungry mountain lions was attempting to pry it open like a can of tuna. The windshield was shattered on the right side, with a deep crack like lightning crossing over to the left. It was obvious it was still intact by sheer luck. The front bumper was bent in, giving the car a narrow look. I plastered a smile on my face before turning back to face the officers.

I grimaced. "See? Not bad."

Oh, it was *terrible*, but I was not going to show it on my face.

Sheer silence filled the garage for what felt like hours. On the other side of the Mini Coop in the two-car garage sat my maroon Jeep SUV with four-wheel drive. The men looked over at the Jeep, then back to the Mini Coop, and then back to me, over and over as if trying to make sense of it all.

Finally, the sheriff asked, concern dripping from the words, "Are you sure you're okay?"

"I'm perfectly fine," I replied, patting myself up and down to prove it for the second time that night.

"Well, ma'am," Sheriff Clark began, tipping his hat back off his forehead as if unsure what to do next. "We'll need to write up an incident report, just in case the farmer wants to file anything to get his fence fixed."

"Do we have to do that?" I began, thinking if anyone should get the incident report, it should be that damn cow. "I will go first thing in the morning with new stakes and wire and fix it like new," I pleaded in a soft voice, one I learned effectively as a child and now used as an adult only when trying to persuade someone not to do whatever it was they were convinced to do. I didn't like my pleading voice, but it was necessary sometimes.

"Sorry, ma'am, but we have to do it," Sheriff Clark responded.

I huffed a sigh and then led them back into the warmth of the house, motioning for them to sit on the couch. "At what time did the incident happen?" the sheriff began. As he spoke, a dimple appeared on his right cheek, something I hadn't noticed before. We walked through the details of the incident once more, his hand scribbling feverishly on the triple-lined copy paper pad.

When we finished, the clock was striking midnight. Sheriff Clark handed the pad to me to sign my acknowledgment of my described events. *I can't believe I am getting a ticket*, I thought, handing the pad back to him. *This was not my fault. That cow better watch out, or it may become the town's Friday-night dinner.*

The sheriff tore a pink copy of the report from his pad, handing it over to me. He then flipped the notepad closed. He and Officer Mike stood, and I quickly followed suit. That night, which started with my first really good first date, was about to end with a pink slip. *Just my luck.*

I walked them to the back door, opening it wide. The officer strode across the back porch into the darkness where the patrol car sat. Sheriff Clark paused, turning back to face me on the porch, slipping his hat down further on his forehead.

"My son said you were a surprising sight tonight, out there in the field," he commented, another dimple forming on his left cheek. "He was the one to give us the license plate. The winters get rough up here, and cattle escape all the time onto the small lane. Be careful. Try not to drive too much at night. And I would retire that Mini Coop for the winter. Seems you have a perfectly good four-wheel vehicle that could be used instead. We've had to pull one too many newcomers out of the river until they become used to Woodland's weather patterns."

Mystery solved.

"Thank you. I appreciate your concern and forewarning," I replied, leaning against the door frame with folded arms, clutching my pink slip. Glancing down, I noticed the gold band on his left hand. With his right hand, he tipped his hat toward me with the edge of his finger. "I'm sure I'll be seeing you around, ma'am. This *is* a pretty small town."

"I'm realizing that, Sheriff," I said, holding in a sigh. "I am definitely realizing that."

CHAPTER SIXTEEN

The wounded Mini Coop seemed to let out an auditory whimper each morning when I glided past it to its counterpart, the Jeep. At least, that's how I imagined it. I would pause, touching its hood upon my return home from the city each day as if to comfort it.

"It will be okay," I'd soothe. "I just need to find someone local here who can fix you. Just hang on a couple more days, and then I'll find a car doctor." Certainly, my Coop was in no condition to be driven down to the valley to my old mechanic. And the cost of towing would cut into my already stretched-thin budget from the remodel.

The first snowstorm was just a memory, having melted quickly away in the crisp November sun. But I knew it was only a warning sign of what would come for the rest of the season, allowing me to prepare better before what might be a treacherous winter ahead.

I had not spoken to my date Jake about the events that followed after our evening. *No jumping cows or anything!* All I did was send him a quick text the following day thanking him for a lovely time. I was trying to determine if the freak accident was a sign. Maybe I had jumped into dating too soon? Or perhaps the universe was trying to tell me not to see Jake again? Or maybe I needed to slow down and not jump too fast at the next shiny object of a man that came along?

Or perhaps I was overthinking *all* of it, and the sign was to get snow tires on my cars and not drive at night whenever possible. Whatever it was, I heeded it on both accounts.

That Saturday, the sun peeked through my bedroom's blinds, casting a sliver of light across my eyes. I opened one eye and fixated it on the clock nestled on the bedside table: 7:46 a.m. *Sooo nice to sleep in*, I thought with a yawn. I rolled onto my back, prying my other eye open and wiping away the crusted residue. I stared up at the brown beam that ran the ceiling length, now adequately insulated. The shapes and patterns swirled as my mind attempted to fully regain consciousness.

My hand fumbled around on the side table, feeling for my cell phone. I pulled it close to my face as I lay in bed.

"Hey, Siri, find mechanics near me," I asked in a crackly voice.

"Okay, I have found mechanics near you," she said in her mechanical tone.

Two mechanic locations appeared on the screen. I clicked on the first option, which produced a picture of a shop with two car bays. Scrolling down to find the number, I saw their hours of operation.

CLOSED SATURDAYS AND SUNDAYS.

Damn.

I closed the tab and scrolled to the other option Siri found. As I clicked on the location, a picture of a large old shop on what appeared to be the backlot of a house materialized. By the looks of the image, it was a single extra-large bay garage. Just big enough to hold an RV, I assumed. Next, I scrolled to the hours of operation: open Saturday from eight to three, closed Sundays.

Tapping the phone icon, I waited until the familiar ringing began.

"You've reached F&T Repair and Towing. For towing, press one. For the repair shop, press two."

Well, it's a two-for-one shop! I will put that in my memory bank for future reference.

Pressing two, I waited.

"F&T Repair," a deep voice resounded back.

"Good morning, my name is Cindy, and, well . . ." I hesitated, clearing my throat and sitting up in bed against the headboard. "I think I live just down the road from your shop. I was wondering if you have time to look at a car of mine today to see if you can fix it this week?"

"Sure, ma'am. What needs fixin'?" he asked, his drawl becoming more apparent.

"Well, I definitely need a new windshield," I began, deciding to keep the description slightly vague. *No need to scare the mechanic off before he sees the car.* "And there are a few dents and scratches, along with the possibility of some undercarriage damage I would like to have checked."

"Sure can, ma'am. Anytime after nine this mornin' will be just fine," he replied with no hesitation. "You know how to get here?"

I pulled the map up on my screen. Zooming in on the shop's location, I discovered, to my surprise, that it appeared to be right by the notorious cow field. *The irony of it.*

"It looks like you're not far from the bend in the road into Woodland from Kamas. I think I can figure it out," I replied, adjusting the map on my phone with my fingertips. As I scrolled through, the entirety of that night flashed before me, and I had an insidious thought.

Maybe the mechanic owns the cow, and he sets her loose at night to crash cars! Drive more business to his shop.

I held in a chuckle. What an absurd thought.

"Alrighty, ma'am, I'll see you when I see you, then." And with that, he hung up.

Shortly before nine, dressed in navy blue sweats with a hoodie, I shuffled to the garage in the crisp morning air. My breathing cascaded light clouds into the sky, resembling abstract shapes you may see in a modern museum. I patted my poor Mini Coop one more time on the hood, which created an alarming creaking sound, before climbing into the driver's door.

"Here we go, baby," I cooed to her. "I promised you, didn't I? We're going to take you to the nice mechanic."

Relieved, the engine roared to life once again. Rolling the window down, I craned my neck out the opening as I backed out. As I turned onto the small lane, driving forward, I stretched my neck out even more to see where I was going. The windshield looked worse than I remembered from the other night driving it home, and the cold air rushed over my face as I tried to keep a semblance of control on the road. *It wouldn't do to have Sheriff Clark see me now, would it?*

It was surprisingly quiet on the road that morning, making my awkward drive on the shoulder with my flashers somewhat easier. I glanced at the empty Camper World. Too cold now for campers, and yet not enough snow for the snowmobilers yet. Those are the two main travelers on this lane, besides the locals. I couldn't even hear the river as I drove, realizing it might be just a trickle this time of year.

I looked up in time to see the small sign before passing it:

F&T Towing & Repair

It was no bigger than a For Sale sign. Easing the car in reverse, I backed up on the road edge, turning into the dirt driveway—something I never would have been able to get away with in the city.

The private road ran alongside a blue ranch home, with a large front porch covered in plastic flowers in worn vases, ceramic gnomes, and a few bright pink flamingos. I continued to drive past the house, where the side of the dirt road became cluttered with broken-down cars and parts strewn on both sides. Ahead of me stood a giant pole barn garage, just like the online picture.

The bay door was wide open. The sound of my car coming down the road must have alerted the mechanic of my arrival since a heavy-set man appeared in the empty space. He looked to be in his late fifties, maybe a little older. His blue jean overalls were covered in dark smears. His hair was untidy, and he was wiping his hands on a rag as he walked out onto the dirt road where I was about to stop.

I parked, got out of the car, and stood close to my driver's side door, watching him closely. I witnessed the moment the man's expression changed when he surveyed the Coop. His initial solemn demeanor suddenly took on a Sherlock Holmes visage, surprised and deeply curious, in fact. He stopped a few feet in front of my car, remaining silent. Then, taking his greasy hand, he ran it through his hair, which explained why it looked untidy.

Without acknowledging me, he walked around the car slowly, without a word. He ran his hand over a few of the spots that were more severely scratched up and dented. As he did so, I could feel my shoulders slump, ashamed of my car's appearance. A part of me also worried he would tell me no, that he couldn't fix my poor little red-and-white Mini.

"Ma'am, what happened?" he finally asked. He bent down over the windshield and hood, tracing his fingers across the scratches and shattered glass. "How did you even drive this here?"

By now, I had a memorized script for my misadventure. Animatedly, I repeated the event's highlights that led my car to be in this condition. I watched the mechanic as he slowly walked around the car as I spoke, now feeling the deeper scratches. He occasionally paused when he came across a significantly damaged area, running his hand through his hair and glancing at me with bewilderment.

He fell silent when I finished my story, his hand resting on his chin. I took a few steps back from the car, waiting for him to tell me there was no way he could fix it. But then . . . he looked over at me and started to laugh.

It was a loud, bellowing laugh that permeated the air with brevity. His response cascaded an easy feeling over me, diminishing my worry. And because he was laughing and kept laughing, I realized how funny and absurd my story was. I couldn't help but join in, laughing with him. Finally, the mechanic walked toward me with his hand outstretched.

"That was quite the story. In all my years of livin' here, I didn't know cows could jump either. I'm Frank," he stated and grasped my hand.

"I'm Cindy," I replied, catching my breath from the sudden outburst, clasping his greasy hand back firmly with my usual aplomb.

"Well, this will take me about a week to get'er done," Frank began, shaking his head. He reached his hand back over to the car's scratched roof, tracing a few lines with his fingertip. "I need to order the windshield and get some paint that'll match the color."

"I am more than fine with that; just grateful you can fix her," I began, relieved that he said yes as if this was a marriage proposal or an equally important decision. "And I am even more grateful your shop is close to my house."

His shop *was* nearby, but I realized it was not close enough that I wanted to walk the five miles back to my house that crisp morning, which had been my plan. I glanced around, then into his shop bay. There was no one around, only a beater car up on the lift.

"So, there is one more thing," I began hesitantly, looking down and kicking at a rock with my shoe. "Is there any way I could get a lift back home? I'm happy to pay your tow fee for the five miles. I live a few miles down the road by Camper World."

As soon as the words left my lips, I realized this was yet another thing that would have never happened in the city: asking a complete stranger for a ride. Instead, I would have grabbed a Lyft or an Uber, none of which were available in this remote town.

A faint smile crossed Frank's face, causing his forehead to wrinkle. "Ha. No need to pay me; it's the neighborly thing to do. Give me a sec to clear the seat in the tow truck. It may be a bit dirty, ma'am, fair warning."

Tow truck? Looking around to the far side of the shop, I noticed the truck, hidden behind a camouflage of parts and broken-down cars. Or what I could see of it, anyway.

"That's fine by me," I said, glad I had decided on sweats that morning.

Frank strode into the shop and grabbed his keys before reappearing. I watched as he opened the tow truck's passenger door and grasped armfuls of old food wrappers and drink containers that he ditched in a nearby barrel before motioning me over.

I hoisted myself into the cab, which smelled just like I expected. *Grease and oil.* I didn't mind. He walked around the hood in front of me. His gait seemed strained as he leaned to the left before plopping himself into the driver's seat, starting the engine, and pulling out onto the dirt road.

"Whereabouts do you live by Camper World?" Frank asked in a curious voice. "I could have sworn I knew everyone around these parts."

"I live on Maple Loop, down from them," I replied, realizing I needed to explain further. "I just moved in a few months ago and don't get out much."

"Well, then," Frank continued. "My missus and I have been living in these parts for over thirty years now."

I noticed a softness to his voice, almost a Santa Claus feel. I liked it. I liked him. Any man who made me laugh that loud and hard was on my A-list, but I rather liked his character, also.

"One of our boys lives to the side of us with his wife and youngins. He helps me at the shop. So you could say Woodland is in our blood."

I smiled over at him as he spoke. *Can you imagine being so connected to a town that it's as if your blood is consumed by it?*

"Be careful during the summer," Frank suddenly warned, keeping his eyes on the road. "That Camper World gets full of out-o'towners walking up and down yer street. Best to keep your doors locked."

I blanched. "Thanks for the warning. I hadn't even thought about how the camping site would affect me." His revelation made me pause and thank God and Charles for the new door locks. I knew they would keep me safe. "Anything else I should be aware of in Woodland?"

"Well, you stated you met the sheriff. I'm sure Clark gave you the winter warning details?" Frank asked.

"Oh yes, and from the boy scoutmasters too. So I am now well-versed in what to expect for the winter," I stated, hoping that maybe the season would be kind this year since it was my first. Possibly drop just ten feet of snow, not the twenty that the men had warned of.

Frank turned onto Maple Loop, needing no direction on how to get to the lane.

"Which one?" he asked instead.

"It's the big white house down to the right," I replied, pointing three houses down to where my luscious tall pines stood, blocking the full view of my house.

"So this one is yours?" he asked curiously. "Everyone in town has been nattering about it since you fixed it up." Frank pulled into my dirt driveway. "Who knew the abandoned blue cabin could be turned into something like this!"

I blushed a little at the comment, realizing I had a vision that it could be this wonderful when I first saw it. However, I was relieved and overjoyed that it turned out even better than I ever expected.

"Well, most of the credit goes to my brother," I admitted. "I am just his assistant."

"This house was so run down," Frank stated as he put the tow truck in park in front of my garage, his eyes focused on the vibrant white exterior of my home in the morning light. "I was sure someone would eventually tear it down since it had more critters livin' in it over the last few years than people!"

"You're not the first to tell me that. It just needed a little TLC," I replied, recalling the number of burials we had for the dead animals. I clasped the passenger door's handle and pushed it open.

"Well, ya did good."

"Thanks, Frank," I said warmly, feeling genuinely grateful for him as I stood in my driveway, speaking through the open passenger door. "And thank you for the lift home." I turned to go. "Wait! I almost forgot to give you my number." I grabbed a scrap piece of paper and pen in the clutter from his dashboard, jotting my number down before handing it over. "Just in case you have questions or issues with my car. Or think of any other tips I should be aware of in Woodland."

"I could write a book of tips on what *not* to do in Woodland," Frank replied with a chuckle. "I'll touch base with you in about a week. Until then, stock up on snow bombs for your roof. The hardware stores sell out of them fast. There is tip one for you."

A laugh left my lips. "Snow bombs, eh?"

"Yeah, they're little round balls of snowmelt," he began, taking his hand and forming a ball with his fingers. "You throw them up on yer roof like a softball, and they melt the snow, so yer roof doesn't cave in from the weight of the snow."

"Thanks, Frank! I'll stock up today," I confirmed gratefully as I closed the passenger door.

Frank waved out his driver's window as he backed out. An eerie feeling came over me at that moment, like a sixth sense urging me to put his number in my phone on speed dial. For some reason, I knew I would be seeing a lot of Frank going forward, not just for tips about Woodland.

After a while, I forgot about the good-natured mechanic from earlier in the morning, anticipating the dinner I had that evening with a friend. Maggie, who needed a weekend away from her back-and-forth relationship with her boyfriend, would stay with me overnight. She, like me, had had to start over, learning how to date in her forties after a tumultuous divorce, and I was looking forward to commiserating.

As soon as Maggie arrived at my house, we decided to head straight to dinner. I changed into something sensible—jeans, a T-shirt, and a blazer.

The moment we arrived at the restaurant, a friendly hostess guided us to a corner table and handed us menus. Maggie and I settled in, taking in the eclectic decor and music playing in the background. "Good evening, ladies. Are you ready to order?" the waitress asked Maggie and me as we perused the menu.

I glanced over at my friend, grateful she was here not only to experience the early December beauty of the mountains but also to save me from first date number fifteen, which would have been my fate tonight. I still couldn't navigate the unbridled waters of the dating world with much skill. Heck, I wouldn't even call myself a novice yet.

A hiatus was what I needed. Plus, I had wanted to try out the local café in town for months but hadn't wanted to come alone. Certainly, I was not about to bring a first date here. It was too close to my home—making it way too close to comfort for me. But a third date . . . well, maybe, if I ever got to a third date with someone.

The café waitress stood before us with her hands clasped professionally at her waist. She appeared to be in her mid-thirties, with a diner logo T-shirt, bold name tag, and black jeans that complemented every curve of her fuller figure. Her blonde hair was tied back in a low ponytail, accenting her round, makeup-free, flawless face.

"Well, Betty, what would you recommend?" I asked, glancing at her name badge before raising an eyebrow inquisitively above my menu.

"All of the pastas are made from scratch daily," she began, her hands becoming animated as she spoke. "The lamb is locally sourced from Kamas and is simmered for hours until tender. The meatloaf is always juicy and the favorite of the locals. Just so you know, the chef's special tonight is a seared halibut with a white wine sauce and asparagus tips."

Betty conveyed each item eloquently and confidently as if she had tried every meal herself to confirm her recommendations.

"I see you also brought a bottle of wine; may I uncork it for you?" Betty asked, yanking a corkscrew from her black apron tied around her waist. I looked up the diner online a few days ago. While scanning their menu, I noticed the fine print at the bottom of the screen: *Have a bottle of wine you enjoy? Bring it with you. The uncorking fee is $10.*

"Yes, please," I replied wholeheartedly as she reached across the table to clasp the bottle. "Your recommendation for entrees sounds incredible. Maggie, what are you thinking?"

She ordered the halibut, and I decided on the chicken piccata as Betty poured equal glasses of the dark red for both of us before walking away.

"Well, this establishment is not so bad, quite cozy, in fact," Maggie stated.

The café from the outside reminded me of an old pizza parlor, one I had visited only on special occasions as a young girl with my grandmother. Earlier, when we entered, we were instantly hit with the mouthwatering aroma of fresh garlic and sauteed tomatoes as we scanned a large bulletin board full of announcements and business cards on one wall.

On the opposite wall of the diner entrance was an opening at shoulder height with a counter for to-go orders and pre-filled glasses of water that the servers could quickly grab for awaiting patrons. A few steps ahead of us sat a sign on a tall stand: *Wait to be seated.* It was perched at the top of three steps leading down into the dining area filled with classic American-style tables and booths.

"Travis wants to know where we are eating," Maggie commented, looking through her texts. "I think he wants to call this restaurant and pay for our dinner and the drinks at the bar afterward."

Travis was Maggie's on-again, off-again boyfriend who lived in Pennsylvania. They had met through work. *Lucky girl.* She hadn't had to deal with the online dating chaos for long.

"Well, if Travis wants to buy us dinner, who are we to stop him?" I replied, and raised my wine glass high and bold to toast her. "To us, and our 'after lives' we are creating."

Maggie picked up her glass, tapping it against the edge of mine, creating a slight clink sound. "To us," she began. "And to a much-needed break from irrational men for a couple of days."

"Here is some warm bread for the table," Betty interrupted, placing a basket covered in a white linen napkin between us. She paused, appearing not to be in a hurry and noticing our air of celebration and humor. "You ladies aren't from around here, are you?"

"You could say I am now," I said, reminding myself how small this town was if you could be spotted this quickly as not being a local. "I moved to Woodland several months ago. My lovely date for the evening is visiting me for the weekend."

On cue, Maggie waved lightly at Betty, who smiled at her.

"What made you move all the way out here?" Betty asked curiously, her eyebrow raised and a quirk to her smile. I replied with a simple overview of my circumstances and how they led me to Woodland.

"Huh. That's definitely one way to start over!" she proclaimed when I finished my story before excusing herself to attend to other customers.

Throughout our evening, Betty ventured over many times to check on us. She started conversing with us as if we were just a bunch of girlfriends versus a waitress and patrons. Betty revealed throughout the small exchanges that she was a mother of three, and working at the diner was her second job; she also worked at the bakery down the road during the day. Her husband was in construction, and the two were doing their best to raise their children away from the big cities, giving them a chance to understand small-town values.

As the meal concluded and Maggie and I finished the last bites of a decadent cherry cheesecake we decided to split, Betty reappeared at our table with a stunned yet enthusiastic expression.

"So the strangest thing just happened," Betty said, holding a white receipt in her left hand. "A man proclaiming to be one of your boyfriends called into the restaurant and paid the entire bill for both of you, including a *very generous* tip for me."

"That would be my boyfriend," Maggie replied, raising her finger nonchalantly. "He hinted to me earlier he may do that. Looks like he was as good as his word . . . for once!"

"Well, I must say, that is the first time I have had anyone do that." Betty placed the receipt in front of Maggie. "On the dating scale, he must rank high up there! I give him points for that. He either is out to impress you, or he is making up for something he did."

We both couldn't hold in the burst of laughter that followed. She nailed it.

"Oh, he is definitely making up for something he did," Maggie answered.

"Well, I hope this goes a long way to mend it. I have been married for over fifteen years and serve a lot of couples here at the diner," Betty said, leaning against the booth wall and folding her arms across her chest. "I can always tell when a man is trying to impress a lady or attempting to buy his way back into good graces. I can also pick out the frauds—you know, those men who are up to no good *and* expect a good time after the meal."

Betty glanced over her shoulder then, hearing the footsteps of new patrons entering the diner. "I gotta tend to the other customers, but I sure hope I see you around here more often."

At that moment, a light bulb went off in my head. "Betty, before you leave, do you work Friday and Saturday nights here at the café?" I asked, my expression filled with intrigue.

"Not all Fridays, but every Saturday. My regulars expect me," she answered, an inquisitive look crossing her face.

"I get the feeling I may see a lot of you, Betty," I replied, a devilish smirk appearing.

She walked away with a bewildered expression. But *I* knew exactly what I was doing. If any possible suitor were to make it past date one, I would bring them here for date two or perhaps date three. Betty would become my secret weapon, gauging the unexpecting dates' intentions throughout the evening and supplying me with her powerfully intuitive insight and mad skills.

This will be how I crack the code to online dating!

The cool, crisp air took my breath away as I raced from the cover of my back porch to the garage. I was still getting used to the extreme temperature shift between Woodland and the city, and I shivered despite the sprint. Today officially marked seven months since I moved into this quaint but quirky town. Tonight would be my *third* date with Tyler, a new *maybe*. This meant we would meet at Mayberry Café in town.

During our initial dates in the city, Tyler and I spoke about home renovations since he was starting his own remodel—a topic I was always eager to engage in. It also didn't hurt that he wasn't that bad-looking, even in person. Sure, he had a crooked smile and his lips were nonexistent on his overly tan face, but the previous conversations had gone well. And he insisted that he pay the bill. Now *that* was something I was still getting used to.

This would be the third time I had asked a suitor to meet me at Mayberry Café over the last six weeks. Betty had become the ace up my sleeve, and I was delighted she was entirely on board with my scheme.

We developed a technique of sorts. I would arrive ten minutes early and take the last booth in the far-right corner, which conveniently stayed dirty until I showed up. I sat on the right side of the booth, facing the direction of the stairs to the entrance. From this angle, I could see Betty easily in the background, watching for any hand signals or gestures she would give me. They were her silent way of telling me the man was either worth another date or to cut him off now, which was always a thumb across the throat movement. My date would sit across from me since there was no side-by-side sitting on date three either, per my yellow pad of rules.

I was earlier than usual tonight, wanting Betty's opinion on the suitor from last week before deciding if date two was the finality of my quest with him. She hadn't slashed her throat, nor had she given me the thumbs-up last week. It may have been due to the bustling crowd of customers that appeared late in the evening.

I pushed my way through the door, dusting the light snow off my shoulders as the familiar garlic-and-tomato scent engulfed me. Walking to the top of the stairs, ignoring the Wait to Be Seated sign, I caught a glimpse of Betty through the counter opening in the wall. I waved at her as if I was Forrest Gump welcoming Lieutenant Dan. She enthusiastically waved back, her lips twitching in a quick smile. I knew she would come over to me momentarily, so I strode down the steps to the predesignated booth I now politely claimed as mine on Saturday nights.

Betty had a handful of water-filled glasses as she walked by my table. "I'll be there in just a minute; I need to get these to table six really quick," she stated before striding to the other side of the dining room wall.

I watched her set the glasses on the table in front of the patrons before extracting the menus she held tightly under her arm and passing them around. I smiled as I heard her faint voice across the room, letting the customers know the specials and that she would take their orders shortly. Then she darted back over to me.

"So," I said as soon as she was within earshot, "what did you think of Jesse last week?"

Betty rested her arm against the bench seat, letting out a slight huff. "He was *handsome*, yet he finished the last of the bottle of wine without offering you any. So, Cindy, that means he will put himself first before you."

As if the answer had been in front of me the whole time and I couldn't see it, I leaned back in the booth, my head resting on the seat, tilting up as if the clouds had just parted and the sun was now able to shine through. "Wow, you're right. You're absolutely right!" I paused, but only momentarily in my gratitude. "So date two will be the last of the Jesse saga."

"So who is it tonight?" Betty asked, her right eyebrow raised with intrigue.

Leaning forward, placing my elbows on the table, I continued in a low voice, "Well, he is a successful realtor and does a local TV show every Sunday. He enjoys robust red wines and passed the first two dates in the city, which I had to reschedule on him twice."

Betty began to chuckle, shaking her head from side to side. "I still don't know how you convince them to come all the way up here from the city for dinner. That is still a mystery to me, but it earns them definite points!"

I thought about that for a second. *How do I convince them?* No one had said no yet when I'd asked. *But I have only asked three so far.* Maybe they saw something in me they wanted to explore further as I did in them?

"It's part of my dating plan, I suppose." I clasped my hands together on the table. "If they accept, I know they are more serious about me. If someone doesn't in the future, that will be my sign that they are not flexible, and I will cut them loose then and there. Plus . . . I value your opinion. You know that."

Betty nodded, a smile crossing her round, flawless face. "A glass of pinot grigio to start?"

"Yes please! And as always, he will ask for me when he gets here," I conveyed, although it was something I was sure I didn't need to say anymore.

"Of course he will, my mistress of the night," she proclaimed mischievously, bending over in a half bow with a slight flip of her arm before turning and walking away to procure my liquid courage.

After Betty brought my wine, she glanced over her shoulder at the sound of the entrance door opening. "That must be him. Excuse me, madam, as I escort him to your table so the evening and the judging can commence," she stated in a melodramatic voice.

Betty strode back within moments, Tyler by her side. I glanced up, forcing a smile as he stared down at me. She motioned for him to sit in the booth across from me. As she began to walk away, she turned around, raising her palm above the top of her head, bouncing it up and down slightly, and mouthed, "What is up with his hair?"

I turned my full attention back to Tyler, whose stick-straight hair was messy, the tips now bleached blond, as if he'd joined a boy band from the 1990s and they had just finished shooting a music video.

I chuckled under my breath, coughing slightly to hide it as Tyler grinned back. He slid into the booth and picked up the menu in front of him. I was almost certain this would be the last date with Tyler. I was a forty-four-year-old woman, not a twenty-something-year-old groupie.

CHAPTER SEVENTEEN

As Sheriff Clark and the Boy Scout leaders predicted, the snow came. It wasn't the light drizzle I had wished for, but a full fury dumping feet upon feet, just as they had foretold through the end of December and into the new year. The eerie feeling I had to put Frank's number on speed dial felt more like intuition now. And it was. Over the last month, Frank had pulled me out of the snowbank twice and fixed the Jeep's radiator after I hit a deer in town. Of course, it wasn't my fault; the blasted thing sprang out from the bushes one late evening in the dark, leaving me no time to stop.

It was just like the big brown cow—my nemesis on the road. On my way home tonight, he took up the entire road, blocking my car.

Not again!

I swerved hard to the right, propelling my newly repaired Mini Coop up the mountainside as I attempted to navigate it over the snow and rocks. My hands were firm on the steering wheel until my knuckles turned white. I could feel the underbelly of the car being torn apart yet again with every forward movement of the vehicle.

Why? What did I do to deserve this kind of luck? The skies had been clear, and I just wanted to save on gas by taking my little baby out instead of the massive Jeep. That's what I get for trying to love Mother Earth.

The car propelled itself twenty feet up the foothill before I could turn the wheel to the left with tremendous force from both arms, thrusting the car to descend back down the other side.

Bam! Pshhh . . . came from the car as it collided with a large boulder, forcing it to stop ten feet above the road's edge. A huff of air left my lungs, releasing the breath I held.

But now, in the safety of the patrol car, I peered over at the Mini Coop on the hill. I imagined it was crying out in faint whimpers, like a scared stray cat, just like it had done after the cow field incident months ago, as it sat in the garage waiting to be repaired. You'd think I would have learned my lesson, huh?

Frank had a hard time controlling his laughter when I called him asking for a tow again after conveying my circumstance to him. Which, in turn, made me laugh.

"God sure does have a sense of humor when it comes to you," Frank proclaimed in a lull of laughter. "I'm finishin' another job; I'll be there as soon as I can. Just hang tight. Get it? Hang tight, on a cliff?"

He's only mildly amusing today.

That was when the sheriff found me and helped me climb down the crag before offering me a seat in the patrol car until Frank came. He'd saved me from sitting in the cold and graciously decided not to give me a citation that time, explaining, "The mountain is not owned by anyone yet."

"I think the cows have a mafia going on up here, and that big brown one, I'm pretty sure she is the ringleader," I revealed to the sheriff as I placed my hands over the vents that were blowing out warm air. "We may need to deploy a special task force for cow gangs, round them up, and put them in a corral they can never get out of."

"Funny. Or maybe," he replied quietly, taking his hat off and setting it on the front dashboard, "a certain newer resident to Woodland, who shall remain nameless, should slow down when taking the sharp turns on the small two-lane road. That's a thought."

He was right, of course; the speed limit during the winter should be no more than fifteen miles per hour on the small lane. Maybe even ten, especially for me. But speed was not the only reason for my predicament that morning, nor was the weather.

I'm pretty certain that big brown cow is out to get me.

"Sheriff," I said, changing the subject. "How long have you been married, if you don't mind me asking?"

As if on cue, we both turned our gaze toward the gold band on his left hand.

"Almost twenty years," he replied, facing me.

"I made it fourteen years this time. Five years the first time," I said, bowing my head as I folded my now warm hands in my lap. "I don't think I am good at being a wife. I just can't seem to get it right."

"Well, in the few months I've known you, I would disagree," he began, slightly shifting in his seat. "You took on that abandoned, dilapidated house, and now it's beautiful. After barreling through the farmer's fence, you fixed it better than new. I've passed you in the grocery store as you bought all the Boy Scout jamboree packets you could and then gave them away. I would say you are one of the kindest and funniest people I have had the pleasure to know. In fact, I dare say you have just not found your match yet."

I could feel my cheeks turn red, embarrassed by the comments and that he saw the small things I did when I thought no one was looking.

"Can I ask you something?" I said, meeting his eyes again. "Do you feel . . . connected to your wife? Not in a way that she can't go anywhere without you, but more in a way that she's the first person you want to tell everything to. That her flaws or habits, if she has any, are endearing and not irritating? That your love has no conditions or limits. It's, I guess you could say, unconditional?"

He looked out the driver's window for a moment. His right thumb and finger shifted to his left hand, and he twirled his wedding band. "Yes, I would say I do. She snorts when she laughs, which is adorable. She spends two days a week at the senior center, on top of caring for our three children and running a small online store selling custom-made signs for kitchens. And she keeps me in my place, reminding me that I am also responsible for house chores. She is my best friend, my companion, and the person I trust most."

As he spoke, I could feel a sense of envy course through me. My stomach began to knot up, causing my saliva to pool in my mouth. The sheriff had precisely what I wanted, what I thought I had with William before everything burned down.

Honesty. Trust. Unconditional love. Acceptance and connection.

I shifted my head to the right, glancing out the passenger window, allowing the moment to lapse. The old, familiar sound of a diesel engine came up from behind us. Looking around, I could see Frank's truck pulling up to the side of the patrol car.

He rolled down the truck's passenger window, and the sheriff rolled down his. " Hey there, Clark. I see the miss has roped you into another run-in with the cow," Frank began, peering at me through the window. "Help me remind her she's down to about six of them nine lives now. At this rate, I'll be able to retire in a few years with all the repairs I'm doin' for her. We may need to ask Barney and Florence to start parking the ambulance in front of Camper World. Have it closer to where it may be most useful soon."

"You do realize I am sitting right here?" I said, leaning my head further to look into Frank's truck.

"I know. Why'd you think I said it so loud? This one will be a doozy," Frank said, looking over at my car on the hill. "I better get started pulling it down and getting it back to the shop. Pass me the keys, will ya?"

I retrieved the keys from my handbag, handing them to the sheriff, who passed them to Frank through the open windows.

"Thank goodness your Jeep is fixed. Clark, you got a sec to take her home? I may be a while with this," Frank asked as if he knew I would need a lift home.

Which I always do.

"Of course, I was planning on it. Just waiting for you, Frank," Clark replied, grasping his hat from the dashboard and placing it back on his head.

"I'll call you when it's ready, ma'am," Frank said, pulling past us to where the Mini Coop sat awaiting its rescuer.

The sheriff and I drove in silence back to my house. He pulled into the snow-covered dirt driveway, putting the car in park. He paused, clearing his throat, looking down at his wedding ring. "Ma'am, give it time, regarding this partner thing. Someday you will find your match, someone that makes you feel the way Alice, my wife, makes me feel. This kind of relationship, the one I have, usually shows up when you least expect it."

I looked over at him, almost wishing he was single for a moment. I wasn't sure I believed him, having been on twenty-six dates and counting. I wasn't in any rush to find my next husband as if they were collector coins. And maybe, just maybe, the sheriff was right. I needed to stop looking and accept what (or who) would show up at the right time.

"Thanks, Sheriff, and thanks for the lift home," I said, grasping the door handle, pulling it open, and lunging out of the car before strolling to the back porch.

I waved as he pulled out, pondering if he was one of the last of a dying breed of husbands, leaving only cast-off men in the dating pool, especially over forty. I wasn't sure what it was, but Ellen's voice from *Finding Nemo* started looping through my mind:

"Just keep swimming, just keep swimming..."

Once the weekend arrived, it brought with it a blizzard. Three feet of heavy, wet snow covered the ground by Saturday morning. No leaves were left on the trees, and the lawn, along with the shrubs, had turned a light yellow on my lot before they became covered in a sheet of white. Charles had called earlier to double-check that I had taken care of everything around the house before the blizzard's wrath was in full force.

"Did you turn the heat tape on for the pipes?" he asked without saying hello when I picked up the house phone.

"Yes," I answered curtly, irritated that he sometimes treated me like a child.

"And the snow bombs, you threw some of those on the roof?"

"Yes, and I have the faucet dripping in the kitchen so it won't freeze, and the thermostat is set at seventy. In about thirty minutes, I will start plowing the driveway. Anything else, Father?" I questioned, sarcasm dripping off the last word.

"Don't break the shovel," he warned, "and don't break my four-wheeler, either. Remember, don't put the shovel all the way down, or you will pick up the rocks and dirt on the driveway. I don't have time to come up today in this storm and fix anything."

"I won't. I know the rules: if I break it, I repair it," I replied through heavy sighs. "Are you done now? I think I have better things to do, like knit sweaters for mice."

"You say that now, but who is the first person you call when something happens?" Charles questioned snidely.

"I know." I took a long sip from my steaming cup of milky brown coffee. The robust aroma filled my nose, cascading a sense of calm down my spine. I knew his advice was based on how much my brother cared for me rather than a scolding. "I'll be careful, I promise. Scout's honor. I'm hanging up now; I have work to do," with that, I clicked the end button.

I didn't have work to do, per se, other than plowing the driveway at some point. I shuffled to the back door and opened it wide, stepping outside. My steaming cup of coffee billowed white puffs as I walked out onto the back porch to gaze for a moment at the enormous flakes that came down in a heavy blanket, adding to the feet of snow that had already covered the ground from the overnight storm.

Everything was white, clean, and void of all noises I would generally hear in the city. In the distance, I made out the occasional snap of tree limbs as the snow pulled them down. I inhaled a large, deep breath of crisp air so pure that my lungs wanted to hold it for a moment longer. When I did exhale, I allowed my breath's steam to float into the morning air.

I glanced up to see a tall, older man walking toward me from the end of my driveway. He wore light blue jeans and a worn navy blue jacket, as far as I could tell through the clouded air. He held a rope attached to a giant Saint Bernard. I waved through the flurry of white snow, recognizing him as he got closer as one of the few full-time residents on this lane: Rich.

"Howdy, neighbor," he thundered over the faint wind as he approached me on the porch. "I wanted to check in on ya, knowing that this is your first winter here." He climbed the step onto my deck, the dog in tow. "She's friendly, wouldn't hurt a flea. Her name is Ladder Day. I gotta cat back at the cabin named Saints. Funny, huh? Latter-Day Saints?"

"Clever," I said with a smile, reaching down slightly to pet the enormous dog's head. All she needed was a small barrel of whiskey under her chin, and she would be the spitting image of the cartoon dog I loved as a child.

"Hey, sweetheart! How are you? Look how sad your eyes look," I resounded in a low, soft voice. It was the tone one only used when speaking to dogs and babies. I continued to pet her head as her massive tail wagged.

Rich appeared to be in his sixties, but I didn't ask. His gray hair was a bit greasy and long overdue for a proper haircut as strands fell into his eyes, coaxing him to sweep them away. His old jeans were stained, and his black sneakers had no laces, but I think that was his preference.

The small road I lived on had six residents who resided there full time. The other homes were occupied occasionally during the warmer months. Charles had updated me on the neighbor situation one summer night after one of the more senior neighbors, Pat, had asked for his help moving a stove into her home.

Pat had lived in Woodland for twenty years on the corner lot with the big barn. She used to live in the house next door to the barn with her then-husband Tom. But he ended up having an affair with a thirty-two-year-old waitress from the next city over. She was known as the crazy young woman in that town due to her ever-changing moods.

Tom fell for the waitress in one of her manic phases of charismatic energy; a thirty-two-year-old woman seemed a prize to him. Pat got most of the land in the divorce, including the large custom barn, the guest house, and all the farm equipment. Tom was left with the house, a small barn, and a deranged new wife whose disposition fluctuated daily. The now ex-waitress's moods were usually influenced by her three obnoxious dogs she brought with her. Pat jokingly remarked to my brother that she got the better end of that deal as he helped her move her stove into the guest house.

Next to Tom was Sandy and her new husband, John. Sandy's ex-husband, Rich, the man now standing on my front porch, lived in a small, eclectic cabin to the right of their house. Rich still cared for Sandy and John's yard and snow removal since, per Pat, Rich was the kindest of all the neighbors on our street.

To the north of my house was Lisa, and like the others, her ex-husband, Stan, lived in a camper on their lot part of the time and the other amount of the time up the hill on his family's ranch. They had four children together, one now grown, leaving the other three at home still, which was the main reason our street got plowed early on school days.

I recalled finding the combination of residents unusual, in fact, rare. I could never imagine living next door to my exes, and yet, here was a street full of them.

Is the pull to stay in Woodland that strong for its residents?

I was brought back from my thoughts as Ladder Day began to lick my hand with her enormous tongue, coaxing me to pet her more. "This weather is beautiful," I replied, straightening from petting the dog and staring out onto the sea of white that covered my wooded lot. "But if I am ever going to get to work this week, I will need to clear a path. Lucky for me, my brother hooked a plow to the front of the four-wheeler."

I could see Rich eyeing my steaming coffee cup as I spoke.

"Would you like to come in for a cup of coffee?" I asked.

"Sure," he replied, redirecting his gaze from my cup to me. "As long as it's no bother?"

"Not at all. Is it okay if we tie up Ladder Day on the porch?" I asked, looking down at the clumps of snow and ice stuck on her fur. They would surely leave pools of water on my new wood floor.

"Of course," Rich said as he took her rope and tied it around one of the poles on the covered porch. I opened the door, gesturing with my free arm for him to enter, before shutting the door behind us. Knowing Rich was the kindest man on the street gave me no hesitation in having him in my house alone with me.

"Right this way." I led him through the foyer, into the open living space, and to the kitchen. "Take a seat anywhere you want at the dining table. How do you like your coffee?"

"Black, please," Rich replied, gingerly pulling out one of the brown, cushioned dining chairs surrounding my large dark table. "You're sure this is no bother? The coffee?"

"Not at all," I replied, placing a pod in the Keurig and pushing it down to start the brewing process.

"I usually plow the front of all the driveways on this road with my truck," Rich began, tapping his fingers absentmindedly on the tabletop. "The plow trucks just pile it up in front of the driveways, creating snow walls, making it hard to get out. That's another reason I stopped by, to make sure you were okay with me plowing your driveway."

"I welcome all the help anyone is willing to offer me," I replied, walking to the table carrying a cup of black, steaming hot coffee. I handed it to him before sitting at the table, sipping from my cup. Rich and I continued to exchange small talk about the weather in Woodland, what essentials are necessary to stock up on, and the hours the county plow is in operation.

He glanced over at my faucet during a lull of our conversation, hearing the fast drip streaming from the spout. "Make sure you keep a little drip going at all times. Don't want the pipes to freeze up on ya'."

I nodded, thinking he and my brother were in cahoots.

Rich took the last big gulp of his coffee before standing. "Well, I better get going. I need to finish walking Ladder Day. Let me give you my phone number, just in case you need anything."

Pat was right; Rich was the nicest neighbor on the street. I extracted my phone from my purse on the kitchen counter. Rich stated the numbers slowly as I entered them into my phone, with the contact's name: "Rich—the nice neighbor."

I walked him to the back door and opened it, allowing him to pass onto the covered porch. Ladder Day stood quickly, her tail wagging with windful force. I crossed the door's threshold, grabbing Ladder Day's head in both hands before giving it a good shake. "You be a good girl for Daddy," I told her in a low-pitched tone.

"One more thing," Rich said as he untied the giant dog. "They won't deliver mail until the snow melts, so you may want to stop in town at the post office and leave a cardboard box with your name and address on it. Shoe box size is fine, as long as you pick up the mail every few weeks."

I shook my head and giggled. *Only in a small town is mail stored in your own cardboard box at the post office.*

CHAPTER EIGHTEEN

"Hey, Betty," I whispered into her ear as I passed behind her, making my way to my booth. She joined me with my usual glass of wine when she had a chance. "So, who is it tonight?"

"Andy. He's a bigger guy with a little pooch, jet-black hair, and full lips. He runs his own fundraising business," I conveyed before taking a sip of wine.

I then remembered what I really needed to share with Betty. It was time for her to know about Sam. "But," I added pointedly, catching Betty's eye, "I will be *bringing* someone to dinner instead of just meeting him here in a few weeks."

Betty stopped mid-wipe of the table. Standing straight up, she placed the wet towel on the tray she had brought and leaned against the side of the booth, raising an eyebrow. "Really?" she asked, her voice questioning yet concerned.

"Really," I confirmed. "There is a guy from work with whom I have had some 'after-hour meetings,' if you get my gist. He lives in California, so we only connect when he travels for work mostly. It's been going on for a month or so, and I'm unsure where it's going. I know we are both seeing other people. He just got out of a relationship, and, well . . . you know my story."

I felt like I was babbling, trying to make excuses for why I had not brought Sam up before in conversation with her. After all, Betty was my official screening service for men I dated. But then I realized I didn't need her opinion about Sam. Sam was Sam, and he would come and go, just like the rest.

Betty cocked her fist to her waist. "But he knows where you live?" she asked, her voice tainted with concern. "Is that safe for you? You do live alone, you realize?"

Sam was as harmless as a fly. I was more ashamed about breaking one of my rules. *Don't date anyone you work with.* That was etched in ink on the yellow-lined pad I had on my desk at home. Technically, he didn't work with me; we didn't share the same office. Our company was a national organization, and this was a national project involving some state participation. That was why I got involved. But I couldn't help feeling a little guilty. The two of us still worked for the same organization and were currently on the same project.

I was starting to feel something for Sam. It wasn't the official "L" word or anything like that; it was just a feeling that left me warm inside and empty. I felt a longing for something more, something Sam could not give me. Whatever the empty feeling was, it made it impossible to see any long-term future with Sam. That was probably another reason I hadn't spoken to Betty about him.

"It's safe, I promise." I placed my elbows on the table, clasping my hands and resting my chin on them.

The day after Valentine's Day, Sam showed up in true Sam fashion at two o'clock in the morning. He crept into the house using a key I had hidden under the mat, climbing the stairs to the second floor. His traveling companion, a chocolate brown lab named Sancho, was in tow with a wagging tail that ricocheted off every wall and door.

I opened an eye when the noise stirred me, finding a wet, warm nose nestled next to my arm. I knew Sam was bringing him, having met him on a weekend visit to California, yet the dog's presence beside my bed caught me by surprise. I instinctively stroked the furry head lightly and willed my other eye to open, clearing the cobwebs.

"Happy Valentine's Day," Sam cooed as he leaned over the bed. "I brought you these." A dozen red roses wrapped in cellophane were in his hand, with a grocery store price tag on them and a giant mylar heart balloon.

My own heart pounded rapidly with appreciation. That was the sweetest thing *any* man had done for me in the last year!

Sam was tall, even when hunched over on the edge of my bed. His six-foot, five-inch frame cast a shadow from the moonlight across me. His Persian features were perfect in the glow, unlike his tousled salt-and-pepper hair and beard that were untidy, opposite of how he wore it for work. His shoulders were mildly broad in his oversized green T-shirt.

"Thank you," I managed to say in a hoarse voice, leaning forward from the bed and pecking his lips, taking in a voluptuous breath of the fragrant flowers. "Can you do me a favor and put these in water downstairs?" I said groggily, turning back on my side. "I'll put them in a vase tomorrow. We both need sleep if we are going snowmobiling in the afternoon."

He trudged down the steps, rustling around in the kitchen before lumbering back up the stairs, instructing Sancho to lie down in the bedroom corner as he climbed into bed next to me.

I knew there would be no sexual relations that night or any night going forward. That part of our relationship had stopped a few weeks ago, as did the transparent conversations. I got the feeling Sam was still not over his ex-girlfriend. But I couldn't be positive because we never spoke about such things. Or should I say *he* never talked about them to me. All I knew for certain was that Sam had become a dear friend, a confidant, and an excellent snuggler to sleep with. And right now, that was enough for me.

Unfortunately, it was *more* than enough because I'd overslept big time. When I glanced at the clock on the side table the next day, it read noon, causing me to jolt straight up. The company hosting our snowmobiling excursion would begin at one sharp, not a minute later.

"Sam, we're going to be late!" I exclaimed as I threw the covers off me, plunging my feet into slippers nestled by the edge of the bed. I hated being late for anything, unlike Sam.

He grunted back at me, "Five more minutes," as he grabbed the covers and pulled them over his head. I hastily pounded down the stairs to let Sancho out and get him food and water. I stalked back up the stairs and over to Sam, still slumbering. Decidedly, I wasn't gentle this time. "Sam, *get up*; we will be late," I stated in a pulsating voice as I pushed and rocked him back and forth.

"All right already!" he roared, flinging the covers off his head as he sat up.

We dressed hastily, layering on snow gear. I made two steaming cups of coffee for the road and packed a container of croissants to eat during our drive through the canyon to Park City.

"Be a good boy while we are gone. Don't wreck any of Cindy's things, okay?" I reminded Sancho before closing the back door. We were greeted by a thick, heavy snowfall with a layer of fog outside. The air was crisp and filled with the scent of wet pine and log fires from nearby chimneys. I was grateful that I would not be driving for once since my Frank-repair-man budget was maxed out that month. Sam's dark blue Toyota sat in my driveway, ready to go.

As we navigated down the small lane, the giant flakes of white multiplied as we got closer to town, and so did the layer of fog. That was uncommon in Utah. The haze was as thick as country gravy, making it hard to see more than a few feet in front of us. I silently prayed that the vindictive cows would take the morning off so we could make our one o'clock deadline without any incidents.

We rambled past the grocery store, hardware store, and lone fast-food establishment, all barely visible through the heavy ground cloud covering. Next, we ascended the hill to drive through the canyon to the excursion location.

The farms and houses to the east were scarcely visible as we climbed the first peak through the gorge. But something caught my eye in the mist and flurry of snow on the right edge of the road.

"Did you see that?" I screeched, whipping my head around. "I could have sworn I just saw someone standing there, waving an arm up and down."

"I saw it too," Sam replied frantically. He pulled over on the edge of the road, peering behind us.

The haze had swallowed whoever it was. Sam slammed the car into reverse, slowly backing up on the shoulder of the road. Within seconds, a dark object appeared in the mist. *So it is a person!* A man, in fact. A sinking feeling formed in my stomach. *Something's wrong with him.*

Sam put the car in park, but I was already out the passenger door, racing toward the stumbling man without hesitation, the nurse in me kicking in. Gone were my worries about making our afternoon deadline; when I saw someone in trouble in such treacherous conditions, I knew I had to help.

"Sir, are you okay?" I bellowed over the whirling storm of sleet that now fell. Panic coursed through my veins, causing my heart to pound against my chest wall. My breaths were forced out in rapid succession.

The man was older, his face etched in wrinkles from a life lived. His white hair stuck out messily from under a veteran ball cap. He wore a long black trench coat, no shirt, stained gray sweatpants, and house slippers. He held his coat together over his bare chest with his right hand.

"I'm sick," he gasped as a wet, hacking cough escaped his lips, causing him to double over. Sam raced to where we stood, grabbing the man under his arms before he tumbled forward.

"Sir, come get into the car." Sam pulled the man's arm over his shoulder as we walked back to Sam's parked vehicle. "It's not safe for you to be out in this blizzard."

I raced in front of them, opening the rear passenger door and pushing wrappers and clothing off the seat to make room for him to sit.

Sam carefully guided the man into the back seat, then rushed to the driver's side. We briefly exchanged glances, our eyes filled with fear and urgency, before climbing back inside.

I turned around in the passenger seat, helping the man sit up while Sam started the car, cranking the heat on and adjusting the vents so that the warm air cascaded to the rear. Every article of clothing on the man was soaked, giving off a scent of stale liquor and musty ammonia as if he had soiled himself. His eyes were sunken in, and his skin was pale, almost translucent, as if he had been sick for a while.

"Is that your house up there on the hill?" I asked as I managed to get a seat belt over him. The fog had begun to lift in the distance, allowing the A-frame house to come into view. It was the closest house to the road, even though it was surrounded by a few acres. It was quaint, with a bank of windows that looked out onto the valley and mountains to the east. Standing in front of the open garage door on the side of the house were two animal shapes. Squinting, I could see they were dogs.

"Yes," the man answered through another coughing fit. "I tried to drive myself to the hospital, but I got stuck in the snow."

In the distance, I could see an old truck that had veered off in the middle of the man's field. Sam hastily pulled out and back onto the highway. I stayed twisted backward, fully engaged in fight-or-flight mode, preparing for the worst.

"Do you live with anyone?" I asked abruptly.

"No, I live alone," he said through mucus-filled coughing. "I need to go to the Veteran's Hospital."

"That is over an hour away," I said with urgency. "I think we need to get you to the closest hospital in Park City. Then, once they stabilize you, they can transfer you to the VA hospital."

"What's your name?" Sam asked, his eyes still focused on the slick road in front of us.

"Ron," he replied.

"I'm Sam, and this is Cindy. Do you have family nearby? Or maybe close friends?"

"No," Ron replied, causing Sam and me to glance at each other. "I have a brother in Texas, even though we don't talk much," Ron answered hesitantly, his voice becoming shallower. "I'll need my phone that I left in the truck. His number's in it."

I took a deep breath, relieved that at least he had a brother.

"Hang on, Ron. We're almost there," Sam proclaimed, giving me a side glance to confirm that we were, in fact, close.

"Just another ten or so minutes," I replied, giving Sam a nod.

I swiftly pointed out turns and stops as Sam raced the car into the emergency room parking lot to the side of the hospital. "Wait here," I told Ron. "We're going to grab a wheelchair and a nurse to help us."

Sam and I rushed into the emergency entrance, the doors opening instantly as we reached them. I was caught off guard by the strong scent of bleach. The lobby was empty, except for a small booth in the far-right corner enclosed in glass. Behind the glass sat a middle-aged woman looking at a computer screen.

"Help! We need help! We have a sick man in our car who we found on the side of the road!" I exclaimed. Sam headed straight for a row of wheelchairs by the side of the door. Grabbing one, he hurried back to the emergency entrance.

The woman swiftly stood up, almost toppling her chair in the process. "Let me grab a nurse, ma'am," she said, lurching through the opening into the emergency room behind her.

Ma'am? I thought through my panic. *Do I really look that old?*

Within moments, two men dressed in light blue scrubs, accompanied by the clerk behind the glass, raced through the door into the waiting room. At the same time, Sam was sprinting back in through the doors with Ron nestled in a wheelchair. In the harsh stare of the hospital lobby lights, I could see how ill my distant neighbor actually was. My years of training told me Ron wouldn't have survived if we hadn't seen him in that blizzard.

I rushed over to Ron and Sam as the rest of the medical staff circled around him. Stethoscopes flew from around their necks, with hands placed on Ron's wrists to gauge his pulse.

"Can you tell us your name, sir?" one of the male nurses asked while counting beats on his wristwatch. I could feel myself counting with him.

"Ron," he uttered between his broken, rattling cough. "And these two are my angels."

I raised my eyebrows at Sam, who looked at me with surprise and a wash of realization. We both knew we'd likely just saved Ron's life.

The staff gave us a few side glances before continuing their questioning. "Do you have any family nearby? Someone we can call?"

"No," Ron uttered before tumbling forward in a hacking fit.

"We need to get oxygen on him, stat. Excuse us," one of the men stated as they moved around the chair, nudging Sam aside and propelling Ron into the back.

The clerk touched my arm. It tingled with empathy. "Do you have a moment for a couple of questions?"

"Of course."

Sam and I spent the next ten minutes reiterating the events, including Ron's conversation in the car. I realized that we were all Ron had for now. There was no one else until we could find this brother Ron spoke of, if the brother even existed. We would have to go back to Ron's house, find his phone, and figure out what to do with the dogs. I knew Sam and his love for animals. He would not leave those dogs abandoned in that house while Ron was in the hospital.

The clerk's pounding of the keys brought my awareness back into the present. "Who should I list as the emergency contact?"

I glanced at Sam, knowing he would return to California within days. I knew what I had to do. "List me, please, for now. I will be his emergency contact."

How can someone not have anyone?

That question kept going through my mind when Sam and I tried to enjoy our snowmobiling. The one o'clock sharp policy appeared to be flexible if the tour guides ran late, which worked in our favor today, even though I fully expected we would not be doing this excursion today when we found Ron.

But the repetition of the question persisted even when we returned to Ron's house, got his phone, moved his truck, and discovered he had two dogs that desperately needed attention. The open garage and the subsequent kitchen of the house were filthy beyond what I had ever seen before with my own eyes. It was as if I had entered a house from the TV show *Hoarders*.

Even though I cringed heavily at the idea of the matted, stinky, unhouse-trained animals soiling my months of hard work at my house, I knew they had to come back with me while Ron was being treated. But first, we had to get back to the hospital before visiting hours were over to give Ron his phone to call his brother. When we entered the hospital room, we were relieved to find him awake and settled into his bed; Ron was even more grateful when he saw us again.

It only took the two practically wild animals a short amount of time to trash the heated garage once Sam and I got them back to my place. Blackie and Sissy, whose names we'd learned from Ron, seemed grateful to have somewhere warm to be with food. Still, they needed bathing if they were ever to come inside at night-fall. So, one disordered bathroom later (and a few tears shed from me), we did our best to clean up both dogs. By then, I was utterly exhausted, and yet, when I lay down, that same repetition of words was waiting for me:

What would it be like to have nobody to call? No one to care that I was hooked up to oxygen machines and IV bags?

CHAPTER NINETEEN

On my way to work early the following day, I placed a call to the hospital for an update on Ron's status. He was stable, but the tremors from the alcohol withdrawal, a finding that surprised me, were getting worse, which required high doses of Ativan to control. He was on ten liters of oxygen, a high amount for anyone. The doctor confirmed that he had acute respiratory failure caused by pneumonia and started him on high doses of antibiotics intravenously.

When one of the nurses told me that Ron hadn't heard back from his brother, I decided to stop by Ron's neighbor's house to see if they could watch the dogs and to inform them that their neighbor was in the hospital. They may be concerned; I would have been if it was my neighbor.

A woman in her late thirties answered the door, a baby hanging from her hip. The minute I described Ron's predicament, her face turned cold. She told me Ron was a mean drunk with destructive dogs that everyone nearby hated. *I was floored.* That sounded like a different man than the Ron I had met, who now lay in a hospital bed.

I could feel a pit form in my stomach. The dogs were a little untamed, but that was due to not being adequately trained. What had Ron done to make his neighbors so bitter toward him? Who was this man who now lay in a hospital bed with no one to care he was there but us? I could only think of one thing to do: go back into his house and look for clues.

Sam and I ventured back to Ron's neglected house after work. Luckily, while digging through the mail in his dirty kitchen, we found an envelope with an attorney's address. Since it was past five, I thought it was best to at least stop by the small office down the road and get the phone number to call first thing in the morning. I also thought I might be able to catch him before he left the office. I had to figure out why the man the neighbors despised was so different from the grateful man we had saved.

The next day, Ron's attorney and I had a chat. I could hear the astonishment in his voice as I relayed the entire situation.

"I just saw him in January! We were finalizing his business affairs and starting to work on his will," he replied after I was finished. "In fact, I do have his brother's name and number. Unfortunately, I can't give it to you due to attorney-client confidentiality. Still, I can contact him and give him your information."

"I would appreciate that," I replied, taking a deep breath before asking, "Was there no one else? No parents, children, maybe a significant other?"

"None that he shared with me. Perhaps his brother has more details. I'll dial him immediately and let you know what he says."

That certainly helped, but what would I do with the dogs? If my garage was an example of what they could do when left alone, I most certainly could not leave them in the house while I went to work. With Sam heading back to California, I pondered my options. The only thing I could think of was to drop them off at Ron's house on my way to work and pick them back up on my way home. At least they would be safe in his house. I would leave fresh water and food for them, they would be out of the weather, and my house would remain intact.

This routine went on for a few days until I received a phone call from Ron's brother. I had just pulled back into my own driveway after picking up the dogs on my way home from work. His low, exacerbated voice caught me off guard as I answered the phone.

We exchanged pleasantries before I brought him up to speed on Ron's condition, including the dogs and the state of his brother's house. His brother was patient as he spoke, his voice just above a whisper, causing me to pay careful attention to his words. But I still couldn't help but feel a gush of sorrow. I had so many unanswered questions about who Ron was.

"Can you tell me about Ron?" I asked cautiously, trying not to sound like a nosy neighbor or a woman out for a reward. I was just curious how this man had come to be alone.

Ron's brother told me how grand his brother had once been. He was a war hero in his early twenties before becoming known as the Waterbed King throughout the '80s and '90s. He then opened one of the most successful barbeque restaurants in Park City. He had been married then until his drinking became out of control. His wife left and took their five-year-old daughter with her to Florida, and he never saw them again. He was never the same after that.

My jaw clenched as my eyes blurred over. The pit in my stomach swelled as I realized the actions that caused Ron to be alone: his own.

"Would it be okay if I tried to find homes for his dogs rather than take them to the shelter?" I couldn't bear to think of Sissy and Blackie tied up in chain-link cages, sleeping on cement floors, hoping someone would want them. I could not let the dogs end up like their owner, with no one.

"Sure. You've already done so much. You really are a saint," he replied, pausing for a moment. "And one more thing: thank you."

Those two words propelled the water blurring my vision to stream down my cheeks. I knew at that moment what unconditional love felt like. It felt like someone accepted you for your flaws and still wanted to be by your side.

The week passed, and I was able to find Blackie a new home. But something made me hesitate to find Sissy a home. An ache in my gut told me I needed her as much as she needed me. Sissy was a great dog, mannered in a way that I could only see when she was alone, not with Blackie. She sat when asked, never strayed far from the driveway when she was let out, and always had a wagging tail to greet me.

It made me realize I had found Sissy a home. With me.

It was late on a Saturday night when I got the call. By then, Ron had been in the hospital for three weeks, hooked up to machines keeping him alive. I was surprised when a woman began to speak on the other line. She explained she was Ron's daughter. Her uncle had told her about her dad's condition the day before, and she had decided it was time to pull the plug. No one would come to bid him farewell; it wasn't worth the ticket price to say goodbye to a father who she felt had abandoned her. As a courtesy, she wanted to let me know since the hospital staff had informed her that I had been visiting.

"I never saw Ron awake again," I said solemnly, fiddling with a piece of twisted wire in my hand. "He died a week ago, and I was the only person by his side."

I'd driven to the city to hold the hand of a dying man as he took his last breath. Frank was beside me as I relayed the end of the story. He placed a firm hand on my shoulder as we leaned against the side of his tow truck. He could tell I was not my jovial self when I called him that morning, asking him to come pull the Mini Coop out of a snowbank. I knew I shouldn't have been driving the small car yet, even though it was the beginning of March and I hadn't seen a snowstorm in days.

Frank had asked about the dog after pulling the car out since he had never seen me with an animal in the past. There was only one way to explain how I came to have a long-haired black-and-white border collie named Sissy: to tell Frank about Ron.

I looked over to Frank as his hand passed lightly over the fur on Sissy's head. His gaze focused on me. His mouth corners were turned down. No more words needed to be said at that moment, nor did he ask for payment that day for his services. His firm hand released from my shoulder as he gazed at me with a look of admiration before climbing back into the cab of his truck.

Sissy and I trudged back onto the porch, peering back at Frank's truck as he drove away.

CHAPTER TWENTY

Winter turned into spring and then into summer. Beyond the trees to the east, the river's edges overflowed from the snowmelt. The rage of the water could be heard easily from my back porch as it crashed against the boulders while cascading downstream. The land came alive with shades of light green. The bare limbs of the trees sprouted tiny buds, and a sweet, musky smell drifted in the breeze. What amazed me most was the sea of yellow wild-flowers that now covered my lot. I could gaze at them for hours from the sanctuary of my wrap-around porch, and most evenings, I did.

Sissy eventually became CC, close enough to her original name, yet with a slight tweak from the previous name that reminded me of the forgotten man who was once her owner. Every morning a warm nose welcomed me into the day at the edge of my bed, waiting for me to get up. And every evening after returning home from work, she was there to greet me, tail wagging out of control, eager to go out.

CC's evening walks had me conversing with every neighbor who happened to be out during that time since CC galloped twenty feet in front of me, greeting them all with an occasional look back to make sure I was still there. I sometimes would tease her and hide behind a bush just to see her stalk back looking for me. Which she always did.

Rich had been working on an eclectic front wall of sorts. Stacks of rocks, glass bottles, and bits of colorful plastic that others would have discarded were now being formed into a usable work of art. The showstopper was the bright red canoe that now sat atop the wall, like a star on a Christmas tree. Some nights we would share a glass of wine at his outdoor table, a gigantic wood spool that had once held an electrical power line conduit. It was now turned on its side for a different use and surrounded by mismatched chairs.

CC especially liked the walks to the river. With her hair cut short, she easily jumped into the shallows of the rushing water, lapping it up as she splashed about. My house was full of paw prints across the dark wood floors that had been pristine and new only months ago. In another life, this would not be acceptable to me. In this life, it brought me comfort.

On the weekends, we went for hikes or four-wheeler rides. CC would instantly jump on the seat of the machine if the third bay garage door was opened, where the ATVs were stored. We explored every trail, meadow, and flawless view of a valley that could only be seen at the top of a peak, looking out onto the wonder of land only mother nature touched.

Dating became an afterthought with CC around. It took work to get ready and pump myself up for the usual first-date questions and small talk. I hated small talk. It was a necessity I dreaded, just to find out at the end of an evening that there was no spark. For once, I wanted to show up to a date in my stained sweats, messy hair in a bun, and a makeup-free face. It would be lovely to just shoot the breeze on topics of substance, like global warming and wars in Iraq.

But that's not how dating works.

At least CC preferred me in my dingy clothes, and when I talked to her about global warming, I swore she understood me. Tilting her head to the side, she peered at me as if waiting for me to tell her how she could help.

She accepts me for me.

The Fourth of July holiday was in a few days, which meant a three-day weekend from work this year. Mathew had plans with his wife, Janelle, and her family. My grandbabies Lia and Silas were to attend their first parade and fireworks show. Lyle would be sleeping, his favorite pastime being a single man of twenty-five with a full-time desk job and no other responsibilities. And Cortland and Melissa were still not traveling with the grandbaby twins yet since they were only four months old.

I had decided to skip the fanfare of the holiday celebration and instead planned to use the time to power-wash the porches and touch up the chipped paint resulting from the first winter after the remodel. It had been nearly a year since I moved in. The house was a far cry from its previous state, now a wondrous country retreat that required just a bit of maintenance here and there.

As I rolled up the washer hose and wheeled the machine back to the garage, after a full day of carefully cleaning each plank and rail, I could hear CC loudly whining at the back door. She'd been locked up in the house all day after I turned the machine on this morning, where she immediately lunged for the water that sprayed out of the hose, trying to bite it in the air. I knew I would get nothing done with her outside but mostly feared the pressure of the spray may cause bruising to her face. And the last thing I needed was a trip to the vet.

She was ready for a walk, even though I was ready for the couch. My worn gray fleece was covered in wet spots from the overspray, and strands of hair fell out of the bun I had piled on top of my head.

"Okay, I hear you!" I called thunderously as I opened the back door. She bolted out, quickly finding a spot to pee as I strode to the refrigerator, grabbing a cold beer bottle. After popping the top, I leisurely walked back outside to see CC standing in the middle of the driveway, waiting for me. She was not in the mood to lie on a couch right now, even if I dragged her back in. She needed to release some energy like a toddler child, and I had to grin and bear it.

The sun had started to set over the east bank of mountains, casting an orange glow over the lane as we began our walk. A chorus of crickets chirped in the distance by the river. I strolled down the street, gulping my beer as CC galloped her usual twenty feet in front of me. Behind me, I could hear the loud thudding of a truck engine, one I recognized.

I peered over my shoulder to find Stan driving slowly up behind me in his truck with his camper in the bed. Stan is the ex-husband of Lisa, my neighbor on the left. The two were the youngest of all the divorcees on the street, with three children still in junior high and high school. So that had to make Stan just a few years younger than me.

I edged my way over to the side of the road even more to allow him to pass. But instead, he pulled up to the side of me, pacing the truck to match my walking speed. Stan and I had exchanged conversations over the last few months since CC forced me out of my house each evening. From our exchanges, I had learned he was an engineer by day and a cowboy by night.

"Hey there. I saw you working on your porch today. Do you need any help?" Stan asked through his rolled-down driver's window. He had his wide-brim black cowboy hat snug on his head and a crisp, blue, long-sleeved button-up shirt—everything in typical cowboy style.

"No. I got all the power washing done. Thanks for asking though. Tomorrow, I'll touch up the paint, and the porch will be as good as new again," I replied nonchalantly, swigging down the last of the beer I was holding.

"You going to the rodeo in town later?" Stan asked in a hopeful tone.

"I don't think so," I replied, slowing my pace down. "That would require me to change from this super-hot outfit I am wearing into some jeans that make you suck in your stomach all night. I'll pass."

"I was thinking the same. Not about the jeans, of course, just about passing on going," Stan said, a hesitancy to his voice. "My ex will be there, and we're not on the best of terms right now." He paused, then continued, "You're welcome to come up to the ranch later with your dog. I'll have a big fire going and a cooler of beers."

I stopped for a moment, and so did Stan and his truck. CC peered back at me, ensuring I was still following her, before careening a few more feet ahead. "Not sure if that's a good idea. What will the neighbors say?" I replied with a wink.

"Nothing like that. Just two people, not alone, in comfy clothes, shooting the shit around a campfire on a Friday night," he replied with a chuckle to his voice. "Here, let me do this." He leaned over his seat to find a scrap piece of paper and pen. He jotted something down on the slip and handed it to me. "Here is my number. If you feel up to it, just send me a text. The ranch is up the other loop, past the buffalo on the east side of the road. Weidler Ranch. You can't miss the sign."

I took the scrap piece of paper, glancing down at the number on it. "I'll think about it," I replied tentatively before stuffing the paper in my pocket. Stan tipped the brim of his hat at me and slowly drove off down the lane.

My house was eerily quiet that evening. I sat on the floor in the dining room and had been throwing stuffed monkeys and rabbits down the long hallway for CC to retrieve for the last thirty minutes. The sound of her nails sliding across the wood surface as she attempted to stop echoed throughout the main floor before she picked up the soggy toy in her mouth and brought it back to me. The crinkling sound the scrap of paper made in my pocket caught my attention between throws. I reached down and pulled the slip out, staring at the number.

What can it hurt?

A few beers and swapping stories over a campfire with a neighbor. My dingy sweats, plain face, and messy bun were the acceptable attire for a night with a possible new friend. I stood, typing a few words on my cell phone. I pressed send before grabbing a leash, a bottle of wine, and a blanket. "Come on, CC. We are going for a ride."

CHAPTER TWENTY-ONE

My Jeep headlights bounced off the signs as I drove by each ranch on the high road loop, passing the large, bouldering shadows of the buffalo. Finally, an old, weathered wood sign came into view with a tattered scene of crops painted on it. The faded black letters on the sign read: Weidler Ranch, established 1905.

I turned down the dark dirt lane that was only partially lit by my car lights and the bright stars beginning to multiply in the sky. In the distance, I could see the flames of a campfire in the clearing, and Stan's truck and camper came into view. I parked by the trailer before climbing out of the car. CC instantly sprinted across the dirt to where Stan sat in a folding chair.

The clearing was an open space about half the size of a football field, covered in low patches of wild grass mixed with dirt spots. Three gigantic old oak trees spaced evenly canvassed the area like umbrellas. Under the hot summer sun, I imagined the trees providing the perfect amount of shade for any family gathering held on the ranch.

The open space was surrounded by crops. In the darkness, it was hard to identify the type of crops as they stood a few feet high in some areas. I pictured what the space may have looked like a hundred years ago: cowboys with their horses tied up, a big pot of stew on the campfire, and rolled-out bedding nearby. This was one of those places I wished could share the stories of its history.

"You made it. I expect it wasn't too hard to find?" Stan asked in his usual deep voice as he finished petting CC and stood. He was still dressed in his formal cowboy getup, minus the hat, which was replaced with a baseball cap. As I approached, I realized he was just a few inches taller than my five-foot-five frame without his wide-brim hat.

He had a medium physique, and when he pulled his hat off for a moment to scratch his head, I could finally see that his thinning hair was a sandy blond, which matched his hazel eyes. "I hope a lawn chair is okay. You have to keep adjusting it a bit, depending on the direction the wind is blowing the smoke. Do you want a beer?"

"No, I brought wine. I know it's poshy, but beer makes me bloated when I drink too much of it," I replied nervously, realizing I had forgotten to bring glasses. "Would you happen to have a spare plastic cup on hand? Maybe two and we can share?"

"Of course. Let me go grab some from the trailer," Stan replied as he strolled over to where his camper sat. His silhouette was that of a cowboy, with a wide-stance walk, tight jeans, and boots tucked neatly under the cuffs.

I threw my blanket over the back of the lawn chair Stan pointed to as I listened to CC sprinting through the trees and crops in the dark. She was chasing something, I guessed, as she frequently did at home. The squirrels and mice were no match for her.

"Here we are!" Stan bellowed as he climbed out of the trailer, strutting back to where I stood, handing me the red plastic cups.

"Thank you. Can I pour you a glass?"

"Maybe in a bit. I have an open beer I need to finish before it gets warm," Stan replied graciously, then sat back in the chair by the fire. "Make yourself comfortable. I see CC is already chasing the rodents that sneak out in the dark. That's a true border collie for you, always herding and chasing."

"I wouldn't know. I've never had a border collie before," I replied sonorously, a feeling of sadness creeping up in my chest. "I rescued her a few months ago. Her owner died."

"I'm sorry to hear that," Stan replied solemnly. "I was wondering how you came to have a dog suddenly. Her owner, was he a friend of yours?"

"Not exactly, but I was the only one he had in the end."

"Really? Do you mind sharing the story?"

I poured myself a tall glass of wine, sipping from its edge as I nestled into the lawn chair, and then began the tale of how CC came to live with me.

Minutes turned into an hour as Stan and I swapped tales of Woodland, our families, and ultimately our divorces. The conversation flowed easily from one subject to the next. Stan's family had settled into these parts in the early 1900s, farming and then ranching, saving enough money to buy the sixty acres we were now sitting on.

He told me stories about his forefathers and the small general store in town that was now a restaurant serving breakfast and lunch to the locals. It was once the only spot for miles to get the supplies needed to last through winter.

When the conversation shifted to our divorces, I could tell he was holding back. He hemmed and hawed a bit as if he was not prepared to divulge a deep, dark secret. Of course, it didn't bother me since I was not ready to share my details.

After a while, it grew quiet between us. CC had come to nestle by me in the dirt, gently playing around with a mouse she had caught. I leaned my head back in the chair, watching the puffs of smoke from the fire float into the night sky that now had small cloud drifts covering half the stars.

The quiet was suddenly interrupted. *Crack. Pop. Crack. Boom!*

Stan and I abruptly stood and turned, facing the town in the distance as the firework show began. The residual glow of reds, blues, and greens could be seen from miles around.

In an instant, CC sprinted off through the field of crops. "CC, stop! Come back. It's just fireworks!" I screamed, dropping the nearly empty cup I held in the chair as I raced after her. I could hear the thudding sound of Stan's boots as he followed me.

"CC, come back! CC, come here, girl!" Stan and I repeatedly called along with blaring whistling as we sprinted through the tall stalks, pushing them aside as we barreled forward.

When we reached the edge of the field that opened onto the high loop road, Stan and I paused, catching our breath. "We lost her," I began, huffing and bent over with my hands on my knees.

"She couldn't have gone far. She's just spooked a little," he replied through exacerbated breaths. "You go to the left, and I'll go down the road's edge to the right."

Pulling out my cell phone, I turned on the flashlight and jogged down the shoulder. I kept shouting her name, hoping my voice would calm her down and let her know she was safe with me. Before long, a light drizzle began where the clouds had pooled together in the sky. It didn't take long before it became a downpour, soaking me straight through. I hurried back to the ranch entrance and noticed Stan was also in the distance.

"Quick, jump into my Jeep! She may have gone far at this point. It's safer if we drive and find her." My body trembled, not from the cold rain but from the feeling of loss. I had lost so much already in the last year. I could not lose CC too.

My stomach knotted as I placed the key in the ignition, revving the engine before pulling out of the dirt opening, my tires spewing rocks in their wake.

Stan and I continued to call out for CC from the rolled-down windows. He scanned the darkness with the light of his cell phone.

"Dammit, I should have put her on the leash!" I roared after the second pass down the road with still no sign of her. "How could I be so stupid? I should know that most dogs don't like fireworks."

Stan reached over to my arm. "Don't be so hard on yourself. Not all dogs are scared by fireworks. You didn't know," he said calmly. I could feel the warmth of his hand through my wet sleeve, causing a surge of electricity up through my spine.

How long has it been since a man did that? I shook the feeling off, refocusing on the road.

The rain was easing up as the minutes passed, trickling down as I drove in the darkness. "There! Did you see that? Over on the edge," Stan gasped, pointing to the left side of the road. I swerved over to the shoulder, allowing my headlights to catch the black sagging tail and hind end of a dark animal galloping along the side of the lane.

It's her!

"CC! Come here, girl!" I called in a high-pitched voice, but she didn't stop or even look back. I slowed the Jeep behind her, carefully keeping her in the view of the headlights as I drove.

I began to grow anxious. "This isn't working," I groaned.

"I have an idea," Stan chimed loudly. "Let me out here. I'll jog behind her, and you pull the car up ahead and block her from going forward. After that, she will either come to you or turn around and come back in my direction. In either case, one of us should be able to grab her."

The idea was not the best, but it was the only one on the table. I put my foot on the brake, allowing Stan to get out. I could see him jog over to the shoulder, the light drizzle bouncing off his cap. I pulled around him, racing past CC enough to block her.

I spun the car around, facing the direction Stan and CC were coming from, allowing the headlights to blare into the distance before jumping out of the Jeep, bracing myself in a quarterback position, ready to tackle her if need be.

Suddenly, she was in the vastness, head down, galloping quietly on the road's edge. Close behind her, Stan jogged steadily, trying to keep his distance, not wanting to spook her away and keep sight of her simultaneously.

She slowed as she approached the headlights, swiftly darting across the road and back toward Stan.

"CC, come here, girl! Please!" I pleaded, running in the direction she was going. The darkness engulfed her and everything else. I could feel my heart sink with the realization that we may not be able to catch her. I might actually lose her. I stopped, panting for air, my head dropping forward as my vision blurred.

In the distance, I could hear the scuttling of feet on the road, bracing myself for Stan to call out, letting me know she got past him.

"I got her!" Stan said in the dark.

He got her. Mary, Joseph, and Peter! Thank you, God!

I stood back up, racing forward as Stan came into view carrying a wet, shaking CC. "You're okay. You're okay," I repeated over and over, grabbing her head and stroking it in Stan's arms. I didn't need to tell Stan what to do next. Instead, we both instinctively strode back to my Jeep.

He kept a firm hold on her as we drove back to his ranch. I was sure he was fearful that if he let go, she would bolt again. "Come into the camper. Let me get some towels to dry us off and a dry shirt for you," Stan suggested as we pulled in.

I was too cold and tired to argue. The camper on the back of Stan's truck was modern, unlike his forefathers' accommodations. The small space was clean, with a neatly organized dining table and a small kitchenette on one wall. A closet and toilet room were on the other. And in front, above the truck cabin, was a queen bed covered in a brown quilt with a cowboy hat sitting square in the middle.

He set CC down on the floor as he reached into the closet, grabbing towels and handing them to me. I sat on the edge of the dining bench right as CC began to shake feverishly. "No, CC, not in here!" I insisted, quickly placing a towel over her and attempting to dry off her wet fur. A pungent odor of wet dog filled the small space, causing my nose to crinkle.

"She's all right. Let her shake. She had quite the fright tonight, along with her owner," Stan replied as he gazed over at me. I could feel the angst that had been brewing in me through the search subside as Stan maneuvered in the small space, pulling a T-shirt out of the closet for me to change into.

"I don't suppose you have a curtain hidden away that I could change behind?"

"Unfortunately, no. If you would like me to step outside, I can, or I can turn around. I promise I won't peek," he replied snidely.

"That's what they all say." I realized sending him out into the rain would be rude, even with it being only a drizzle. "Fine, turn around. And close those eyes tightly shut."

He did as instructed. I hastily removed my wet sweatshirt, tossing it aside before slipping into the dry gray shirt. "Done," I announced.

Stan squinted sideways at me with one eye. A smile crossed his lips as he saw me sitting in his shirt.

"Better?" I asked.

"Yes. Dryer is better," he replied, taking his cap off momentarily to dry his hair. "Let me pour us a drink. That should help warm us up." He extracted a bottle of whiskey from a cabinet, along with two glasses, filling them both a fourth of the way full before he slid one in front of me on the small dining table.

"Cheers. Here's to new friends, rescuing a dog for the second time in its life, and a twenty-year-old bottle of whiskey," Stan proclaimed, raising his glass in a toast. I cupped the glass in my hand, raising it up and clicking it to his rim.

"Thank you," I said softly, savoring the warmth of the liquid as it cascaded down my throat with a lingering burn. "For everything tonight. To say all of this, and you, were unexpected is an understatement."

I slid into the booth more, allowing him space to sit. His closeness made the hair on the back of my neck stand at attention. His musky scent drifted between us. I inhaled a deep breath, letting it linger in my lungs before exhaling.

"Why do you live in the camper?" I asked, breaking the silence as I sipped the whiskey from the rim of the glass. "Why not get a place in town?"

"Can't afford it, really," he replied, gulping the last of his drink before pouring another. "I pay for the house my ex and kids live in and its upkeep. Along with whatever the kids need and the animals. Horses aren't cheap anymore. I still wanted to have a little fun and not be too far from the children. I opted for this. It suits me; just hard to date when you live in a camper. My friends tell me when I find a woman willing to come back here after a date or two, I'll know she is the one."

I laughed. "Well, they're right. Finding someone who will accept you for you, in all its camping glory, is like finding a needle in a haystack, as the saying goes."

"What about you? What does your needle in the haystack look like?" Stan asked as he filled my glass with more whiskey.

I let out a big sigh, thinking for a moment. "I'm not sure yet. I have been on over thirty first dates, and I still don't know." I thought back on the barrage of men over the last year, and a couple of them were still on a shortlist of plus-one options when I needed them. But none of them made me stop in my tracks. I supposed I still needed time. There were many waves to ride when it came to grieving a past life before discovering what I wanted in this new one.

"Thirty first dates?" Stan said, surprised. "You have gone on thirty first dates and *still* haven't found what you are looking for? Are you just really picky?"

I chuckled at that comment, swirling the contents of my glass. "Maybe. I think I'll feel something when it's the right one. Something will draw me to that person, allowing them to linger in my thoughts throughout the day without me even trying. I guess that's what I'm looking for."

"I admire your tenacity. Hell, I can't even make it past first date number three, let alone thirty," Stan replied before looking down at CC. "Let me get her a bit of water. All that running has to have made her thirsty."

Stan stood and pulled a paper bowl out of a top cabinet before grabbing a jug of drinking water off the counter. He filled the bowl and placed it in front of CC. She began to lap up the water, stopping when the bowl was almost empty, before lying on her damp towel with a grunt.

"She's a good dog. You're lucky," he stated, leaning back against the small kitchen counter facing me.

An uneasy silence fell between us. Stan stood there, staring down at me for what seemed like minutes. Then he reached down with his free hand, cupping my chin and tilting my head up. He bent down and kissed me softly. His lips were warm. Inviting. They were not in a hurry to move, and they stayed on mine, slowly shifting until our lips parted and the tip of his tongue traced the bottom inside of my lip.

The heat rose in my chest, along with a yearning. It was an ache I knew would drive me to do something I shouldn't do. Not here, not with my neighbor.

CC shook at that moment, breaking the trance I was in. "I should go," I quickly said, pulling my face away from his. I knocked back another large swallow of whiskey before reaching down and grabbing hold of CC firmly in both arms. I darted past Stan and out the camper door, racing to my Jeep under the now cloudless sky.

Tossing CC into the back, I climbed into the driver's seat and started the engine. Stan stood in the doorway of his camper, peering over at me with a surprised expression, I assumed, as I barreled out of the clearing and back onto the road.

I shouldn't have allowed that to happen.

In my gut, I still knew there was more to his story, something not quite right surrounding his divorce that he skirted around earlier in the evening around the fire. I reached up, touching my lips, the sensation of the kiss still tingling on them. An uneasy feeling washed over me, one that screamed to never do that again. And yet, the desire to kiss him once more pulsated through me.

CHAPTER TWENTY-TWO

I spent the next two days priming and painting the wrap-around porch, but what I was really doing was avoiding Stan. My walks with CC occurred only when Stan's truck and camper were not in sight. He had sent me a text later that night on the Fourth of July after I sped away. For longer than necessary, I stared at the ten simple words: **Please let me know if you made it home okay.**

I had finally replied with a simple, **We did.**

I'm not sure why I felt so guilty about allowing Stan to kiss me. There was no law that stated a single neighbor could not kiss another neighbor who was also single. In fact, I was sure it happened all the time . . . it just didn't happen to me.

I was grateful for the distraction of returning to work that week, something to take my mind off the events from the weekend. As I pulled into my dirt driveway on Wednesday, with the halfway mark of the workweek almost done, I could see Stan pull out of his ex-wife's driveway simultaneously.

Whew. Another bullet dodged.

I opened the house's back door, allowing CC to sprint out as I plopped my work bag and purse on the bench in the foyer. I strode back out and down the driveway, stopping at the mailbox.

"Hey there, neighbor!" Lisa boomed as she marched toward me and her mailbox, causing my breath to catch with surprise. "I know we have not officially met. Sorry about that; I usually hole up through the winter in these parts."

A feeling of shame coursed through my body. Unsure what to do or how to reply, I froze, mail in hand. Lisa was neither skinny nor fat and stood six inches shorter than me as she closed in the space between us. Her hair was a light golden brown and cascaded in curls slightly past her shoulders, with the top pulled up in a small clip. She wore a cream-colored blouse with a long brown skirt and a pair of shiny tan cowgirl boots.

I swallowed the lump that had formed in my throat. "It's all right. I did about the same. I'm Cindy, and you must be Lisa." I moved the mail over to my left hand, outstretching my right hand for a handshake. She grasped it in less than a firm hold, causing me to loosen mine.

"Stan said you're really nice. I know he and my boy have helped you from time to time. We should go out sometime, hit the Notch up for some drinks. Living out here, you don't find too many single younger women, or older women, for that fact. Not counting Carol, of course; she'll remain single just to spite her ex-husband. Cash in those alimony checks as long as she can."

I paused, thinking about Carol, who lived at the end of the lane. Last summer, she had informed Charles about each of the neighbors when he helped her move a stove. I didn't picture Carol as a person who would stick it to anyone, but rather as someone heartbroken about the end of her marriage and unwilling to do it again.

"That would . . . be nice," I lied with unease. It felt weird talking to Lisa casually since I had kissed her ex-husband less than a week ago. "I've been to the Notch once. Quaint little bar. The crowd seemed a little young. The few that were there, anyways."

"They may be young, but that's the good part, right?" she replied with a wink as if everyone enjoyed a young crowd. I assumed Lisa had to be ten years younger than me since she had one child who was still in elementary school. That would put her somewhere in her mid-thirties. "It's not like the fancy clubs in Park City, but the Notch has a live country band on Saturday nights. There's nothing like a little swing dancing with a hot young cowboy to take the edge off a week." She paused, taking a breath, crossing her arms across her chest. "So, how long have you been divorced? Stan and I have been divorced six years now, not counting the couple hookups here and there."

Somehow, I managed to keep a straight face as I met her eyes. *She knows. She knows I kissed him, and now she is tormenting me.*

"I've been divorced about a year now," I replied, my palm starting to sweat, dampening the envelopes I held. Why was it so hard to swallow all of a sudden?

"I finally had to kick him out after the last drunken outburst he had," Lisa continued, uncrossing her arms while kicking around at a rock. "He pulled a gun on me. And one of our daughters was right by my side. He was shitty drunk, like always, and as usual, we were fightin' about it. My daughter and I tore through the house to the garage, barricading the back door. We were in the car backing out when he stormed out and climbed on the car's hood. I gunned it, causing his drunk ass to fall off into the gravel. Then I called the police. He got arrested and spent time in jail for that stint. That was . . . probably five years ago?"

It took everything in me to make sure my jaw did not drop. Instead, I focused on my expression, hoping it came across as empathetic and not shocked. Maybe I was wrong. Perhaps Lisa didn't know that I had allowed her ex-husband to kiss me. But now I understood why Stan hemmed and hawed when we spoke about being divorced.

It isn't adding up though. Stan was over at Lisa's place all the time. Why would she allow him to be there if what she described was true?

Lisa continued, "Stan and I would brawl. Fistfight, in fact, for years. He never hit me as hard as I hit him . . . But enough about me! Why did you get divorced?"

I stood there, speechless, attempting to understand the story she had just dumped on me. It made no sense. I shook my head ever so slightly to bring me back to her loaded question, *Why did I get divorced?* My customary answer of "our paths were no longer aligning" would not suffice in this situation. Yet I was not about to share the intimate details with a woman I had just met.

"Well . . ." I paused, thinking about what I would share. "He, unfortunately, got addicted to drugs and just could not stop." Not a lie, but not the entire truth.

"Damn these men and their stupid addictions. I could never get Stan to stop drinking, even when I threatened him. So . . . do you like rodeos?"

We exchanged small talk for what seemed like hours, but it was only five or so more minutes as we stood next to the mailboxes. I kept my responses brief since a feeling of unease loomed over me. When she asked for my number at the end of our exchange, I hesitated. I didn't want her to have it, and I definitely didn't want to go to the bar or the rodeo with her. Scoping out young men in their tight jeans wasn't my scene. But I also didn't want to come across as the she-thinks-she-is-better-than-everyone city-girl neighbor. So, I gave her my number, praying I would be out of town for work if she ever decided to use it.

As CC and I strode back into the house, closing and locking the back door behind us, I couldn't help the uneasy feeling that something was not quite right about her story. Stan was kind, even chivalrous. I wondered if Stan knew that his ex-wife told people this story . . . not just people, but people she just met!

What I was more curious about, though, was whether the story she shared about Stan was true or not. If it was, was a person's past mistakes a reflection of their future self? Or can people change? An eerie feeling washed over me, along with images of individuals in my mind. Stan. Ron. William. Me.

I shook my head, realizing I had been standing in a daze in the house's foyer, CC staring blankly up at me from the living room. "CC, what we need is dinner and answers. I'll work on dinner if you work on the answers," I cooed in a high-pitched voice as she tilted her head from side to side, wagging her tail.

As the night wore on, I found myself on the front porch curled up on the brown wicker cushioned couch, a glass of wine cupped in my left hand. My mind had drifted from one thought to another all night, bouncing between my past life, my current life, and the people who had been a part of both. Then, my phone started to buzz on the patio side table where I had left it. I reached for it, turning the screen toward my face.

I wanted to make sure you were okay and to apologize. I should not have kissed you. I'm sorry. I understand if you don't want to speak to me again since I noticed you have been avoiding me all week, but I have your shirt and the rest of your wine. Before I drink the rest of this bottle while inhaling the scent of you from your shirt (that's a joke, by the way), I wanted to bring them back to you.

I stared down at the text message, rereading it several times. The answer to the question that had been swirling around in my head all evening was right in front of me, and yet, it wasn't. *Can a person change?*

Yes . . . they can.

Swiping over the keys on my cell phone with my right hand, I responded.

No need to apologize, but thank you all the same. I'm not avoiding you, just deep in thought the last few days. Would it be okay if I swing by tomorrow night and pick up my things?

The three blue dots in the text exchange started to move, signaling he was typing. I really didn't care about my things; what I wanted was a moment to talk to Stan. I wasn't sure what I would say, and I didn't want to divulge everything his ex-wife had told me about him. Maybe I just needed to know for my peace of mind that he was not the monster Lisa claimed him to be.

The bouncing dots stopped.

Yes, that should work, anytime after six.

A shiver cascaded through my body, leaving my lips tingling. I instinctively reached up, touching my bottom lip, recalling his kiss and the sensation it left me with that night. Lisa was wrong. I just knew it.

The next evening, I turned down the dirt lane on Stan's ranch. It looked even bigger in the light of day. The three large oak trees produced shade in abundance. Stan's truck and camper were parked in the same spot, just off to the side of the trees. The fire pit was blackened, and the lawn chairs were folded, leaning against one of the trees.

Stan appeared out of the camper door as I parked. "You made it," he remarked as I closed the driver's door. He looked sharp, sporting a navy blue button-up shirt with white trim on the edges, dark denim blue jeans with a large silver buckle, and worn brown boots. Perched on his head was a black, wide-brim cowboy hat.

"I did. Hard to miss in the light," I replied, unsure of what I would say to Stan now that I was in front of him. "You really need to touch up that sign, though, if the ranch is ever to become famous."

"The last thing we want is fame," he replied, hopping down from the camper into the dirt, causing a slight cloud of dust to swirl around him. "Can I grab you a beer?"

"No thanks, I can't stay long," I replied, realizing there was no easy way to ask him about the conversation I'd had with his ex except to just blurt it out. I leaned my back against the Jeep side, bracing myself before starting. "I met your ex-wife the other day, Lisa. She is interesting. She shared some stories with me about your relationship, which surprised me. She described things that seemed out of character for you."

He paced over to me, his head tilted down before leaning against the side of my Jeep a few feet away from me. Removing his hat, he ran his hand through his thin hair. "Lisa and I fed off each other, and not in a good way," he began, shuffling his boot in the dirt. "It got very hostile between us at times. She brought out the worst in me, and I suppose I did the same for her. So whatever she said about me, which is really none of my business, is in some way true. I even spent some time in jail, which gave me time to think. It made me realize we were not good together and that if I was ever going to be a better version of myself, I had to do it away from her."

I let a long sigh out. I didn't need to tell Stan exactly what Lisa said, and I got the impression he didn't want to know.

He continued, "Look, Cindy, I am not proud of some of the things I have done in my past. I will be the first to admit it. But I have worked hard and continue to strive to be better than that version of me. Unfortunately, Lisa will always see me as my past self, since that is who I was to her . . . but that's not who I am anymore."

I thought about younger versions of myself and the mistakes I had made. I, too, worked hard not to make those mistakes again.

"I admire you, Stan, for choosing to be better than you once were. It's not easy," I replied solemnly, tilting my head up to the sky, peering at the vastness of blue. I could feel his eyes on me as if the next move was mine. I let the stillness be between us, deep in thought of everyone in my life who had been a variation of themselves that no longer fit in my life. In my mind, I wondered what version they were all displaying now.

Stan cleared his throat. "So . . . does this mean we can't be friends anymore?" he questioned hesitantly.

A small chuckle left my lips, realizing that was what Stan was worried about. "Of course, we can still be friends, silly. I only know this version of you, not the other one. And this version is a great storyteller, keen dog finder, and expert listener. But you better fetch what's left of that wine of mine and two glasses. I feel a toast is in order, to say goodbye to old versions of ourselves and hello to the work in progress we all are as humans on this planet."

With that, Stan pushed off the side of the Jeep, a wide grin on his face.

CHAPTER TWENTY-THREE

"Betty, what's your going rate for counseling today?" I whispered over her left shoulder as she stood at the counter at the café entrance with a handful of water glasses in her hands.

"My last table, in the section I am assigned to today, tipped me twenty-five dollars," she replied sarcastically.

"I'll double that if you serve me on the patio tonight."

A chuckle left her lips as she nodded her head toward the patio door. "Geez, I'll be there in a minute."

I sat at a small table in the patio corner where I could truly enjoy every bit of summer that the café's outdoor area offered. The courtyard was encased in a dark brown wooden fence, embracing all the little iron tables in privacy. With my pause in dating, I had not seen my waitress friend for a few months, and I felt the need to catch her up on my life's events. But, boy, did her face light up when she finally made it to the patio area and it was just the two of us, catching up like old school friends.

First, I shared what had happened to Ron, how CC was now my partner in crime, and how I'd nearly lost her. That, of course, brought me to Stan. I paused, sighing, glancing at the potted orange-and-yellow geraniums across the tables and around the edges of the patio and pergola. Then, stalling a bit, I felt Betty's expectant gaze on me as I grabbed a piece of warm bread from the basket on my table and shoved a good chunk into my mouth.

"So . . . ?" Betty prompted mercilessly. The golden streaks of her hair were pulled up in the front, falling in loose curls down her back. They shifted as she leaned toward me. "Have you seen him since then? After you spoke to the crazy ex-wife?"

I washed down the bread with a long, slow draw of pinot grigio that Betty had brought me. Two weeks had gone by since then. Slowly, I nodded at my friend. "Actually . . ." My fingers toyed with the stem of the wine glass. "Stan and I have been spending time together at his ranch, away from Lisa. Last week, after a few glasses of wine, I was the one who leaned in and kissed him."

"Cindy!" Betty exclaimed, her jaw dropping slightly in surprise.

I smiled. Stan hadn't stopped me, but I was riddled with guilt. I certainly wasn't looking for any long-term relationship with Stan. But it was lovely having someone geographically close to me in this little town that I could chat with, share goals with, and feel comfortable around. Inside, I felt like a teenage girl sneaking around with a boy behind her mother's back. Except Lisa wasn't my mother, and I wasn't a teenager.

I knew I didn't need Lisa's permission to see Stan, but something in me felt like I did. I couldn't quite put my finger on it, but I had a feeling that something was off. Stan had confided in one of our late-night talks that he thought she had a screw loose somewhere, along with a short fuse and a fiery temper.

Am I scared of her?

That couldn't be it. I had battled with the best in the corporate world, not backing down from any executive who thought I should do things their way when I knew we could do better in my heart. I had stood up to any bully I encountered who treated other people as less than, but Lisa gave off a different vibe that left me feeling guilty for kissing her ex-husband and worrying about what she would do to me if she found out.

In my mind, I had two choices: one, tell Lisa that I was slightly more than just friends with her ex-husband and take whatever wrath she dished out, or, two, stop being friends with

Stan. Of course, I hated both ideas, leading me to option three: ask Betty for advice.

"What are you smiling for?" Betty asked in the silence.

I realized I had a grin on my face at that moment because, deep in my heart, I was coming to a pretty big understanding. Even though the weight of my predicament and the recounting of my recent life events to Betty started to weigh on me, my problems were trivial in the grand scheme of things. I was worried about telling a neighbor that I had kissed her ex-husband, even though it was none of her business. World hunger and wars still ravaged other countries. First-world problems, I supposed, were what I faced. Petty and unimportant.

I sat up in my chair as Betty watched me curiously. Then, finally, I decided that I needed to stop overthinking this. I needed to stop worrying about what others thought or didn't think about me. That was none of my business.

People would make their own conclusions about me no matter what I did. As long as I lived by the Ten Commandments, everything else I decided was at my discretion. I was a grown-ass woman and didn't need anyone's permission on what I wanted to do, nor did I need to apologize for any of my decisions.

"Earth to Cindy," Betty spoke up, waving a hand in front of my face. "I haven't even given you advice yet, and you may not like what I'm about to tell you."

"It doesn't matter," I replied confidently. "I just made up my own mind on what to do."

I'm having a birthday party on Saturday, you should come. My mom makes a killer apple pie.

Stan's text arrived late Tuesday evening. I had been working late in my home office, with deadlines approaching for audit work. I was still in my work clothes, a pair of gray dress slacks and a form-fitting short-sleeve black sweater.

I set down my phone after reading the invitation. Then, standing, I stretched my arms up and over my head, causing CC to stir from her resting area at the top of the stairs in the loft. She galloped over to me, pushing her nose under my hand, her cue to let me know she wanted to be petted. I ran my hand up and down her head firmly, looking out into the iridescent sky from my office window before picking my phone back up from the desk.

For three days now, I had been making decisions based on what I wanted, not what others or society thought a woman should be or do. I had scheduled an appointment for the following month to get the slight bags under my eyes tightened, an inherited gift from my mother, not caring what others thought of cosmetic procedures.

Let them comment. It was my face and my decision. I had sat on the couch Sunday evening binge-watching documentaries of wars and influential leaders while eating ice cream straight from the tub. And both nights after work, I sat sidesaddle on the four-wheelers in my perfectly pressed pencil skirt, button-up blouse, and high heels as I drove up and down the street while CC chased after me, running off the built-up energy she had stored while lounging around the house all day. No need to change into more appropriate clothes to ride an ATV. My work clothes were just fine.

I had been kinder at work but firm. Every day, I complimented my team for a job well done while steadfastly defining expectations for the next project. For better or worse, this was me now.

I stared back down at the text from Stan. He and I were nothing more than friends, with some slight benefits. I knew our friendship may lead to full benefits if I let it. But I wasn't ready to meet anyone's family, being introduced awkwardly as someone's *friend*. That was something I wasn't sure I would ever be ready for again. And the thirty-plus dates I had been on were proof of that.

How about I come and celebrate with you after the family party? Just you and me. I'll bring your favorite whiskey, and you can save me a piece of apple pie.

That sounds even better, Stan texted back. I'll text you once everyone leaves.

A smile crossed my lips as I responded with a thumbs-up emoji. Another decision was made just for me. Trudging down the stairs in my bare feet with CC scampering behind me, I opened the back door, letting her outside one more time before calling it a night. I made my way to the kitchen, refilling my wine glass from the chilled box in the fridge.

Maybe I would let Stan have the full benefits of our friendship this weekend. Besides Mr. Chivalry, Darren, who had consistently become my plus-one for events in the city at this point, along with a release of physical frustrations every now and then, I hadn't been with anyone else in that way in months.

The hiatus from the swipe left or right features was a break I needed after CC became a full-time resident in my home. It allowed me the time I needed to catch up on work and finish a degree I had put on hold at the end of my marriage. Plus, I had CC to keep me company, and now . . . Stan.

Is it what I want, though? Is having a friendship with benefits in this bewildered little town a good idea?

I took a deep breath and sipped my wine as CC bounded through the back door and into the kitchen, where I was leaning against the island. She stood in front of me, tail wagging. I knew what she wanted: a chew bone, something I gave her every night before I went to bed, leaving her to nestle on the rug under the dark oak dining table, gnawing away for hours. I retrieved the rawhide stick and handed it to her before she quickly scampered to her spot.

I turned off the lights and locked the back door in the foyer before climbing the stairs to the loft. The sounds of clicks from lamps and switches echoed through the quiet house with just a light gnawing sound from CC in the distance.

I settled into bed, setting the glass of wine on my nightstand. Saturday night would come, and I would decide how far I wanted to take my friendship with Stan. I reached over, turning the lamp off on my nightstand.

Click.

CHAPTER TWENTY-FOUR

The coast is clear. See you in a few minutes?

Saturday night, from the sofa on my front porch, I read the text message from Stan. For some reason, an uneasy feeling shivered through me. Shaking it off, I stood up from the couch, chalking it up to nerves. I was ready to head out wearing jeans and one of my favorite comfy shirts. Striding into the house, I retrieved a chew bone for CC, handing it to her before retrieving the bottles of whiskey and wine from the icebox and making my way to the garage.

The bay door eased open with the click of the button, revealing the evening dusk. I backed out discreetly, easing onto the road as I flipped the car headlights on. I would have to pass Lisa's house and then onto the main lane before taking the loop toward the ranches.

But there, in the headlights, on the edge of the road, stood Lisa and three of her children. Her younger boys were playfully wrestling with their barking brown lab. Lisa and her daughter, who looked around sixteen, leaned against the car, holding plates covered in foil.

A surge of panic raced through me, mainly because I thought they would have been home for a while by now. It felt like I was sneaking out of the house behind my parents' back instead of being one-half of two single consenting adults having a drink together. Of course, I wasn't doing anything wrong; they had been divorced for years.

So why does it feel like I am?

It was too late to turn around and drive in the opposite direction; they had all seen me. The youngest boy waved when he saw me, since I'd hired him to mow and trim my lawn over the last few weeks, thanks to Stan.

As I slowly drove past the family, I rolled down my window, not wanting to be rude. "I heard it was someone's birthday today. Looks like you all celebrated 'til the sun went down," I commented, trying to swallow the forming lump in my throat.

"We did. We have a lot of leftovers. Are you hungry?" Lisa asked, extending a plate toward me as she walked a few feet closer to my driver's window.

"No thank you," I stammered. "I have someone I'm meeting . . . for drinks just over in town."

It was not a complete lie. I was meeting someone for drinks, just not in town. Plus, it really wasn't any of her business.

I could see her eyes shift in the glow of the car lights as if giving me the once-over before the corners of her mouth turned flat. "Well, have a good time," she replied tightly. She scanned the empty backseat of the Jeep before looking back at me.

"I will, thank you," I replied before rolling up my window and slowly pulling away. I could see Lisa standing in the middle of the road in the rearview mirror, holding a plate covered in tinfoil, eyeing me.

Ten minutes later, I was entering Stan's ranch. There was no campfire, which I thought was unusual. Only plumes of gray smoke cascaded up through the center of the three giant oak trees where it once was ablaze. Besides the light that glowed through the shades of the camper windows, the world had succumbed to darkness, and the stars began to appear as if the sparkling white lights of a Christmas tree stand were being turned on.

My tires crunched over the gravel as I parked beside the truck and camper. Cradling two bottles in my arms, I got out and heard the loud click of the camper door opening. Stan stood in the doorway.

His arms were above his head, holding onto the top of the door frame. He wore a white T-shirt and basketball shorts, with sandals and no hat. I had never seen him this way, out of his cowboy gear and slightly unsteady. Yet a pleasant twinge of anticipation rippled through me as a smile crossed his lips.

"Are you drunk already?" I asked, balancing the bottles on my hip as I observed him.

"I've had a few beers," he conceded with a slight hiccup. "Just enough to take the edge off having the ex here this afternoon."

"You know you can always just not invite her. Totally an option," I replied snidely.

"And unleash the wrath of the dragon lady?" He leaned to one side of the door frame to balance himself. "Not in a million years . . . or until the kids are grown. I like seeing those small humans I helped create, especially those boys."

I bit back the reply I wanted to launch back at him. I had a perfectly prepared rant about how visitation was court-ordered and protected. Women who used children as pawns after a divorce were a mockery to all single mothers who would give anything to have their children's fathers be involved in their kids' lives. But today was Stan's birthday, and the last thing he needed was a tirade from me.

"So, are you going to invite me in?" I held up the bottles in my hand, realizing our celebration would not be under the stars tonight. "I brought the good stuff."

"Where are my manners?" Stan said with a slight slur, stepping to the edge of the truck gate. "Hand those up. Do you need me to let the ladder down, or are you in the mood to hoist yourself up tonight?"

I didn't reply immediately and just handed him the bottles before lifting myself onto the tailgate. "I got this. Just slide out of the doorway a bit so I can get past. Apparently, I have some catching up with you on alcohol consumption." I moved past him into the small space, reaching up and opening the cabinets above the kitchen sink.

"The one to the left," Stan pointed, closing the camper door before placing the bottles on the table. He squeezed past me to extract glasses from the cupboard. My body became keenly aware of his closeness, sending goosebumps cascading up and down my arms and neck.

I unscrewed the bottle of whiskey, pouring each glass a quarter full and handing one over to him. "Cheers," I said, raising my glass in the air. "Some people drink from a glass half empty, and some drink from a glass half full. It's your birthday, so drink as many glasses as you want."

With that, we clinked the edges of the tumblers before downing the brown, nutty liquid. I instantly squinted as my mouth puckered. The harsh liquor tumbled down the back of my throat in a burn.

"Ack! That is strong," I gasped through coughs. "Hand me the bottle of wine. I need a chaser."

He reached across the table, sliding the bottle toward me. I slid into the bench seat and opened the wine, pouring a full glass before guzzling a third of it down.

"Not sure what you're tasting, but this whiskey is smooth like butter," he replied, tipping to the left slightly. "My lady," he asked with a slurred British accent, "would you care to slide over a bit? Allow some room for the birthday boy to sit and enjoy another glass with you?"

"It would be my honor, sir," I replied. "For 'tis your birthday today, and ye shall have a place to sit, drink, and be merry."

I moved further into the U-shaped booth, allowing Stan the space to slide in next to me. Heat rose within me, though I was unsure if it was from the liquor or his proximity. It was likely a combination of both. Grasping my glass, I took another sip from the edge as the room began to swirl slightly.

"So how was your family celebration today?" I asked, facing him as he poured another glass of whiskey.

"It was good," he said, tracing the rim of the glass with his forefinger. "Would have been better if you were here. But—oh, that reminds me! I saved you some pie."

Without standing, Stan reached over to the counter by the sink, grabbed a tinfoil-covered plate, and placed it on the table before extracting a fork from the drawer under the counter.

"Is this the famous apple pie I've heard so much about?"

"It is. I was lucky to save this piece for you. Everyone wanted seconds and thirds," he replied richly.

"Well then . . ." I lifted the foil from the plate to uncover a crispy, golden-brown slice of pie, with apple filling dusted in cinnamon oozing out of each side of the flaky crust. I picked up the fork, wasting no time diving into the front triangle, pulling it eagerly to my mouth.

"Oooh! Ummm, wow, this is good," I replied sweetly, cutting another piece of the pie off with my fork.

"I told you. My mother's apple pie cannot be beaten. That's a blue-ribbon pie in the county fair right there."

"I can't argue with that," I mumbled through another mouthful. "I'll make you a deal. I will eat the rest of this pie if you tell me about your party."

"Deal," he agreed, and leaned back so our shoulders nearly touched. "My day started with an amazing dirt bike ride with my boys up the trails to the east . . ."

The conversation flowed like a river, long past my pie consumption. Stan was right, it was delicious. Maybe I did need to meet his mother, if only to get her recipe. But even in my inebriated state, I knew that wouldn't happen. There was still something more between Stan and Lisa, which kept gnawing at me like a slight stomachache.

There was a lull in the conversation, and he peered at me yearningly. I knew what he wanted, and with a nearly empty bottle of wine and a half-full bottle of whiskey in front of us, I guess I wanted it too.

He slid closer to me on the bench until his face met mine, and we began to kiss. It was slow and easy at first; then, as if all our walls tumbled down and indiscretions burned away, our mouths consumed each other.

Soon, our shirts were off, and he stood, reaching out to me while balancing himself with his other hand on the counter. He motioned to the bed on top of the cabin front with his eyes.

I stood awkwardly, the force of the alcohol now coursing through my veins with my pounding heart. Stan took me by the waist and heaved me onto the bunk before climbing up himself. Our mouths became intertwined again as he reached behind my back, unclasping the hooks of my bra.

Small explosions tingled over my body, fueling a desire I had not felt in months. My mind flashed back to moments with William and the overwhelming rejection I'd felt at the end of it all when he found solace in another woman. But here, in this instant, and many times over the last year that I allowed similar events to occur, I realized that men could still want me. They wanted my mind, my body, and my company. That's how it felt, anyway: that I was wanted.

But if my thirty-odd dates had taught me anything, it was that this feeling wouldn't last long, and once it was gone, I would be too. Stan, like the others, would be just a lost memory. It was as if I was an addict, and the feeling these men gave me was my drug.

I felt Stan ease his hand under my bra, cupping my breast firmly. I pulled the straps down my arms so our bare torsos could fuse into each other. My head was spinning, and so was the trailer as our mouths sought comfort from being intwined. Stan's hands were hasty and clumsy over my heated skin, something I was not used to.

Then, in the distance, I heard the crunch of gravel. It was getting louder, coming closer. Until it stopped.

"Stan," I swiftly whispered with an edge of panic in my voice. "I think someone is here. I heard a car pull up just now."

Stan crawled over to the side window on the top camper bunk, pulling the curtain aside to peer out into the starlit darkness.

"Who is it?" I asked hesitantly. I was back to being a sixteen-year-old girl, and my parents had just gotten home from work, catching me in the act.

"Wait here," he suggested hoarsely as he climbed down from the bunk, pulling his T-shirt back on.

The sound of a car door slamming vibrated through the cabin, followed swiftly by banging on the camper door. Stan fixed his hair. In two long strides, he was at the door, opening it a crack, blocking whoever was out there from seeing inside.

Before words were even uttered, I knew who it was.

"What do you want, Lisa?" Stan demanded, causing me to pull a corner of the blankets across me to cover my naked top half.

"I know you are in there, slut!" she screamed. The once-dizzy camper came back into focus, realizing that what I feared was true: there was still something more between Stan and Lisa.

"Lisa, you need to leave," Stan stated low and firmly. "This is none of your business."

"It is my business. I'm making it so!" she shrieked, her tone dripping with jealousy and fury.

It was as if she had just caught me sleeping with her husband instead of her ex-husband. I was suddenly grateful that we were not in the center of town in the back of my buzzed brain. We were not close to anything or anyone who could hear her protests.

"Did you tell her you tried to get me to sleep with you just hours ago?" Lisa's question stuck like barbs in the bare skin of my back. "Did you?"

"Lisa, please, go home," Stan pleaded.

My breathing began in shallow gulps as I pulled the blanket further up my neck. The strong woman I knew myself to be was cowering under layers of cloth, too scared to move for fear of what this woman would do to me. I would have stood chin to chin with her in any other situation, but at that moment, and with her past mention of a gun altercation, I was afraid.

I am so stupid. So goddamn, bloody stupid!

"Does she know you have been trying to get me back for the last year?" Lisa continued to howl. "That you beg me every day to take you back? How you want us to be a family again? Does she? Does she also know you held a gun on me in front of our daughter and spent time in jail for abuse? That you are a raging alcoholic and drink even at work? Does she know this? Do you, SLUT?"

Her words seemed to permeate my flesh, immobilizing me in shame and fear.

"Do you know this about him? Miss Professional Woman? Do you? You're a fake, a phony, trying to pretend that you have your shit together. You're nothing more than a bitch."

"Lisa, you need to leave. NOW!" Stan replied. Even though he emphasized the last word, he kept his tone low as he spoke through the crack in the door.

"I'm not leaving," Lisa insisted. "Not until she comes out and faces *me*! Miss Goody Two-Shoes, who thinks it's okay to be nice to my face as she sneaks around with you behind my back."

I lay there, my body absorbing every verbal blow she threw at me. I started to shake as a lump formed in my throat. *Is this what I have become? A woman who joneses for moments of being wanted by someone, anyone, just so I can feel that I'm still worth something?*

I could feel a dark shadow cast over me as Stan and Lisa argued through the door. The apple pie and liquor turned sour in my stomach, and I now wanted to pull the blanket up and over my head. *Oh my God . . .* The sudden irony of the whole situation was no longer lost on me.

I thought my life had hit rock bottom when I discovered William's affair, and again when I realized he was still seeing her . . . a woman I, too, had called a slut.

But that wasn't my rock bottom.

This was.

In a camper, half-clothed, I lay, with a deranged ex-wife screaming at me from outside and a drunk man I barely knew trying to hold her back. I didn't really know Stan; he could be a serial killer. And I had no clue what Lisa was fully capable of either, but I knew she was clever and hurtful from the stories Stan shared.

Trapped in a hell of my own making, I yanked the blanket tighter around me, realizing I had become a shell of the woman I once was. Where was the lady who had determinedly jumped over a hole in the floor of her foyer? What had happened to that feisty soul who made a pact with an old, worn-down house and loved and healed it while she loved and healed herself?

Stan finally closed the door on Lisa after telling her again that she needed to go home. I could hear her get into her car, slam the door, and peel out on the dirt road as she left the ranch.

Stan climbed back up on the bunk next to me. "Sorry about that. I told you she was fiery and a little psychotic."

My jaw dropped slightly in the dark space. *Really?*

His hand sifted through my long, auburn hair. I wasn't sure if he could tell I was trembling.

"Where were we?" He rested his lips on mine.

We kissed again, but my mind and body screamed in protest. *Don't do this!*

"I'm sorry. I can't . . . I can't do this," I groaned out between kisses. Hastily reaching for my bra, I climbed down from the bunk, located my shirt, and pulled it over my head. "This was a mistake. A horrible mistake. I have to go."

I opened the camper door with a loud clank before jumping down into the dirt. I scurried to my Jeep, starting the engine and racing out of the ranch into the Woodland starlit night.

CHAPTER TWENTY-FIVE

You are a phony. You think you have your fucking act together, but you don't.

Walking around in your business suits. You ran from one addict to another. To a man who pulled a gun on his family. He spent time in jail because of his acts. Did you know I had a restraining order against him for years?

Stay away from him. Don't call or text him, don't show up at the house or the ranch. Don't ever speak to him again or me. And don't come near our children. They will no longer be helping you in any way.

Stan and I are going to try to make it work again. So leave us alone, bitch!

I reread the message, letting every word sink in. The barrage of texts from Lisa had started early this morning. After I had blocked her on my phone, she found me through social media sites and continued her rant. Like all the others, I deleted it.

I glanced at the clock on the nightstand: 11:34 a.m. stared back at me. I pulled the blankets tighter around my chin, hoping that if I stayed in bed long enough, the outside world would disappear, including my mistake from last night.

Maybe Lisa was right. Perhaps I was just a phony. If I genuinely had my act together, a stupid, shameful thing like last night wouldn't have happened. Instead, sheer recollections sent another anxious shiver through my body, causing me to ball up in a fetal position. I could feel the water as it pooled in my eyes and then the coldness as the silent tears trickled down my cheek onto the pillow.

It was as if the last year and a half of my new life had taught me nothing. I wasn't any closer to figuring out who I was after William; in fact, it was as if the previous evening's events had set me back years. I had been on over thirty dates, had a black book of men to call on depending on my mood, and worked close to seventy hours a week, and the person I counted on the most had four legs.

At least through CC, I had found unbridled trust, genuine connection, and acceptance.

But when it came to my heart, I was no closer to finding those elusive feelings than I had been almost two years ago. I teetered on the sharp edge of accepting that Lisa's words held harsh but undeniable truths. Maybe I couldn't have those things, except with my children and CC. But I had felt them before, years ago.

Why couldn't I find them again?

Am I no longer worthy? What am I doing wrong?

That morning, the reel of images from CC's walk played through my head. I was dressed in worn sweats, a cup of coffee in hand, as CC and I strolled down the lane. A light breeze helped cool the air as the rising July sun took hold. The sound of the river's low rush cascaded over the brush line to the east. The lane was void of people until I heard a car coming behind me. I didn't look up but kept walking with my head down, still reeling with humiliation.

Shrill voices overcame me as the car sped by. "You're just a slut! Stay away from our father, you cunt!" a young woman's voice boomed from the car window.

A crumpled wrapper hit me on the side of the head. My attention snapped upward, and I felt disgrace coursing through my veins like hot lava. I watched the car of teenagers, two of them being Stan and Lisa's children, drive away. I had never been called a slut in my entire life, and now in the span of twenty-four hours, I had been called it several times.

I had hit my deepest low. *But how did I get here?*

Turning quickly, I raced back home, CC following close on my heels. Barreling through the back door, I thrust it closed behind me, bolting all the locks. Running through the house, I closed every blind and curtain, only wanting darkness, a form of safety for me, a way to shut out the exterior world.

And now I lay curled in my bed, tears running onto my pillow. CC was coiled up in the corner on the floor next to me. Everything I had accomplished over the last two years had turned to dust. All my triumphs with the house, independence, and self-acceptance had melted underneath some alcohol and one stupid mistake. Now, I was left feeling emptier than I had ever felt. I let out a weak whimper. There was no coming back from a wound this deep.

It would be much simpler if I weren't here anymore.

My kids would miss me, but they would be okay eventually. Plus, they would come out much wealthier in the end, what with my insurance policies and retirement account. How many times in jest had I told them they would be set if anything happened to me? But never in my life had I seriously considered not being there for my children and grandchildren. Still, the thoughts pervaded.

I could easily find CC a new home; she was a good dog. After that, I just needed to wrap up a few things at work, ensure my finances were in place, and sell the home I'd worked so hard to restore. Then I could go up to the meadow beyond the mountains, the one CC and I hiked through often, far from the view of everyone, with a rope . . . and a bottle of sleeping pills.

The image of me hanging from a tree caused another wave of panic. I was awash in a fresh set of tears, which turned into heaving sobs. I rolled onto my back, stretching out my legs. Still sobbing, I wiped my runny nose on the edge of my sleeve as the quiet space flooded with the sound of a wounded cat in the wilderness.

It wasn't a cat though; it was me.

Softly, I whispered to myself, "That is not the answer, Cindy. That can never be the answer. If you do that, you only transfer the despair you feel onto others."

It was not even noon, but I no longer wanted to be awake. I was exhausted. Exhausted from last night's events and that morning's accusations and name-calling, but mostly, I was exhausted with life. Still, slumber would just not find me. *No rest for the wicked.*

I eased out of bed, wrapping a robe tightly around me before plunging my feet into slippers. CC quickly jumped to her feet and strode to my side, tail wagging. I smiled down at her through my swollen eyes, knowing she at least loved and accepted me.

I trod down the open loft stairs and staggered to the front door to let CC out to do her business before floundering weakly into the kitchen. Extracting a cup from the glass cabinet, I poured a tall glass of wine and gulped it down before pouring another. There wasn't even a hint of a hangover from the previous night's drinking. Still, the emotional battering I'd taken was worse than a typical headache and dehydration. I had to take the edge off somehow.

CC strode back through the cracked door, which I raced to close and relock. Not only was I trying to keep others out, but I was also keeping myself in.

Within my four walls, I couldn't cause anyone angst, not even myself. I climbed the stairs back up to the loft and back to the master bathroom. Grabbing pill bottles from the cabinet, I opened them all, placing several in my hand before swallowing them down with wine.

I wanted to sleep, realizing not forever, but for a very long time.

When I woke up, the room was dark. My body felt heavy as it wrestled to break free from the tangled blankets. My eyes were crusted with particles and swollen as I reached up to rub them. The clock flashed 2:34 a.m. I had been asleep for over twelve hours, yet I felt even more tired than I did the day before. CC eagerly jumped up from her spot on the carpet by the side of the bed when she heard me move, making me realize she had not been outside to relieve herself since I lay down yesterday.

Climbing out of bed, I hastily went to the dark bathroom to empty my bladder before wrapping a blanket around my shoulders and making my way down to the front porch. The night was crisp yet warm. The smell of campfires drifted in the wind.

CC raced into the trees with a rustle. I wandered to the porch steps that led into the wooded yard, found my familiar place, and sat. There was not a cloud in the sky, just the vastness of the stars that seemed so close that I could reach up and touch them. I grew still, gazing at the lights as they grew bright and dimmed. I imagined the vivid ones to be planets, or suns, orbiting in another galaxy.

At that moment, I felt small.

I was just a speck in the much broader scheme of the universe, a woman with trivial problems compared to others who, on that same night, may be hiding in war-torn countries praying for their lives to be spared, or perhaps a young father fighting for his life after a horrible accident.

My problems were trivial. But they were still my problems.

"God, if you can hear me, I need your help," I whispered, cinching the blanket tighter around my shoulders. I thrust my gaze back up into the stars. "I know you have a plan for me, because if you didn't, I would have died a half a dozen times over in the multiple car accidents the last couple of years."

"Still . . . I need a hint about what that plan is. I need to know I *am* meant to be more. That I have a purpose yet to be fulfilled. That someday, I will be content again. Please. God, or Higher

Power, whatever you are, help me. Help me find my way. Help me be the person I am meant to be. Show me the path, I beg of you. For tonight . . . I am lost."

CC appeared in the small clearing of grass in front of the porch. She stood still as if she could hear something rustling close by. Her ears were perked up, her tail frozen in mid-wag, and she peered at me or through me. I could see her as clear as day from the brightness of the stars.

I hesitated to turn, worried that if there was someone behind me, it could be Lisa, wanting to seek revenge. Tonight, I was a sitting duck. I watched as CC wagged her tail happily as if she realized whatever she saw behind me was good and trusted. I rotated slowly, peering over my shoulder into the darkness, but nothing was there.

A swift breeze picked up at that moment, pushing a gust of wind behind me and into the yard in front of me. CC let out a small bark, then lowered her ears, wagging her tail furiously as she pounced toward me.

I embraced her, a bit bewildered. "What did you see, girl? What was it?" I asked in a low voice as she nuzzled her nose under my chin. She turned away from me and galloped off, back into the bushes.

Just then, it felt like a spider web cascaded over the back of my left hand. Looking down, I was met with a surprise. I could make out a single white feather in the star's glow.

My mother was there at that moment. She was the white feather. I could feel her very presence.

She was behind me; that was who CC was looking at. I took a breath and allowed my mother's presence to remind me I had a purpose. In due time, it would eventually unfold before me. I took another breath in before exhaling slowly. That time, it felt as if I was breathing out my fears, along with my worries, regrets, and disappointments.

I am the only one holding myself back.

I kept everyone at arm's length for fear of being hurt again. I needed to first learn to love myself unconditionally, through all my mistakes and misgivings, before I could love any partner the same way. I needed to listen and trust my gut, follow it, and, in turn, learn to trust others again. I needed to learn to accept the person I was and the one I was becoming, including my imperfections and failures. I needed to stop labeling myself and just be the best person I knew how to be.

Taking the feather in my right hand, I swirled it around with my thumb and middle finger. The Woodland stars always had the answer.

I just needed to listen.

CHAPTER TWENTY-SIX

I went to my place, where the vastness of the valley from the hilltop resembled an exquisite painting. The meadow was littered with long grasses and yellow shrubs that cascaded into the rolling hills before hitting the base of the small mountains. A deep forest green covered the background, offset by shades of emerald and shamrock in the foreground. Dark and light were present, with hints of yellow and orange appearing in the shadows as the season began to change.

Up a trail that few knew, behind the smaller mountains, sat the grand Uinta Basin. The peaks shot up through the sky, embracing the wafting cloud of dust. The air was thick with pine, and the trees rustled in the background with each small gust of wind. I felt it was only proper to call this "my place" because it was where I went when things were at their worst.

It was also where I went when I was ready to change those things.

CC sat in front of me on the four-wheeler, the mode of transportation required to reach this view. We'd been here often over the last several weeks. It was tranquil and vast in a lonely way, yet full of possibilities that I now accepted I was worthy of reaching for.

It had been eight weeks since the eventful night with Stan and Lisa. Since then, I avoided them—and mostly all their drama—at all costs. Their children stopped screaming profanities at me a few days after that night. I suspected the novelty of it had worn off. The messages also stopped from Lisa, resulting directly from the blocking features on my cell phone and social media accounts.

CC jumped down from the four-wheeler, eager to sniff around in the brush. Over the weeks, my mind would wander back as I gazed at the valley below on my visits. My obscure search for unconditional love, trust, and acceptance, which started after I moved to Woodland, was in front of me the entire time, just like the vale below.

Or rather, it was within me. The answers came to me a week after the white feather. It began with a dream.

In my dream, I was a young girl walking down the side of a highway near my childhood home. In the distance stood my mother. She wasn't the way I remembered her, a girth of a woman at her passing when I was just twenty-four. In this vision, she was perhaps younger, in her mid-thirties, and wearing a form-fitting polyester teal dress with long sleeves and a hem that cascaded down to her ankles. She wasn't thin, but not her size when she passed. Her brown hair was short, curled at the top, and straighter on the sides and back. Peeking out from under the dress were brown, lace-up patent leather dress shoes.

My mother glanced back at me over her shoulder in my dream. Her soft green eyes were full of hope, love, acceptance, and trust. She looked at my younger self while my present self floated above. Her eyes then shifted up to where I was hovering.

"Go within," she mouthed.

She turned back around and continued walking down the road's shoulder before disappearing. I stared down at my younger self, standing on the road's edge. My big brown eyes focused forward to where my mother once stood. I knew what that young girl felt: scared, unsure, lost. I had felt those feelings the weeks after my mother had passed.

But at that moment, I realized what Mom was trying to tell me. What I sought and fought so hard for must first be found internally. Only then could it manifest externally. Mom shared that I needed to love myself unconditionally through all my failures and missteps, my wins and losses. True acceptance and trust started inward, not outward from others.

Driven in my career.

William.

The Woodland house.

The slew of dates over the last year and a half.

As I gazed at the peaceful display of nature before me, I realized I had been doing it all wrong. *God, give me grace. Teach me how to do it differently. I'm ready.*

Getting off the four-wheeler, I climbed the boulder that hung on the cliff's edge in front of me. I sat with my legs crossed before closing my eyes and inhaling deeply. The waft of fragrances that Mother Nature created permeated my nose. I held them there for as long as I could before exhaling. I did this over and over until I could taste them. Eventually, my mind was empty, and the only thing I was consumed with was my breathing.

I could hear the leaves rustling and CC scurrying around in the brush. Soft moos rose in the wind from the cattle in the distance. The songs of birds crept in, along with the buzzing of insects as they flew by. The boulder was warm, having been baking in the sun all day. Its heat radiated through my pants and onto my skin.

I let every sound, smell, and touch sink into my soul. It was in those moments that I became connected with myself—the one person I should have been with all along. I once lost her to external controls and desires that left her feeling empty. But I wasn't going to lose her again. I needed to continue to find her every day.

I opened my eyes, blinking several times against the bright sun. CC had stopped rustling around and was now sitting at attention next to the boulder, her gaze out over the meadow.

"Come on, girl. I've got work to do!" I bellowed as I climbed down from the rock, hoisting myself back on the four-wheeler.

On cue, CC lunged back to her spot between my legs at the front of the machine. It roared to life quickly with the turn of a switch and a rev of the gas on the right handle. Within moments, CC and I were flying back down the trail, leaving a cloud of dust behind us.

CHAPTER TWENTY-SEVEN

At work, I started excelling beyond expectations. Everything seemed to be falling in total alignment. Solutions to problems flowed, understanding the bigger picture became easy, and the team I was leading multiplied, and so did the results they were delivering. I was more present with people and much more patient with myself and others. Soon, I was able to accomplish goals I had never dreamed of professionally.

Saving the company thirty million dollars seemed impossible, yet it happened with initiatives my team had executed. That led to a prestigious award within the Fortune 500 company. The ceremony itself felt like I was at the Oscars or Grammys. Walking across a stage with lights focused solely on me was something I had never dreamed of.

And then there was dating. I had a renewed sense of direction. I inherently had discovered something vital: if I wanted to find a partner I could trust, who accepted me just as I was and was open to building a love that had no conditions, I had to give that to myself first. After weeks of sitting on the warm boulder that overlooked the vale, I was doing just that—learning to love, accept, and trust myself. Inherently, searching for your true self can only lead to finding others who are doing the same.

With different intentions, I took my time choosing men from the reactivated dating app on my phone. I selected bios dripping with acceptance of who they were, pictures showcasing love and affection, and, of course, hints of sass, my love language.

Within several weeks, the few whittled down to one: Moses. I put him through my usual challenges and tests, seeing if his sass, wit, and patience could stand up to my barrage of unusual dating techniques. One test included a picture of me with puffy, swollen eyes after my recent eye procedure. It was the first picture and message I had sent him outside of the dating app. Talk about putting your best foot forward. His reply to the picture sealed the deal.

I would hate to see what the other guy looks like. I'm sure you came out the winner.

This experiment was already turning out differently. *How can you not love a guy who responds like that when you look like an emoji?*

One thing I was sure of: I was in no rush to meet him. Instead, I embodied the characters from the movie *Shallow Hal*, first understanding him from the inside out.

A couple of months passed before Moses and I met face-to-face. It wasn't for lack of trying; our schedules never aligned, or something would come up unexpectedly last minute for one of us. We never took it personally, nor did it stop our communication exchanges in other ways. In the past, this type of man would have been crossed off my dating list. But now, with my renewed sense of acceptance and love for myself, he was exactly what I needed. *I wonder if we canceled on each other on purpose?* The ease and flow of our talking and messages were perfect. Too perfect, in fact. Something I had never felt from anyone else over the last year and a half.

His low, sultry voice through phone conversations was kind, patient, and empathetic. His laugh was infectious, making me smile each time I heard it. As he spoke about family and friends, I could feel the kindness and patience for them in every word he uttered. We could talk for hours on end, and yet the moment we would hang up, I was left with a desire for more. I also worried. Would it be ruined if we met? Surely, it wouldn't, but for two months, I wasn't ready to test that theory. I was content in our exchanges as they were.

It was a cool late fall evening in Park City. Snow was a month away, leaving the uncrowded streets with bustling locals versus tourists. I had picked a quaint restaurant on Main Street for Moses and my first meeting. We had confirmed several times via text throughout the day that we were both *actually* going to show up. And in each exchange, the answer was always a resounding yes.

I said a quick prayer as I pulled into the first parking stall I could find. *Please, God, Mom, whoever, let him be just as wonderful in person as he has been over the last two months.*

In the small modern eatery, I was seated in the last booth along a wall lined with them. Being a few minutes early, I ordered a glass of wine. The drink wasn't to calm my nerves, though, since I had none. For the first time in my dating saga, I had no nerves. Was it because I had truly learned to love, accept, and trust myself first? Or was it because of the ease of Moses and my conversations and communication over the last two months? Or maybe it was a combination of both?

Whatever it was, I felt like I was about to have dinner with an old friend versus a first date. I shot Moses a quick message, letting him know I had arrived and where I was sitting. He replied that he had taken the wrong exit and would be just a few minutes late.

A few minutes turned into fifteen, leaving me fidgeting in my seat. The polite waiter offered me more bread and water as he tried not to glance at me with pity each time he passed. *Maybe Moses changed his mind about our meeting?* Perhaps he also felt that our magic would be lost if we met. A connection unlike any other that we had grown over the last couple of months online and through phone conversations and texting would suddenly alter somehow. At least, that was how I felt about us. *I wonder if he thought the same, or was this all in my head?*

Whatever it was, maybe Moses was too good to be true, I supposed. I grabbed my purse off the bench seat, too embarrassed to sit alone any longer with the constant looks from the staff in my direction as they passed by me.

"Well, hellooo," Moses cooed in his smooth, deep voice as he swung around behind me, his hand holding the floor-to-ceiling pillar anchored on the booth's edge. *I would have recognized that voice anywhere.* The low, soft, sultry sound was enough to melt me back into the booth I was about to leave.

Our eyes locked as a smile spread across both our faces. Instantly, I was put at ease. I placed my purse back on the seat, hoping he hadn't noticed that I was preparing to depart.

As Moses stood in front of me, the overhead light bounced off his chocolate-brown skin. He wore a newsboy cap that perfectly matched his blue sweater and jeans. I stood and embraced him with excitement and relief. It was the kind of hug you exchanged with someone you have known for a while, not someone you are meeting for the first time. An all-encompassing hug, not just a light one-armed with a slight pat on the back kind. His frame was solid and firm under my arms; his height was perfect, just a few inches taller than me.

"We finally meet," I said sweetly as we took our seats. My pulse picked up pace with excitement.

"We finally do," he replied smoothly.

We stared at each other for what seemed like hours but were mere moments. If I doubted that Moses would be different in person, it promptly washed away in those initial heartbeats we shared.

But what was it? Why did my heart feel so much comfort with this man? Why was he so different?

When dinner concluded, I was filled with disappointment. I didn't want the evening to end, and I felt Moses didn't either. I grabbed his hand as we exited the restaurant, electricity instantly coursing through me. Our hands fit together like a pair of perfectly matched gloves. With ease, I steered him across the street toward a small saloon.

The saloon was primarily empty for a Friday evening—a rarity in this town. We settled into a back booth, where the conversation picked up right where we had left it in the restaurant. We talked and danced into the early morning hours. It was like I was twenty-one again, instead of a forty-something grandma. And when he looked over at me with yearning during a lull in our conversation, I knew what he wanted because I wanted it too. But my want was not fueled by an emptiness I had been attempting to fill for the last couple of years. It was a desire, instead, to connect our energy into one. His lips slid over mine, and the current coursed between us.

As we kissed, I imagined taking my yellow-lined notebook full of first-date rules I had worked hard on forever a year and tossing it into the garbage. None of those rules seemed to apply to Moses.

One date led to two, then three. They flowed just the same as the first, in perfect harmony. Before I knew it, I asked him to spend a Saturday night in my guest room and have dinner with me at the Mayberry Café. I was ready for Betty to pass one of my dates with flying colors for the first time.

After ordering, Moses headed to the men's room, and Betty came to our booth. Before I could speak, she blurted out, "You don't need my advice tonight."

Bewildered, I gave her a sideways glance with a raised eyebrow. "Of course I do. Why would you say that?"

"Because *you're* different. For the first time, I can see you are no longer dating with your head, basing it off a perfectly planned checklist. Instead, today I see you sitting here with this man, finally dating with your heart. You don't need my advice; you already know the answer."

I let her words sink in as she smiled, before walking away.

She was right. Moses didn't check all my perfectly planned boxes, yet I was drawn to him like a bee to a flower. The way our conversations flowed, the energy that surged through me when his dark brown skin touched mine . . . his gentle, subtle way of approaching me. He was a light wind that blew in without me even noticing, causing a windstorm of emotions. *No one has done that in years, if ever.*

Looking up, I could see Moses skipping down the center steps of the café, passing Betty with a nod, down into the dining room toward our table in the far back right corner. I had designated that table as mine on many a Friday and Saturday night for almost two years. But now I realized I no longer needed it.

"So, where were we?" Moses asked as he glided back into his side of the booth. My eyes lingered on him as he slid a slice of bread out of the basket between us.

"What . . . ?" he asked as I stared at him without answering his question. "Do I have something on my face?" He raised his napkin up to his face and began to wipe.

This was our fifth date, yet it felt like I had been with him for years.

CHAPTER TWENTY-EIGHT

"Hey, Frank. I have a problem," I moaned as soon as he picked up the line, skipping any pleasantries.

It was a clear Wednesday in December. Not a cloud in the sky. The roads had not seen a drop of snow on them in over a week. I imagined right now Frank was pondering what trouble I could have gotten myself into on a day like today.

"I just drove by the cow herd in the field. The fences were perfectly fine," he said, sarcasm dripping from his words. "The sheriff's car was parked in front of the station, and we ain't got enough snow for you to be stuck in any drift. So whatever this is, it did not involve your usual suspects."

I couldn't help but let out a laugh. I leaned against the side of my poor red Mini Coop. The smoke that had been pouring out in dark black plumes from under the hood was now just puffs of gray. An hour ago, I had started ascending the roads through the mountains of the first canyon on my way home from work. Then, my baby spat and hesitated before the sharp snap of a backfire vibrated through the whole car.

Smoke billowed from the hood and through the vents. I raced the car through the lanes of the highway to the far right so I could take the exit that was fast approaching.

After safely maneuvering it into a nearby parking lot, I turned the engine off. Getting out and pacing a few yards away from the smoke, I let it sit for a time, thinking maybe it would cool down and then I could slowly drive the rest of the way through the canyons and safely to Frank's shop. When the smoke had finally subsided enough, I climbed back in my Mini and turned the key in the ignition. Nothing happened. No click or sputter. Just silence.

"Well, Mr. Comedian, it is none of the above," I mockingly replied before coughing. "Hold on, I need to move away from the smoke."

"There's smoke this time? That is a new one. Are you okay?" Frank asked with concern.

"Yeah. But the Mini Coop, well . . . let's just say she needs to go to the nearest car ICU and be hooked up to life support. She may need a heart or lung transplant at this point."

"When was the last time you checked your oil?" Frank questioned curiously, not even rebutting my spot-on medical humor.

"Um . . ." I squinted my left eye as I tried to remember. "Don't you do that when I bring it to you? You know, while fixing other things, just ensure the car's vital signs are okay?"

"Cindy, we are mechanics, not doctors. We only do exactly what the customer wants," he replied low and slow. "It's quite possible you blew your engine. Unfortunately, that is the one thing I cannot fix for you. I have no experience replacing a Mini Coop engine. Now, if ya had a Ford or a Chevy, I'm your man."

I let my head drop, the phone still snug against my left ear. I reached my right hand up and pinched the bridge of my nose with my thumb and index finger.

"Are you still there, Cindy?" Frank asked in the silence.

"Yup. Just thinking about what I'm going to do next," I said, realizing I had to call on an old mechanic friend in the city. "Sorry to have to do this to you, Frank, but I will have to cheat on you with another mechanic."

"You can do it with my blessing this one time," he replied with a humorous tone. "Are you going to be able to get home okay?"

"I'll be fine. My brother will come to get me. You go have dinner with your family. It's about closing time for you."

With that, we ended the call, and I opened up the Uber app to request a ride. No need to bother my brother or Moses. Then, I placed a second call.

"Brook's Auto," the mechanic's niece replied into the phone. I recognized her voice from the years I'd taken our vehicles to their shop, back when William and I were still married.

"Hey, Kristy, it's me . . . Cindy. Long time no talk." I paced around my smoldering car as I spoke. "I need your help with my Mini Coop. Can you call your tow guy and have him come pick it up?"

The bells chimed on the grease-stained glass door to the reception area at the side of the mechanic's shop when I opened it. The room held an old desk and mismatched chairs covered in stains. The air was thick with the smell of gasoline and oil. I had been in this room dozens of times over the last two decades but had not stepped foot in here since moving to Woodland. This had been our family mechanic shop for years, and it felt like stepping back in time to another life.

Brent, my old mechanic, called me the day after the Mini Coop was towed to his shop, confirming Frank's assumption. The engine was bone dry of oil, causing it to seize and stop.

I had blown the engine. *How could I be so stupid as to not check the oil?*

Brent had been able to secure a rebuilt engine and spent the last two weeks replacing it. The shop's receptionist, his niece Kristy, called to let me know it was ready to be picked up. I secured a ride to the shop in the city from my brother, which was an inconvenience for him, and one he would no doubt remind me of for months. I now stood in the dark, small room full of nostalgia.

A side door opened off the reception area. A medium-built girl, hair pulled up in a messy ponytail, came sauntering out.

Kristy.

"I thought I heard something. Haven't seen you in a while," she said, passing in front of me in the small space behind the desk, retrieving paperwork from a row of files on the wall. "I heard you and William got divorced. That's what your brother said a few months ago, anyway."

I nodded in the silence, keeping a pleasant enough smile.

"That makes sense as to why some other lady came in to check on his BMW last week," Kristy added.

I felt my smile falter a bit. *William's car is here? Now?* A surge of angst seared through me, causing my palms to be moist. I didn't expect that, at least not at this point when I'd done so well moving beyond him.

"You heard right," I replied flatly, not wanting to dive into the past with her, knowing she kept nothing confidential. Instead, I just wanted to get my car and drive home.

But Kristy didn't seem to get the hint. Instead, she set down the file on the desk and leaned forward on her elbows as if she somehow got the idea that I wanted to gossip. "The last two checks William wrote bounced, so we make him bring cash in now. We've been trying to fix his engine after someone poured sugar in his gas tank."

Now my interest was piqued. *Why would someone pour sugar into his gas tank?*

As if reading my mind, Kristy continued, "He said he was out at a club. Why he'd be doing that at his age, I don't know. He said his car was parked by the door so the valet could keep an eye on it. He said someone was jealous of his BMW 6 series, so they keyed the side and poured sugar in the tank."

I thought about his precious car, which he'd bought without conversing with me at the tail end of our marriage. He told me they'd traded him straight across at the dealership for the other BMW we had picked together. He always had to drive a BMW, which we could not afford on my salary alone.

What I found out later was that it was just another lie. His old buddy Marco, who took almost everything we had in the Ponzi scheme, had given William the money for the rest. *Hush money.* My money, it turned out to be in the end. I hated that car but knew that if someone poured sugar into the tank and keyed it, it was not a random act of jealousy. The car's security system wouldn't have allowed it. It was done out of spite by someone close to him who had access to his keys.

"Well, that's unfortunate. I'm glad it's not me footing the bill anymore," I replied snidely. I knew Kristy would repeat my words as hot gossip to everyone, but I didn't care.

"We always knew you were the smart one," she shared. "That it was you who supported the family. He always tried to pass it off as if he was the successful one. We saw right through it. Hence why we won't take his checks anymore. She rustled through the papers before her, stamping "PAID" on each page. After a moment, she met my eyes again.

"And then," she continued, "this skanky middle-aged woman showed up with stringy black hair and too-tight clothes. She cussed between every other word, and her shirt was so tight and small you could see her tramp stamp above her butt on her back, along with the top of her underwear. She claimed to be William's 'assistant,' but I highly doubt that."

I crossed my arms over my chest. *The tramp stamp. It was her. He was still seeing her.*

I expected to feel a wave of betrayal wash through me again, but instead, all I felt was relief. *His lies no longer hurt me.* I couldn't help but let a little chuckle escape my lips as I shook my head. For years, I thought that no one saw through William except me, that the façade he put on fooled everyone. Apparently, I was wrong. People did see through him; they just didn't talk about it.

I felt a tinge of sadness creep up at how my ex-husband's life had turned out. Apparently, he felt so uncomfortable being himself that he continued to hide behind a smokescreen. He wasn't fooling anyone but himself, but maybe that's how he liked it. All I knew for certain was it no longer involved me. I wasn't about to discuss Williams's affair and drugs with Kristy. That was petty. I let words linger in my mind silently, then let them go.

I made the right decision to leave William and choose me instead.

I glanced at Kristy as she typed numbers into a ten-key. I didn't need any more details of Williams's current life; it no longer was any of my business. "So," I began solemnly, "how much do I owe you?"

CHAPTER TWENTY-NINE

"Kids, the meat is ready!" I yelled through the open window on the porch into the living room of my Woodland home. The succulent smell of spices drifted through the air from the grill. Behind me was a carpet of yellow wildflowers covering the lot and the surrounding mountains. It was the end of May, and the air was warm and sweet like honey.

My middle son, Lyle, placed the perfectly grilled carne asada on trays before I helped him carry them into the house. Matthew, my oldest son, was finishing the rice on the stove while Cortland, the youngest, and Melissa, his wife, were putting the finishing touches on the side dishes spread across the kitchen island.

Three of Moses's boys were playing an indoor basketball game with a rubber ball using a small hoop placed on top of the closet door in the dining area by the hall. Meanwhile, the younger children, including Moses's daughter and my grandchildren, chased CC up and down the hall, throwing small stuffed toys for her to retrieve.

I was grateful at that moment that the air in the house was a mix of sweet and spicy versus the pungent smell it was a couple of months ago. The side wall between the foyer and kitchen in the living space now sat empty. It was once covered by a dark brown walnut armoire—that was until CC had trapped a baby skunk under it. The frightened creature spent the entire night and the next day spraying the sulfuric scent repeatedly.

It had taken hours for the exterminator and me to finally trap the black-and-white furball in a box so it could be returned to the wild. But the damage had already been done. The entire house, including CC and me, smelled like rotten eggs.

The armoire took the brunt of it though. Eventually, I had to throw it out since the smell had permeated the wood beyond my ability to remove it. That night, my growing connection with Moses was solidified, and the words, "I love you," were uttered. After fumigating the entire house, leaving the windows open to air out, I drove to Moses's on one of our off nights to shower and sleep.

I recalled his expression and his hand clasping over his nose and mouth as he opened his garage door as I got out of my Mini. It was the kind of gesture one does only when the air is truly wretched.

But instead of turning me away, he gingerly helped me shower with skunk-be-gone soaps and sprayed all of my belongings with skunk deodorizer. As he combed the last of the spray gently through my hair, I knew that I had found a partner who accepted me for me.

The family dinners I dreamed would take place in this house over two years ago came true. They turned out to be even better than I had envisioned. The once-abandoned space, with roller coaster floors and lava walls, was now full of life.

This family spread out through the open dining, living, and kitchen space boomed with excitement and energy, leaving me feeling elated and full of hope. Not the hope that I had once felt when I found this house and the thoughts of William and me growing old in it, but a feeling that made me realize that my new life was just beginning.

I watched as the family grabbed plates and circled around the kitchen island, heaping piles of rice and vegetables before spearing chunks of beef with their forks. Warm tortillas were passed as everyone took their spots at tables throughout the dining and living room areas.

My house, which had been mostly quiet over the last two years, was overflowing with laughter and bantering. Moses and his five children, mostly teenagers, nestled at the dining room table. Their resounding voices ricocheted off the four walls as the sporting event highlights from the week were recalled and debated. Over the last five months, his youngest four had spent every other weekend here in Woodland with Moses and me. To them, this would be where it all started: this house gave birth to the relationship between their father and me and my relationship with them.

This dinner was special. It would be the last one we shared as a family in this home. Ten months had passed since Moses and I exchanged our first messages through a dating app; now, we were ready to move in together. The dread that every Sunday night brought us, knowing we would not see each other for a few days, became more than we could bear.

This meal, and all the people sharing it, marked the end of a journey and the beginning of a new one.

A momentary wave of angst overcame me when I woke up that morning. Was I ready to leave this part of my life behind? To leave Woodland and this house? Had I indeed found what I was so desperately seeking?

Gazing around my bedroom at dawn, I could remember how it looked: stained shag carpet, bare beams with insulation protruding, and a giant hornet's nest. Back then, I had felt just as damaged and neglected as the home was. It took a lot to refurbish my wounded heart, like chipping away the layers of ugly rock on the downstairs walls. Now, the beauty beneath it all showed brightly in the daylight, and I felt at peace in a way I never thought possible a few years ago.

Acceptance. Unconditional love. Trust.

I looked at the sea of family and guests huddled together in the remodeled space. My home had become their home. I had realized earlier I was missing a few crucial visitors for this final gathering. Yet I could still feel their presence.

If Frank were here, he would be sitting on the far end of the dark dining table, while Betty would be nestled between the kids at the kitchen island bar. They would be in fits of laughter as they enlightened the children on the adventures we shared over the last couple of years.

Sheriff Clark would sit on the couch, a plate of food on his lap as he cooed at the recent addition of twin grandbabies rolling around on the rug in front of him. Ron would have been most comfortable in the armchair, soaking in the bond we all shared, which now included him.

My mother was there. I could feel it. She sat alongside my father at one of the folding tables, along with her now-grown grandchildren and great-grandchildren.

I visualized Rich tapping on the vibrant red back door as soon as Ladder Day was tied to a pole on the porch. He would sit next to Matt and talk about art and painting. The two would compare techniques to capture the perfect sparkle in someone's eye on a canvas. Yes. This was the perfect farewell.

Taking my seat at the folding table next to Charles, I spread my napkin across my lap before scooping up a mound of rice and inserting it into my mouth.

"I think you should keep the house," Charles interrupted as I was about to take another bite. "We could use it as a vacation home for the family, a place to get away when the smog gets too bad in the city."

Chuckling at his comment, I couldn't help but recall that was the only way I could get him up here almost two years ago to see the run-down place. He had tried to talk me out of buying it at that time. Now getting rid of it was the last thing he wanted to do.

I had considered keeping the Woodland home. This home held my heart. It had been my protective bubble when I needed it most. It had saved me just as I had saved it. The decision to sell it was one of the hardest decisions I had to make.

Still, the responsibility of two houses was something I couldn't currently navigate, along with a new relationship and expanding job duties. Plus, the expense would stretch my new director of medical management salary too thin.

It was time. As sad as it was to sell my home, it was just too far for Moses's work commute and the weekly responsibilities of his children, which were well over an hour from here. Moving forward in life also meant saying goodbye to this treasure. The house Charles and I rebuilt, which rebuilt me, had done its job. It was now ready for another phase of life, just like me, one that consisted of a young couple who would soon fill the home with children and build their family.

But part of my heart would always be here. In this house, in this town. As I would take part of its soul with me.

"Well, it's a little too late for that," I replied with a tinge of regret as I looked around the open space filled with laughter and chattering. "The real estate contract has been signed, the moving trucks are reserved, and the lease on the rental in the city is complete. And unless you won the lottery lately, we can't quite afford it right now."

I didn't feel I needed to go into detail about how the house and the people in the small town had already saved me. Now, what I needed most was to get back to living. My transformation was apparent, or at least for me, it was. The house's magic had worked.

I was no longer the shell of a woman I was two years ago. Back then, I'd walked through the knee-high weeds up to its chipped blue façade. I'd suppressed my feelings of betrayal in light of hope while peeling a layer of paint away with my fingernail, hoping to discover what was underneath.

Like a beacon of light shining through an ocean of fog, the house that had called to me had kept its part of our bargain. I would save the house if, in return, it would save me. It had done just that.

I let the silence settle between my brother and me as recent memories glided through my thoughts. Moses had come into my life like a soft breeze, the kind that brings subtle fragrances and coolness without interrupting anything you may be doing but instead making it better. The holiday party six months ago had allowed him the opportunity to meet my family. It was as if he slid right into place like the missing crayon lining up in the box to complete the set.

I knew this new life would not have been possible if it had not been for this house and evenings under the Woodland Stars. There, beneath their vast glow, answers to my elusive questions revealed themselves.

To find what you desire, you must first go within. While Moses lay next to me and the sunrise made its appearance, the angst and questioning that had drifted into my mind earlier that morning evaporated just as quickly as it appeared. I had gone within, learning to trust, accept, and love myself unconditionally, and in turn, it manifested itself in my relationship with others.

I looked out over the sea of people as the corners of my mouth turned upward, along with a surge of acceptance and contentment. I then glanced down at my feet, where CC lay curled up, peering at me with her big brown eyes, full of trust. Across the room, Moses caught my gaze as he smiled and nodded back at me before mouthing, *I love you.*

I had found what I was looking for, and it was always there. I had just been searching in the wrong place.